Objectivity
Subjectivity
in Social Research

Objectivity and Subjectivity in Social Research

Gayle Letherby
John Scott and
Malcolm Williams

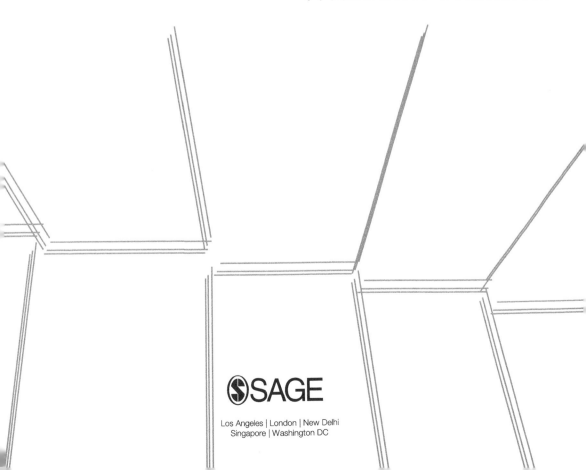

⑤SAGE

Los Angeles | London | New Delhi
Singapore | Washington DC

Los Angeles | London | New Delhi
Singapore | Washington DC

SAGE Publications Ltd
1 Oliver's Yard
55 City Road
London EC1Y 1SP

SAGE Publications Inc.
2455 Teller Road
Thousand Oaks, California 91320

SAGE Publications India Pvt Ltd
B 1/I 1 Mohan Cooperative Industrial Area
Mathura Road
New Delhi 110 044

SAGE Publications Asia-Pacific Pte Ltd
3 Church Street
#10-04 Samsung Hub
Singapore 049483

Editor: Katie Metzler
Assistant editor: Anna Horvai
Production editor: Ian Antcliff
Copyeditor: Sarah Bury
Proofreader: Kate Harrison
Marketing manager: Ben Griffin-Sherwood
Cover design: Jennifer Crisp
Typeset by: C&M Digitals (P) Ltd, Chennai, India
Printed by: MPG Books Group, Bodmin, Cornwall

MIX
Paper from
responsible sources
FSC® C018575
www.fsc.org

First published 2013

Library of Congress Control Number: 2012931554

British Library Cataloguing in Publication data

A catalogue record for this book is available from the British Library

ISBN 978-0-85702-840-2
ISBN 978-0-85702-841-9 (pbk)

Contents

About the Authors

Gayle Letherby, BA (Hons), PhD, AcSS is Professor of Sociology and Director of the Institute of Health and Community at Plymouth University. She researches and writes in a variety of areas including reproductive and non/parental identity; working and learning in higher education; crime and deviance and travel mobilities. She is also interested in all things methodological, particularly feminist approaches, auto/biography and wider concerns relating to the politics of the research process and product. Publications focusing on issues of method, methodology and epistemology include *Feminist Research in Theory and Practice* (Open University, 2003); Letherby, G. and Bywaters, P. (eds) *Extending Social Research: Application, Implementation, Presentation* (Open University, 2007); 'Feminist Methodology' in Williams M. and Vogt P. (eds) *The Sage Handbook of Methodological Innovation* (Sage, 2011); and various contributions to Jupp, V. (ed) *The Sage Dictionary of Social Research* (Sage, 2006).

John Scott is Professor of Sociology and Pro Vice-Chancellor for Research at Plymouth University. He was previously Professor of Sociology at Essex University and Leicester University. He is a Fellow of the British Academy, an Academician of the Academy of Learned Societies in the Social Sciences, and a Fellow of the Royal Society of Arts. An active member of the British Sociological Association, he has held the posts of Secretary, Treasurer, Chairperson, and President. His most recent publications are *Conceptualising the Social World* (Cambridge University Press, 2011), T*he Sage Handbook of Social Network Analysis* (edited with Peter Carrington, Sage, 2011), and *Sociology* (with James Fulcher, Oxford University Press, 2011). His current work on the history of British sociology will appear as *Envisioning Sociology. Victor Branford, Patrick Geddes, and the Quest for Social Reconstruction* (with Ray Bromley, SUNY Press, 2013).

Malcolm Williams is a Professor and Director of the School of Social Sciences at Cardiff University. Though primarily a sociologist, his work draws on social statistics and philosophy of science. His primary research interests are methodological, particularly probability, causality and the counting of rare and elusive populations. He was the first researcher to use the method of mark-recapture to measure homeless populations. His empirical research has included work on household formation and dissolution, housing need and more recently issues of pedagogy in the teaching of quantitative methods. He has published/edited nine books/collections. His most recent are *Teaching Quantitative Methods* (with Geoff Payne, Sage, 2011) and *The Sage Handbook of Innovation in Social Research Methods* (with W. Paul Vogt, Sage, 2011).

ONE
Introduction

The widely accepted view of science is that it is the means of securing truth in knowledge about the world. It is for this reason that many sociologists have taken the view that sociology, along with other social sciences, should follow the scientific method: it should be a science of society. This view has been challenged by those who see society as closer to the arts and humanities than to the sciences: they argue that sociology is a humanistic discipline in which the subjectivity of the individual sociologist is central to the knowledge produced. The most radical variants of this argument see social investigation as totally relativistic.

The implications of this go beyond sociology, and the view of science as an objective basis for truth has been challenged. Those working in social studies of science have developed a view – often characterised as 'social constructionism' – that appears to challenge the objectivity of science and its claims to produce 'true' knowledge. Scientific knowledge, they argue, is a product of the constructive practices of scientists and cannot be seen as an unproblematic reflection of a world external to science.

This is the basis from which we address the question of objectivity and subjectivity in social research. We each believe that this debate is significant for sociologists and other social scientists but challenge some of the simplistic understandings of and values attached to so-called 'objective scientific' approaches and 'politically subjective' ones. We come to this debate from different directions, and these shape the differing conclusions and emphases in the arguments presented in this work. Before continuing with our introduction of the main issues and outlining the structure and organisation of the rest of the book we begin by each introducing ourselves through brief biographical snapshots of our intellectual influences and starting points.

Influences and starting points

——Gayle ————————————————————————————————

MY INTEREST IN OBJECTIVITY AND subjectivity, the relationship between them, and in methodology and epistemology more generally began when I was an undergraduate. In my first year of study I wrote an essay which required me to consider the political aspects of the process and product of sociological study and used the work of Max Weber, C. Wright Mills, Howard Becker, Alvin Gouldner and others. Browsing through the library bookshelves in year two, I found the first edition of *Breaking Out* by Liz Stanley and Sue Wise (1983), and although feminist epistemology was not officially on the curriculum until year three, for me this added to my already growing interest in the status of the claims we can and cannot make from research and our relationship with and responsibility to respondents and the academic community. This interest, indeed fascination, with accountability remains.

In a paper written in 1999, Liz Stanley described herself as a 'child of her time', suggesting that intellectual/academic socialisation affects our interests and approaches. I too am a 'child of my time' and one consequence of the development of my sociological imagination (Mills 1959), alongside the awakenings of my feminist consciousness, has been a constant concern with the relationship between the process and the product(s) of research; how what we do affects what we get. Some of my substantive research and writing interests – which include reproductive and non/parental identities, working and learning in higher education and travel mobilities – also relate to experiences and influences inside *and* outside the academy. For my first piece of individual research (as a third-year undergraduate) I chose to study women's meanings of miscarriage (Letherby 1993), an event I had myself experienced four years earlier. In 1990, when I began my PhD on identity and definition with reference to 'infertility' and 'involuntary childlessness' (which I write in single quotation marks to highlight the tensions in meaning), I fit the medical definition of 'infertile' and was at that time 'involuntarily childless' (e.g. Letherby 1999, 2002a, 2003a; Exley and Letherby 2001). In the mid-1990s I became a 'step-parent', which influenced other writings, including a recent piece focusing on experiences of social motherhood (Kirkman and Letherby 2008). Thus, some of my work in this area (I have also undertaken research in the area of foster caring, teenage pregnancy and young parenthood, and long-term conditions in pregnancy) relates to my own autobiography and throughout my career I have been concerned to reflect on the significance of my own experience to my work. All of the projects I have worked on, whether close to my own experience or not, have had an impact on me both intellectually and personally. I've been interested, pleased, angry, sad, and so on. Research is an endeavour characterised by politics, power and emotion, and it is important to reflect on the implications of this.

Obviously, it is not always possible *or* indeed desirable to research issues close to our own experience. I do not believe that identification should be seen as a prerequisite to 'good' research and it is inaccurate to assume that *all* research is grounded in the autobiography of researchers. Furthermore, researchers do not always identify with respondents and vice versa, even when they share an experience and/or identity, and involvement at any level brings its own challenges and problems within research. Neither do I believe that researchers must always reveal all in their research and research writings. However, I do believe that the life experience and identities of researchers are present at some level in all that we do and that it is important to acknowledge this.

With all of this in mind, I argue that critical reference to the knowing/doing relationship is an essential aspect of all research. In my previous writings in this area I have tried to work towards a position that challenges traditional claims to objectivity and recognises both the personhood of the researcher and the complexity of the researcher/respondent relationship and yet allows for useful things to be said (e.g. Letherby 2003b, 2004, 2011b). For me, then, what we need to do is focus on the theorisation of the subjective (which includes the researcher's motivation and practice and the respondent's expectations and behaviour) and its significance to knowledge production. My starting point thus recognises the values (both positive and negative) of the subjective, the significance of experience, but is not a rejection of the need to be critical, rigorous and accurate.

——Malcolm

I BECAME CONCERNED WITH ISSUES of objectivity through applied social research. My own inclinations are towards a left liberalism, indeed my political background was (and remains to a great extent) libertarian socialist. A concern for social problems, particularly severe housing need, brought me to the social sciences. As a mature student and later a researcher of homelessness, I came to realise that the latter was politicised not just at the level of tackling it, but also in matters of explaining and even measuring it. People on the left wanted to 'prove' how prevalent homelessness was and were often prepared to use methods and rhetoric to achieve this. Meanwhile those on the right believed that homelessness was overestimated and due to the fecklessness of individuals. They preferred not to research it at all. Both sides were concerned to show they were correct, regardless of the number of homeless people there actually were. I wanted to tackle homelessness, but I also first wanted to know what the reality of homelessness was.

This led me to a general question, which has remained with me – 'how can social scientists be committed to progressive change, but remain rigorous investigators?' My intellectual journey to try to answer this question led me to a critical engagement with scientific method. In the 1970s and 1980s the left was sceptical of science, for it had brought us nuclear weapons, nuclear power and pollution. Moreover, the writings of Thomas Kuhn, Paul Feyerabend and their followers, had convinced many that scientific method was simply a rhetoric of persuasion, a cultural and social artefact, a story among other stories about the world. The social sciences were inhabited by people of the left, who possibly as a result of a rejection of science, but also as a result of embracing the emergent philosophies of poststructuralism and postmodernism, turned against the more traditional modes of 'scientific' enquiry in social science.

In some ways these new 'turns' to the cultural, the linguistic, humanistic produced new insights, sociologically and methodologically. Books like Cicourel's *Method and Measurement in Sociology* (1964) demonstrated that there were limits to the more traditional forms of measurement and explanation in social science. Scepticism about science was often sophisticated (see, for example, Brian Appleyard's *Understanding the Present* (1992)) as was the attack on 'positivism' in social science, but they left us with a big and a small question. The big question was: if we see current science as a tool of ideology and methodologically flawed, what if anything do we envisage replacing it? In rejecting the technology we disapprove of, do we reject all technology and the scientific endeavours that produce it? Do we give the same epistemological weight to shamanism as we do to the laws of physics? The small question was: if social 'science' itself rejects science and its methods, how can we provide reliable and valid data that will help us to tackle social ills?

In my view, the political and methodological critique of science had gone too far – it was illogical and hypocritical. Similarly, the rejection of science in social science was so often based upon a mythical science that was value free, always (claimed to be) truthful and accurate. The philosophy and history of science I read taught me that science was a social enterprise, a faltering, sometimes successful search for the truth about the world. It was always ideologically driven, but so often (Galileo comes to mind) it was able to overthrow an ideology by showing that the world was different from that which had hitherto been believed. There were Eureka moments, but mostly the progress of science towards more accurate explanations of the world had to be seen in the long historical view.

Around 12 years ago I worked on a method of counting homeless people that would allow local authorities and NGOs to know approximately how many homeless people lived in particular locations. The method 'capture–recapture' was adopted from biology and was originally used to count penguins, but some adaptation could be used on transient human populations. The method had (and still has) its flaws, partly because of the difficulties of defining homelessness and partly because of the counting methods being less reliable than the statistical method they support. Indeed, at one conference, where I had given a no-holds-barred critique of our capture–recapture work, I was berated for introducing a method of counting the homeless that was 'flawed'. I admitted to this, but my question was how can we do better? At the time we could not and I truly believed it was the best way to count such populations. It is still good, but I'm glad to say new methods that rely on multilevel modelling are challenging it.

Yet, 'how can we do better?' is not a bad credo for social science, both as a tool for improving the lives of our fellow citizens, but also as a tool of investigation. I believe that objectivity and recognition of our subjectivity and of the intersubjective nature of social science are crucial issues in our quest to do better.

────|John──

MY ENTRY INTO SOCIOLOGY WAS directly from school. Unlike Gayle and Malcolm, I did not have a prior work life, apart from weekend and vacation jobs. For this reason, perhaps, I did not experience any great conflict between practical concerns and the academic life. Being male, there was also little discrepancy between my personal, subjective experience and the demands and expectations placed on me by university study. After a conventional education at a boy's grammar school, the idea that knowledge comprises both an objective representation of the way the world actually is and a true account of how it came to be that way did not seem at all problematic.

I began my studies in 1968, when the idea that sociology is 'the science of society' seemed unproblematic to the established teachers of the subject. The views of Auguste Comte were taken as the founding statements of this 'positive' science, and the word 'positivism' had not yet attracted the unfortunate – and very misleading – pejorative connotations that it was later to acquire. The course that I took in 'Theories and Methods of Sociology' presented me with standard arguments from the philosophy of science to buttress this view of the scientific status of sociology.

Yet 1968 was also, of course, the high point of student radicalism, when 'bourgeois' science was being challenged by a rediscovered Marxism and all orthodoxy was subjected to 'critical' reassessment in the light of practical, political concerns. Even a College of Technology in suburban London – not yet a polytechnic, let alone a university – could escape such ideas. I had been brought up in a Labour-voting family of the first-generation middle class, and the politics of the student movement resonated with me and brought home a realisation that sociology cannot be separated from practical concerns with inequality and injustice.

The young teachers recruited to teach sociology were also influenced by the intellectual and political climate of the times, and this influenced the way in which they delivered the established curriculum. Peter Winch's *Idea of a Social Science* (1958) was an established text and was read as a justification for a radical cultural relativism and, therefore, a questioning of the objectivity of western social science. Kuhn's *Structure of Scientific Revolutions* (1962) was also taken up as a manifesto justifying a view that no scientific perspective could be accorded absolute status and all were subject to degeneration and change. I began to encounter the view that there is a variety of competing perspectives in sociology and that diversity is to be encouraged and embraced: sociological understanding rests on 'values' that differ from one social group to another and so sociological theories must be equally diverse. Howard Becker's question, 'whose side are we on?' (1967), became the watchword.

By the time that I began to teach sociology myself, I had begun to wonder how these contrasting views – objectivity and partisanship – could be reconciled. I drew on the arguments of Alisdair MacIntyre (1967), encountered in a course on 'Ethics and Social Philosophy', and found myself attracted to the argument that Stephen Toulmin was putting forward in the first (and only) volume of his work on human understanding (Toulmin 1972). Both MacIntyre and Toulmin put forward the view that concepts are rooted in culturally diverse historical traditions, yet they argued also that principles of rational discourse can be employed within each tradition and can mediate between traditions. For Toulmin, in particular, the possibility existed that both natural and social science could be seen in developmental terms as moving away from misunderstanding and towards improved – but never perfect – understanding.

My views on how this 'improvement' in knowledge was to be demonstrated was sharpened by the publication of Roy Bhaskar's *Realist Theory of Science* (1975), which brought into focus the ideas that I had discovered in Rom Harré (1972). Bhaskar recognised that knowledge developed in a 'transitive' dimension of cultural and historical variability but that the reality to which scientific knowledge referred was 'intransitive' and provided the ultimate basis for judging the adequacy of knowledge. This was the basis on which I felt I could reconsider the various views that I had encountered and could reconcile their ostensibly divergent claims.

I concluded that all sociological work originates in personal and political standpoints that orient us by providing distinctive perspectives on the world, but also concluded that the rational discourse and methods shared with other intellectual disciplines allow us to incorporate divergent perspectives in a more comprehensive account that more adequately grasps the real objects that lie behind all knowledge. Sociological knowledge, that is to say, can be 'objective knowledge'.

Understanding factual descriptions

So, if we all agree on the need for and the possibility of an approach that is both accountable and has value, if not objective in the traditional sense, how are we to defend this view and convince our readers that this is the direction that social science should take? This is our task in the rest of this book. We present a view that concludes that social science can be trusted to produce robust knowledge capable of reliably guiding practical decisions. (Social) science does not provide absolutely certain knowledge, but it can provide evidential support for its claims – even if this support can always be undermined by new evidence. Science faces the constant threat of revision and so is inherently uncertain. Nevertheless, science is the most reliable source of knowledge and has, therefore, been remarkably successful in its practical applications. This is the basis of scientific authority and expertise in the policy sphere. We will show, however, that the values and subjectivity of the scientist, far from being extraneous to science, are integral elements in its claims to objectivity and expertise, accountability and value.

Our descriptions of the world are always partial, selected and filtered by our perceptual apparatus, by the assumptions that we bring to our observations, and by the particular perspective or standpoint from which we view the world. The ways in which we interpret these observations and formulate them into statements that can be communicated with others, are, furthermore, dependent on the particular language that we use. Both our perceptions of the world and our descriptions of those perceptions are linguistically mediated. A language is always the collective property of a particular population or social group. It both constitutes and reflects the assumptions, experience, and history of that group or population. Both the vocabulary and the syntax of our language structure our observational reports. This adds a further selective mechanism to our attempts to describe the world. In all of these respects, then, observations are to be regarded as *cultural* constructions that depend also on the physical perceptual apparatus that we, by virtue of our 'natural' human characteristics, bring to our observations.

Statements of fact, then, bear a logically indeterminate relationship to the external and independently existing reality within which we live and that we observe. 'Reality' as perceived and described in statements of 'fact' may not correspond to reality 'as it actually is' independently of those descriptions. The important question, therefore, concerns what can be said about the 'truth' of observational statements and the accounts that we give of those observations.

The conventional scientific response to this has been, in the words of Sir Isaac Newton, that descriptions are, nevertheless, 'very nearly true' (Newton 1687/1969: Vol. 2: 456). Accepting neither a dogmatic absolutism of factual truth nor a sceptical relativism that reduces fact to opinion, most scientists have held that empirical reports are unlikely to be too far short of 'the truth' so long as scientists strive to eliminate bias and preconceptions and ensure that observations are as technically accurate as possible. Similarly, the objectivity of historiography has been claimed on the grounds that historical accounts that are presented undogmatically can be corrected by technically more reliable observations. For both physical scientists and historians, then, technical reliability provides the route to validity.

Such a position was also set out in the founding statement of sociological method by Auguste Comte in his outline of 'positivism'. Positive knowledge, Comte argued, is a product of the methods of investigation introduced in the Enlightenment and the scientific renewal that it initiated. Scientific methods provide a guarantee for the truth of scientific statements. This was the position that was largely taken over by Emile Durkheim in his *Rules of the Sociological Method* (1895), and applied in his study of *Suicide* (1897), a study that was adopted as the paradigmatic model of sociological research for much of the twentieth century.

For many, however, this is no solution at all. Marxism, Feminism, Postcolonialism, and a number of other radical alternatives to mainstream social science have resurrected and reinforced the spectre of relativism and a denial that anything even approximating to this commonsense view of truth can ever be sustained except by political fiat. If 'might makes right', then, perhaps, might also makes truth.

Developing a similar view in relation to the physical sciences, Thomas Kuhn (1962) argued that all paradigms of scientific description and explanation are subject to radical overthrow by the advocates of alternative paradigms. A successful paradigm is that which is able to attract the largest number of adherents, for whatever reason and certainly not for logical, intellectual reasons alone. Factual knowledge generated through the application of the paradigm remains ultimately contingent.

We argue against the relativistic implications of this point of view in order to defend an idea of scientific truth that respects the autonomy and importance of divergent values and standpoints.

Understanding Value Judgements

The conventional view of both physical and social science is based on an assumption of value freedom. While some take this to mean that science should only ever be undertaken 'for its own sake' and without any regard for its implications for human concerns and values, the core of the position is simply that science is *impartial*: its evaluation of evidence takes account only of cognitive values and does not – or should not – be influenced by moral values. On this basis, science is not so much 'value free' as free from *moral* values. Science can provide technical or instrumental knowledge and an assessment of the consequences of different policy proposals, but the scientist has no moral authority or superiority within the policy sphere.

This was at the heart of the sociological method set out by Max Weber and was developed by Robert Merton (1942) in his view that scientific activity was governed by values and practices of scientific communalism, universalism, disinterestedness, and organised scepticism. He recognised, like Weber, that scientists may have their own moral values and policy preferences, but he held these to be separable from scientific activity itself. Nevertheless, science and policy making have become ever more entangled as policy makers seek technical solutions to physical and social problems. The idea of value freedom is, therefore, more difficult to sustain: how is the technical authority of science in the policy sphere to be maintained if scientists are to be detached from policy debates and agnostic about moral values?

The growing role of science in policy, through its integration with government and commercial interests, has highlighted this question in relation to the moral responsibility of the scientist. Can the scientist evade responsibility for the uses to which that knowledge is put? Wernher von Braun, the German rocket bomb scientist, was famously parodied for holding this position by the satirical singer Tom Lehrer:

Don't say that he's hypocritical
Say rather that he's apolitical
'Once the rockets are up, who cares where they come down
That's not my department,' says Wernher von Braun.

This view holds that the scientists, concerned exclusively with purely factual and technical considerations, need not be at all concerned with the social consequences of scientific discourses and their application. The implications of this position were highlighted in debates over Robert Oppenheimer's Manhattan Project on the development of the atom bomb during the Cold War. Despite his own left-wing views and saying, on the explosion of the first atomic bomb, 'Now I am become Death, the destroyer of worlds', Oppenheimer continued to take a technocratic view of the applications of his scientific ideas and never openly challenged American nuclear policy.

In social science, similar moral issues have arisen in relation to the Project Camelot, in which political sociologists studied rebellion and revolutionary processes in Latin America as part of a project financed by the US State Department and with the express intent of suppressing radical social change in US client states such as Chile. Many participants chose to ignore the intended uses of the research, but Johan Galtung spoke out against it and the project was abandoned (see Horowitz 1967).

We argue that social scientists cannot evade issues of moral responsibility. While science may not privilege any particular value judgements, and while value positions cannot be put forward in the name of science, all scientists must reflect on the actual and potential uses of their research. They must make clear in public debate their personal, moral assessments of the dangers (and benefits) consequent upon the application of their research. They must participate in the public sphere, adding their voice to its debates. They must make clear their expertise, and its boundaries and limitations, and they must argue – as citizens and not as scientists – about the uses to which that expertise is put. One moment in the role of the sociologist, therefore, is to act as a 'public intellectual', stepping beyond the production of impartial knowledge and standing back from involvement in its policy applications, to engage in political discourse concerning the formulation of public policy.

Structure and Organisation of the Rest of the Book

The rest of this book represents the debate between us. Each of us is the primary author for Chapters 2–7, although each chapter begins with a jointly written introduction and each chapter ends with some discussion between us. We have indicated individual authorship, as in this chapter, by using our first names and ragged right text. Collectively written text is set as justified text. We continue our debate in Chapter 8, which is written as a *trialogue* – reflecting email and face-to-face discussions between us – although, for us at least, this is not the end of the debate but simply represents the moment in time at which we wrote our final words.

Chapter 2: 'The Philosophical Basis of Objectivity and Relativity', primarily authored by John, explores the philosophical basis of these debates from their beginnings in the Kantian position on the nature of knowledge. Despite Kant's own concern for objectivity and absolute knowledge, contemporary relativist views have also derived support from his argument. These debates are traced through Nietzsche and perspectivism to Weber's classic position on objectivity and value freedom, and on to contemporary standpoint and postmodernist theories.

Chapter 3: 'Relationism and Dynamic Synthesis', primarily authored by John, looks at the ways in which Karl Mannheim took up the arguments of Weber and provided an answer that also resolved the diversity of standpoint theories. The distinction between relativism and relationism is drawn out as a central element and it is shown that Mannheim proposed a relationist strategy of 'dynamic synthesis', arguing that objectivity results from genuine debate and dialogue among contending positions with the social researcher attempting to incorporate divergent but authentic standpoints in an overall synthesis. This is related to the arguments of Habermas on the emergence of consensus in an ideal speech community and Popper's argument that truth emerges in an 'open society'.

Chapter 4: 'Situated Objectivity in Sociology', primarily authored by Malcolm, picks up the discussion of value freedom and the disputes over whether social science is to be 'value free' or is to base its investigations on particular value positions. It is argued that the search for the truth about the physical and social world is a value position but, nevertheless, one that can produce actionable knowledge. While a freedom from values is untenable, this need not preclude the value of objectivity as a purposeful search for the truth about objects. This search is socially situated and will prioritise particular scientific goals at different times.

Chapter 5: 'Theorised Subjectivity', primarily authored by Gayle, attends to a recognition that, while there is a 'reality' 'out there', the political complexities of subjectivities, and their inevitable involvement in the research process, make a final and definitive 'objective' statement impracticable. Theorised subjectivity recognises the values – positive and negative – of the subject studied, but holds that this should not be automatically equated with involvement or partisanship. Reference to the similarities and differences between theorised subjectivity and 'strong objectivity' and feminist fractured foundationalism will be made.

Chapter 6: 'Social Objects and Realism', primarily authored by Malcolm, argues that the pursuit of conceptual synthesis must be complemented by an understanding of the adequacy of the conceptual objects synthesised. Objectivity and subjectivity imply the existence of social objects that exist as 'things in the world' and that we must inevitably see oneself in relation to these. It is held that social research is a search for explanatory adequacy at the level of cause and meaning, and that explanatory adequacy requires ontological assumptions about the composition of the social world as the outcome of contingent causal processes.

Chapter 7: 'Objectivity and Subjectivity in Practice', primarily authored by Gayle, explores issues of the moral and political responsibility of social scientists as they have been explored in debates in and around arguments for 'public intellectualism' and 'impact'. Political aspects of the research process and praxis as a goal will be considered with reference to the issues of accountability in light of the claims and counter-claims made for objectivity and subjectivity in the earlier chapters of this book.

In the final, concluding chapter, 'Objectivity Established? A Trialogue', we return to the divergent autobiographical reflections with which we began this chapter and we consider, in the form of a trialogue, the extent to which the explorations in the body of the book have resulted, or not, in a coherent account of objectivity and subjectivity and their place in contemporary sociological practice.

TWO

The Philosophical Basis of Objectivity and Relativity

This chapter sets the scene for our later discussions by exploring the philosophical arguments over knowledge and the basis of disputes over the 'truth' of observational and theoretical statements.

Arguments for the objectivity of sociology as a 'scientific' discipline have tended to rest on the claim that this can be achieved simply by invoking 'facts'. It is assumed that observational statements about the social world are unproblematic reports on the way that things actually are. We have shown in Chapter 1, however, that statements about the world cannot simply be detached from the values held by individual scientists and scientific communities and that these values influence many aspects of scientific practice. This has led many critics of the scientific claims of sociology to see sociological theories as irretrievably bound into the moral and political positions of their advocates. On this basis, there can be no objective 'factual' descriptions of the social world, and theoretical accounts cannot but reflect the clash and contention of values. This controversy over the relationship of values to 'facts' raises the question of the extent to which knowledge can be a reliable – 'objective' – report on the world that can be assessed by criteria of 'truth' or 'falsity'.

The view in the natural sciences – in physics, chemistry and biology – was, until recently, that true knowledge is attainable and provides an accurate and objective report on the world: knowledge is a mental representation of the way the world really is.[1] This was also the claim made for the idea of a 'scientific sociology'. According to this point of view, a true statement is one that corresponds to reality; falsity is a result of error, ignorance or deliberate distortion on the part of the scientist. There was an acceptance of David Hume's (1772) assertion that there is a fundamental gulf between statements of fact and judgements of

---

[1]Some parts of the argument in Chapters 2 and 3 were first outlined in J. Scott (1998).

value. Value judgements, Hume argued, are founded in expressions of emotion and so are arbitrary and idiosyncratic. Statements of fact, on the other hand, are direct and unmediated reflections of a world that exists quite independently of human beings.

For others, however, the role of values in the production of knowledge is such that they cannot be ignored and all claims to truth and objectivity must be challenged. Such 'relativists' hold that any ostensibly factual statement must actually be seen as relative to the standpoint of the observer. There is no impartial or absolute standpoint from which the world can be seen 'as it really is': all observers are located at particular positions *within* the world and so must, inevitably, see the world from a particular point of view. Relativists hold that there can be different, but equally legitimate, ways of seeing the world. They prefer to talk about 'truths' in the plural rather than truth in the singular, and – more radically – they may reject the very idea of truth and recognise only a plurality of illusions.

Since the work of Thomas Kuhn (1962), the conventional natural-science view of knowledge has been thrown into question. Kuhn held that all scientific knowledge is rooted in non-scientific worldviews and that this knowledge cannot be seen as reproducing an external reality. Scientific knowledge may 'work' in providing a reliable guide to interventions in the world, but this reliability may be short-lived and any body of knowledge is likely to be superseded by one that works better in practical contexts. Radical thinkers influenced by Kuhn drew the strong relativistic conclusion that if there is no neutral basis from which it is possible to decide between two conflicting theoretical views, then any intellectual debate is pointless: all that matters is practical success in changing the world.

This conclusion is almost the situation parodied in the lyrics of the songwriter Cole Porter. Commenting on changes in women's clothing and behaviour, Porter held that 'In olden days a glimpse of stocking was thought of as something shocking. / Now, heaven knows – anything goes' (Porter 1934). In science, a glimpse of relativity used to be thought of as something shocking, as evidence of prejudice, bias and distortion. Now, heaven knows, diversity is embraced and 'anything goes' (Feyerabend 1975).

This is the argument that underpinned many of the criticisms levelled against the scientific status of sociology. The social world, for these critics, seems even more ineffable than the natural world and our attempts to grasp it in knowledge are inevitably doomed to failure. This relativistic conclusion finds its strongest expression in postmodernist writers (see Lyotard 1979), for whom intellectual works are no different from literary works of fiction, and their sole rationale must be the enjoyment of producing and reading them. They tell us nothing about a world that exists independently of them and so cannot be taken as rational guides to action. Social life must be seen as a kaleidoscopic interplay of diverse social constructions in which the particular 'story' that we choose to tell is a matter of individual creativity and should not be seen as a contribution to any larger project of understanding or explanation (Baudrillard 1977).

In this chapter we trace the philosophical underpinnings of the contending claims for absolute truth and relative fictions. This will show the basis for our discussions of situated objectivity and theorised subjectivity in Chapters 4 and 5.

———John's argument

THE CONTEMPORARY DEBATE OVER KNOWLEDGE owes everything to the way in which Immanuel Kant (1781) formulated the problem of knowledge, and an understanding of his argument is essential for any attempt to resolve the opposition of absolutism and relativism. Kant rejected the rather naïve basis on which Hume had asserted the simple certainty of observational descriptions, aiming to provide a more secure basis for knowledge. His arguments were mainly concerned with human knowledge of the natural or physical world – a world that human beings live in but come to know 'from the outside'. He explored the specifically human world, in which people are actively involved from the 'inside', mainly in relation to questions of morality (Kant 1788). Later Kantians, most notably Heinrich Rickert and Max Weber, took the crucial step of extending Kant's epistemological considerations to the specifically human aspects of reality.

Kant drew a sharp distinction between the 'phenomena' of human mental experience and the 'noumena' of the world as it actually is. Noumenal objects exist outside and independently of any particular human observer and so can never be grasped as objects within empirical knowledge. A noumenon is 'a thing which must be cogitated not as an object of science, but as a thing in itself' (Kant 1781: 188). Noumenal reality can be postulated as a necessary condition for experience, but the objects of this experience themselves are conceptual constructions. As phenomena of experience they are quite distinct from the noumenal objects that exist as things in themselves. Human beings are able to apprehend that noumena exist as fundamental conditions for their knowledge of the world, but they can never grasp or comprehend their true nature. There is a logical gulf between noumena and phenomena, as the mind can work only on phenomena.

The world of the noumena – the world as it really is – remains completely unknowable. Any particular noumenon must be regarded simply as 'an unknown something' (Kant 1781: 189). So far as human observers are concerned, the noumenal world of things in themselves is 'a chaotic, meaningless, and irrational world without concepts and language to give it any semblance of being or purpose' (McCarthy 2001: 133). This noumenal world was depicted by Rickert (1902) as an infinite manifold or 'heterogeneous continuum'. Weber used similar terms, referring to it as an 'absolute infinitude', an 'infinite reality', an 'infinitely manifold stream of events', or a 'vast chaotic stream of events' (Weber 1904: 72, 111). The external world is the source of all human experience, but it is an inexhaustibly chaotic source and is capable of 'inexhaustible differentiation' by human observers:

as soon as we attempt to reflect about the way in which life confronts us in immediate concrete situations, it presents an infinite multiplicity of successively and co-existently emerging and disappearing events, both 'within' and 'outside' ourselves. (Weber 1904: 72)

These ideas are difficult to grasp. Kant's fundamental point was that human observers and the world they try to observe are separated by an unbridgeable gulf. It is as if they are separated by an invisible but opaque screen that responds to the pressure of the noumena upon it and acts as a flexible membrane to present these impressions to human observers. People can see, touch, hear and taste the impressions, but they can only guess at the nature of the things behind the membrane that cause these impressions. There is, of course, no actual membrane. The gulf between observers and the world is a feature of the human body and its sensory apparatus. Knowledge begins from observations based on sensory impressions, the unmediated observation of noumena being impossible. It is sensory impressions, then, that provide the 'appearances' that are the basis of all human experience and knowledge.

The dependence of observational knowledge on the human sensory apparatus can be illustrated by considering the case of vision. Because human beings, like other primates, have three-colour vision (the neurones in their retinas are sensitive to red, yellow and blue light), they normally report grass as being 'green'. Many animals, however, have two-colour vision, some have one-colour vision (monochrome or 'black and white' vision), while others have four-colour vision. Each kind of animal sees the grass as a different colour, and there is no sense in asking which of them sees it 'correctly'. Each of them can see it only in the ways that their visual apparatus allows them to see it. To ask whether grass is really green, independently of our observations, is to ask a meaningless and unanswerable question. Similar considerations apply in respect of perceptions of depth and distance, and in the impressions received through the auditory, taste and other senses. Specific taste perceptions, for example, depend on the construction of the taste receptors, and perceptions of sound depend on the construction of the cochlea.

The perception of objects, then, involves the reception of sensuous impressions through the particular sensory apparatuses possessed by human observers. It is for this reason that it is never possible to know what things are like independently of human presence and specifically human characteristics. In this respect, at least, Kant would agree with Bishop George Berkeley (1709), who asked whether a tree that crashes to the ground in a forest makes a sound if there is no one present to hear it. His point was not that there would be 'silence' in the absence of a human observer, but that the effects of the event in an environment without human observers cannot be described using perceptual terms such as 'sound': sound is a property of the observer, not of the object.

However, empirical knowledge is not simply a matter of sensory impressions, which are merely the raw materials of knowledge. Kant rejected the idea that the human mind can be considered as an empty slate that passively receives knowledge from the outside. Specifically, he rejected Hume's view that knowledge results directly from the impact of sense impressions on the mind. Kant did not see the mind as a camera: ideas do not 'reflect' reality in any strict mechanical way. Rather, the human mind actively constructs its knowledge of the world. With its innate ideas and its sensory apparatus, the mind produces knowledge through the processing of the 'sensuous impressions' of perception. Perceptions are always *particular*, and are formed into knowledge when related to *general* ideas through the mental faculty of 'understanding' or thinking.

This faculty of understanding operates with a priori ideas and principles that organise perceptions cognitively. Kant identified three types of idea involved in this pure, cognitive understanding: the *categories of sensibility*, the *categories of understanding*, and *general concepts*. The categories of sensibility comprise the ideas of space and time that make perception or sensible experience possible. The categories of understanding are fundamental ideas – such as those of substance, causation and totality – that are necessary for attributing materiality and permanence to the objects of experience. Using these categories, the mind can transform sense impressions into objects of experience. In addition to the categories, knowledge and understanding involve also the use of general concepts that serve as labels for describing the various aspects of the world of experience. It is through abstractions such as the concepts of cat, dog, hard, and green that distinct objects of knowledge can be constructed from the phenomena of experience. While the phenomena of experience are singular reports of sense impressions, theoretical representations are built from concepts that are general in character. They are general because they are not limited in their application to particular cases but define whole classes of phenomena. Science involves the construction of objects of knowledge from perceptual observations, using general categories and concepts. It is the analytical manipulation of such objects that yields theoretical or explanatory understandings.

Cultural reality and value relevance

This argument was not much pursued beyond the scientific study of material objects until Rickert (1902) extended the Kantian framework to investigate the socio-cultural world of 'history'. Rickert's crucial point was that noumenal reality should not be seen as purely inert and meaningless. As history, it is the world of human beings themselves and is constituted by the meanings that humans give to their actions and to the events around them. These meanings comprise the 'cultural' objects that are studied by the cultural sciences.[2] These sciences have as their task the production of knowledge concerning an already meaningful reality. While the natural sciences impose a meaning on inert and infinitely chaotic noumena,

---

[2]Rickert used the term 'cultural sciences' (*Kulturwissenschaften*) where Dilthey (1883) had preferred 'spiritual sciences' (*Geisteswissenschaften*). These are both used as equivalents to J.S. Mill's (1843) 'moral sciences'.

the cultural sciences must take account of the pre-existing meanings given to the world by human beings as they live their day-to-day lives: they must be concerned with the values and ideas of the human participants as they live their history.

The actual meanings that permeate the noumenal world of history cannot, of course, be directly known, any more than can the physical aspects of noumenal reality. In this respect, meanings must be understood and interpreted in the same way as is necessary in the study of nature. Nevertheless, Rickert held, the logic of concept formation differs between the natural sciences and the cultural sciences. The natural sciences follow a generalising strategy, while the cultural sciences must follow an individualising strategy. That is to say, reality is interpreted as 'natural' in so far as it can be subsumed under general concepts that can be used to form empirical generalisations. This means that the features that a scientist defines as being of interest are law-like, or 'nomological'. The individuality and distinctiveness of experiences are disregarded in favour of abstract generality. Attention is focused on the recurrence and predictability of observations that enhance the technical, instrumental control that can be exercised over reality by identifying those aspects of a situation that can be treated as means or conditions for the attainment of desired ends (Oakes 1988: 22).

Reality is interpreted as 'cultural', on the other hand, in so far as our scientific interest lies in the individuality and concrete distinctiveness of experiences in the light of our values. Attention is focused on those aspects of reality that are regarded as essential or significant in relation to these values. In Max Weber's words: 'Empirical reality becomes "culture" to us because and insofar as we relate it to value ideas' (1904: 76). The objects that comprise a knowledge of history or culture are, therefore, 'value relevant' or value-related. Aspects of reality are cultural when they are identified by their value-relevant meaning (Oakes 1980: 10, 1988: 26; Schluchter 1989: 18–19). They are, in this way, defined as 'a finite segment of the meaningless infinity' (Weber 1904: 81). General concepts, then, select and organise elements of experience as 'natural' objects of particular types; value concepts select and organise them as 'historical' objects (McCarthy 2001: 44).

Cultural sciences follow the natural science method in so far as they must involve the use of the categories of sensibility and understanding to report perceptual observations. They differ from natural science, however, in that they relate these sensuous impressions to value concepts, rather than to abstract general concepts. Perceptual phenomena, then, must be assigned an appropriate meaning if they are to become objects of a cultural science. The cultural scientist must relate the raw materials of historical investigation to the practical value orientations of the participants (Bruun 1972: 91). For example, auditory impressions that are related to concepts of loudness, frequency, tone, etc., are constructed into objects for the natural sciences. When those same impressions are regarded as linguistic expressions and are related to values such as rationality, democracy and love, they are constituted into objects of the cultural sciences. The construction of these cultural objects involves using values to understand the meanings that are conveyed in the linguistic expressions. In relating impressions to values, their subsumption under general concepts and laws is put to one side and attention is given to their 'uniqueness'. They are treated as objects whose meanings can be understood or interpreted rather than merely given a causal explanation (Weber 1907).

General concepts are extrinsic. They are completely external to sensuous impressions and their use involves a strategy of generalisation aimed at the formulation of universal laws. It is precisely because natural objects can be considered independently of meaning that it is possible to generalise about them. Value concepts, on the other hand, are intrinsically related to the intuitively grasped, meaningful aspects of human reality. Like general concepts, however, value concepts are a priori. They are logically independent of experience, and are brought to experience from outside. According to Rickert, the values that are used as principles of selection and organisation in historical research are general values. As in the case of general concepts, they have a universal validity and make it possible for historical objects to have a similar theoretical status to natural objects.

Weber modified Rickert's position somewhat, as he rejected the view that there could be any axiomatic eternally valid values. For Weber, values are logically independent of and prior to experience (hence they are a priori), but they may not be substantively independent of that experience in so far as they reflect or have an affinity with particular historical circumstances and experiences. Values are hypothetical points of departure for scientific investigation, but they are, nevertheless, every bit as general as concepts. The cultural scientist, according to Weber, must relate the observable value elements that inhere in a historical situation to the values prevailing in the scientist's own historical milieu, recognising that the observable value elements are merely impressions of the actual, and ultimately unknowable value choices made by participants (see also Simmel 1892).

The values of any particular epoch or society are general cultural ideals that do not depend on particular individuals for their reality. Individuals may choose to accept or to reject particular values, but the values themselves are independent of their particular uses in the same way that the general concept of 'dog', for example, is independent of any particular application of it to perceptions. A historical object 'is significant because it reveals relationships which are important to us due to their connection with our values' (Weber 1904: 76), but this does not mean that they involve the making of individual value judgements. They are the bases on which value judgements are made, the recognised standards to which individual choices relate, but they are not themselves value judgements. Just as a natural scientist may or may not like 'dogs' and may or may not approve of 'climate change', a cultural scientist may describe a course of action as rational or democratic without necessarily endorsing or condemning it. Values, then, are general cultural standards to which particular aspects of reality may be related and, thereby, constituted as cultural objects (Runciman 1972).

There is, then, a fundamental distinction between factual statements and value judgements. Kant saw value judgements in terms of the 'practical understanding' that informs moral agency, separating this from the pure or theoretical understanding involved in factual knowledge. Weber emphasised that such practical reasoning draws on cultural values in order to judge phenomena as good or bad. Value judgements might claim exclusive validity, but they are merely expressions of individual faith or emotional commitment. Value judgements, and the policy proposals and programmes of action that derive from them, are matters of 'normative knowledge' that are inherently contestable. They are acts of *will* that involve weighing and choosing from among various possible value standpoints according to a person's 'conscience' and 'personal view of the world' (Weber 1904: 53). They can never be justified in terms of the purely factual, existential knowledge produced by scientists: 'it can never be the task of an empirical science to provide binding norms and ideals from which directives for immediate practical activity can be derived' (ibid.: 52).

Are there intellectual guarantees of truth?

Kant's general position seemed, to many people, to have established a more or less certain basis for social scientific knowledge. Whether the social sciences be regarded as natural sciences or cultural sciences, their knowledge can be assessed by criteria of truth and objectivity. Unfortunately, things are not quite that straightforward. The problem is that both the natural and the cultural sciences rest on a residual uncertainty about the precise relationship between phenomena and noumena. Kant was clear that this was not a determinate, one-to-one relationship of correspondence and so he left open the possibility that knowledge may tell us more about the mind of the knowing subject than it does about the properties of the external world. The fundamental problem of knowledge is the question of what, if anything, can be said about the relationship between 'appearances' and 'reality': 'How can the mind come into secure possession of an authentic truth about a reality that is altogether independent of its own activities?' (Rescher 2000: 11). That is, can we have any certainty that the phenomena of experience are, in any sense, 'true' representations of the noumena? Many scientists turned a blind eye to this problem. Glossing the distinction between sense impressions and conceptual objects, they implicitly assumed the very correspondence theory of truth that Kant had identified – and rejected – in Hume.

Kant had recognised that his epistemology did not go far enough. He had shown that it is never possible to know whether we have adequately grasped the true nature of the noumenal world. There is no way of checking our empirical knowledge against 'reality' except through the acquisition of further empirical knowledge, and this can be accepted as valid only if it, too, has been checked against yet more knowledge: and so the process continues. Direct knowledge of the noumena recedes as rapidly as we think we may be approaching it. The relationship that exists between phenomena and noumena can never itself become an object of human experience, and so it is not a matter to which the usual ideas of truth and falsity can be applied.

Kant did not himself draw strong relativistic conclusions from this argument. The categories of the mind, he argued, are universal – they are the same for all people in all societies and at all historical periods. This is because they are innate, inborn. The knowledge that results from the use of the categories, then, is independent of any particular observer, as any physiologically and psychologically competent observer would have the same experiences and would construct the same theoretical objects from them. Knowledge is relative to the human condition – this is what makes it 'human knowledge' – but it is not relative to *particular* human observers. At a deeper level, however, Kant recognised that the problem remained: we may all see the same things, but we may all be mistaken. Kant resorted to what he called a 'transcendental' solution to this problem. He held that knowledge is not limited by the physiological characteristics of individual knowing subjects because these are *designed* to give humans an accurate picture of the world. There is a transcendental subject – God – who created human beings with precisely the kind of mental and physiological apparatus that would allow them to acquire objective and true knowledge of the rest of his creation. God can be presumed not to wish to mislead individuals about the nature of reality and so human knowledge – thanks to its transcendental subjectivity – can be relied on as *certain* knowledge.

This transcendental argument has been less attractive to later writers because of its logical difficulties. In grounding the acquisition of knowledge in the existence of God, Kant was caught in a dilemma. Any such God must occupy the noumenal world, and knowledge of this God is limited in exactly the same way as any other knowledge. This limitation cannot be escaped by invoking the existence of a God with specific characteristics, as this would be an assertion from faith rather than a true empirical report.[3] The existence of God is a matter of belief and faith,

---

[3]But see William James (1902), who tried to use subjective religious experiences as evidence for spiritual existence.

and anyone who lacks such a prior belief will not find the transcendental argument convincing. Thus, the spectre of relativity haunted the Kantian approach, despite the apparent solution that he provided.

Weber – famously irreligious – justified his claims for objectivity and truth through reliance on the formal properties of scientific enquiry, arguing that these can allow both the natural sciences and the cultural sciences to achieve the maximum possible objectivity. He held that value-relevant knowledge can be objective knowledge so long as social scientists adhere to the impersonal standards of scientific enquiry to handle their factual evidence (Weber 1904: 66–71). Objectivity, therefore, is ensured by the formal, technical rationality of the scientific method: by careful observation and measurement, appropriate quantification, conceptual precision, clear operationalisation, and logical procedures of analysis, deduction and inference. This solution rested on the assumption that the noumenal world may not be directly reflected in our concepts but it does, nevertheless, *constrain* the possible constructions that can be placed upon it. If an observer follows the scientific procedures of rational, critical enquiry, the conjectural knowledge produced is tested against an independently existing reality and so can be regarded as 'objective', as adequate enough to grasp key features of the world for all practical purposes. We will return to consider the adequacy of this argument later in this book.

Talcott Parsons was principally responsible for establishing the Kantian position as the implicit and unquestioned basis of theory in the social sciences. Although the Kantian intellectual scaffolding was often ignored by those who pursued a scientific sociology, the conclusions that Parsons drew from it were, from the 1930s to the 1960s, at the heart of what it meant to do sociology. In his commentary on the Kantian tradition, Parsons (1937) identified the close relationship between concepts and values as general principles of selection. Factual statements are descriptive statements about sensuous impressions, about the phenomena of experience, and are cast in terms of a value-relevant conceptual scheme (Parsons 1937: 28, 41–2; see also Henderson 1932). Such conceptual schemes are frames of reference that comprise the categories of sensibility, the concepts of understanding, and the general and/or value concepts that allow scientific description. Parsons argued that all work in social science – including Weber's own substantive sociology – combines the two principles of selection. The infinite and unknowable character of noumenal reality means that the application of the cognitive interests cannot be arbitrarily limited, and both generalising and individualising strategies have their part to play in any science. Sociology, he argued, has both its *analytical* and its *historical* dimensions, and neither can be privileged above the other (Parsons 1937: 595). The analytical aspects of social science involve the use of general concepts to formulate theoretical explanations, while the historical aspects use value concepts to formulate historical descriptions. Parsons found examples of analytical work in the social sciences in the attempts by economists to formulate general laws of economic action at both the macro- and the micro-levels and the parallel attempts of political scientists and sociologists to formulate laws and generalisations about the systematically organised properties of action (see his own examples in Parsons and Smelser 1956; Parsons 1963a, 1963b). He recognised, however, that any such laws hold only under specific historical conditions and that social scientists also had to construct descriptive accounts of particular societies and the historical processes through which they change (Parsons 1966, 1971). Parsons saw Weber's study of the Protestant ethic and capitalism – which he was the first to translate into English (Parsons 1930) – as the central example of such historical work. Durkheim's *Suicide* (1897), on the other hand, was a classic example of analytical work in sociology. These two studies came to be the unproblematic exemplars or paradigms of sociological research for a whole generation of sociologists.

Thus, we always find the coexistence of intellectual matrices in any science or specialism, and these will be marked by a particular power balance among their adherents (Foucault 1966, 1971) – successful matrices of normal science attract research funding, publications, etc. Within any science, however, there will be a messy pattern of development in which there will be areas of normal science exhibiting progress as well as non-paradigmatic matrices within which less focused research takes place. Such matrices are often mutually incommensurable. They may not be incompatible and may overlap in numerous respects, so this complicates it...

The Kantian approach to knowledge seemed to provide a partial basis for the construction of objective scientific knowledge. Within the mainstream of sociology, the conclusions of this debate for methodological practice were accepted, though the basis in Kantian philosophy was often ignored or unrecognised, and many advocates of this mainstream position reverted to naïve forms of scientific realism whenever a philosophical justification was felt to be necessary. Such assertions of simplistic correspondence theories of truth were the basis of the view of its critics that the mainstream was naïvely 'positivistic' (Keat and Urry 1975). On this basis, the mainstream sociology of the 1950s and 1960s felt that relativism had been vanquished and diverse theoretical positions could be compared and assessed through factual investigation alone.

Perspectives and plurality

The unresolved logical problems of the Kantian position made many uneasy and meant that sociology was periodically challenged by critical positions that reasserted the radical diversity of social knowledge. This tendency was strengthened after Kuhn's work (Kuhn 1962) had appeared to challenge the objectivity and truth claims of the natural sciences. Kuhn held that any tradition of research is based around a specific intellectual matrix[4] that comprises the core assumptions, concepts and methods around which scientific activity is organised. The intellectual matrix comprises 'the entire constellation of beliefs, values, techniques, and so on shared by members of a given community' (Kuhn 1970: 175). For those who choose to work within that tradition, epistemological uncertainties can be bracketed off and their scientific work can continue unhindered as 'normal science'. Normal science is the routinised, institutionalised science of an ongoing and self-confident specialism or discipline and its 'research programme' (Lakatos 1970).

Normal science is highly directed and focused research. It is 'an attempt to force nature into the preformed and relatively inflexible box that the paradigm supplies' and allows 'an articulation of those phenomena and theories that the paradigm already supplies' (Kuhn 1962: 24). Normal scientific research involves the measurement and determination of critical facts and the testing of factual predictions, and the theoretical articulation of established concepts in such a way as to increase the scope of the paradigm and the precision with which it can be applied. It consists of 'puzzle solving': searching into problems that are assumed to have a solution. The practitioners of normal science 'concentrate on problems that only their own lack of ingenuity should keep them from solving' (Kuhn 1962: 37).

Consolidation around a particular intellectual matrix and its paradigms breaks down when the matrix can no longer sustain the ongoing practices of normal science. This process is driven by anomalies. An anomaly exists as 'the recognition that nature has somehow violated the paradigm-induced expectations that govern normal science' (Kuhn 1962: 52–3). That is, the attempt to use existing categories and concepts to construct sense impressions into anticipated phenomena is confounded by discrepant or inexplicable observations. If anomalous observations and unresolved puzzles accumulate, members of a scientific group may come to question the comprehensiveness and generality of their matrix and working assumptions. They search for an alternative and may be more open to rival, emergent or submerged theoretical views. The shift from one matrix to another is a 'scientific revolution' (Kuhn 1962: 90, 92ff.): 'The transition from a paradigm in crisis to a new one from which a new tradition of normal science can emerge is far from a cumulative process, one achieved by an articulation or extension of the old paradigm. Rather it is a reconstruction of the field from new

---

[4]Kuhn's term is 'disciplinary matrix' (Kuhn 1970: 182; and see Masterman 1970), introduced to resolve some ambiguity in his use of the term 'paradigm'. This term, however, is too closely tied to the idea of a scientific discipline or specialism, and the proposed term 'intellectual matrix' is more general.

fundamentals' (Kuhn 1962: 84–5). In such a revolution, a new intellectual matrix is adopted and practitioners come to see the world differently.

The change from one theoretical standpoint to another is not a purely cognitive process. One theory cannot be assessed as 'better' than another but simply as 'different' and as offering greater practical power. Theoretical choice is, therefore, a 'political' matter in the broadest sense. The fact that social science relied on the use of value-relevant concepts made this argument especially appealing to many of those who held doubts about the scientific status of sociology. Some drew the conclusion that sociology was condemned to an eternal and irresolvable clash of rival principles of explanation among which choices were to be made on moral and political grounds (Friedrichs 1970).

It was increasingly argued that the divergent values of observers – values rooted in differences of class, gender, ethnicity and nationality – required an embrace of plurality and the abandonment of any conception of objectivity and truth. Particularly important in these claims was a rediscovery of the ideas of Friedrich Nietzsche, who had recognised problems in the Kantian position and had articulated a view of the situational determination of knowledge into a full-blown perspectival model of knowledge.

Artur Schopenhauer (1818) had been the first to radicalise the Kantian idea of the world as representation. Accepting Kant's argument that perceptions and knowledge are fundamentally grounded in human subjectivity, rather than in any external reality, Schopenhauer argued that the thinking subject must be seen as a psychological subject, as a living, embodied agent with no universal characteristics. The body is a natural object that comes to know the world through purposive action (Schopenhauer 1818: 119). As purpose – 'will' – is the undetermined force that drives all knowledge and experience, all knowledge must be regarded as 'deception' or illusion, as nothingness.

Nietzsche (1887) pursued this idea of the embodied subject. He held that Kant's fundamental mistake had been to detach the human self both from its body and from the world in which it lives. A thinking self is *embodied* in a human organism and *embedded* in history. It follows that there can be no universal or objective categories, concepts or values, but only ideas that embodied and embedded agents project in their purposive thoughts and actions.[5] All knowledge is situated knowledge and gives a view of the world from the particular situation of the subject. There can be no anonymous or ungrounded point of view: there is no 'view from nowhere', as all knowledge must be a view from somewhere. Knowledge is always and necessarily grounded in the particular viewpoints constituted by the bodily and historical location of particular knowing subjects.

---

[5]The embodied perspective in Nietzsche has parallels with Bourdieu's (1972, 1980) idea of bodily 'habitus' and its association with structured dispositions and tendencies of thought and action.

The subjectivity of knowledge, for Nietzsche, is grounded in the will of the subject. The human subject is a cluster of more or less fragmented and contradictory
drives and willed impulses, and human wills must be understood as combina-
tions of feelings and thoughts, of emotions and interpretations. Each human subject, therefore, comprises a specific diversity of historically conditioned impulses.
The drives and wills of a subject may be co-ordinated, to a greater or lesser
degree, through a commanding or leading drive that is expressed in its purposive,
practical agency and that forms the subject as a unified entity. Nietzsche called
this leading drive the 'will to power'. Humans act on ideas in order to achieve
particular goals, and those ideas that enhance their power to achieve those goals
are retained and reinforce their drive to pursue their interests. The will to power
develops whenever it sustains feelings of power and autonomous agency. The
channelling of bodily drives into specific patterns of orientation and action
produces a 'cultural complex' that shapes the values and ideas of subjects and
defines their particular 'perspective' on knowledge. A perspective is a complex
network of concepts and ideas that sets 'a field of visibility bonded by a perceptual horizon' (Owen 1995: 34). A perspective derives from the practical interests,
both cognitive and affective, that define a person's point of view and that are the
basis of the will to power (Clark 1990). Knowledge is reformulated when it no
longer allows people to satisfy their cognitive and affective interests. Knowledge
and agency are inextricably and reciprocally linked. Knowledge allows people to
define or 'recognise' themselves as particular kinds of agents with specific capacities for action, and the ways in which they act provide them with the perspective
from which they construct their knowledge.

This argument had a great influence on Weber, and inspired more radical
readings of Weber's arguments that stress Weber's claim that there are multiple value standpoints from which cultural meanings can be constructed and
that no pattern or purpose to cultural reality can be grasped independently of
the standpoints of the individual human beings who constitute it. Weber had
argued that the cultural sciences are undertaken from particular value-relevant
points of view and that there is a specific 'focus of attention on reality under
the guidance of values which lend it significance' (Weber 1904: 77). 'All knowledge of cultural reality ... is always knowledge from particular points of view'
(ibid.: 81, emphasis removed). It is the perspective that determines the limits
and possibilities for all knowledge. All science is subjective interpretation: there
are no 'facts', only interpretations. Purposive activity constitutes a perspective
for the will and gives it its centre of gravity.

This was the position that led Nietzsche to his radical relativism. Perspectives,
he held, not only differ from one individual to another, but also differ over time
for particular individuals. During the course of their lives, and even over very
short periods, people occupy many different locations. Each location gives them

a different point of view and therefore generates a different body of knowledge. As they move around the physical world, they see it and experience it from successively different positions, and it is only when identical locations are occupied that identical bodies of knowledge are generated. Similarly, social movement and social circulation ensure that any individual will see and interpret the world from a variety of social locations, each of which provides specific practical interests for the acquisition of knowledge and so yields particular constructions of knowledge.

Nietzsche saw, however, certain limits to this radical relativity. Each individual possesses a continuity of self through the various locations occupied, and so a person will construct his or her knowledge in a way that reflects the particular biographical trajectory or combination of locations that they have occupied. In this way, situational knowledges are brought together into synthetic worldviews for each individual and even for particular categories of individual who show similar patterns of movement. Such worldviews, however, may not be coherent or fully integrated, as life trajectories are neither coherent nor integrated. Bodies of knowledge, which may be to a greater or lesser extent mutually contradictory, may be combined together in the mind of any particular individual or the minds of a group of individuals.

Nietzsche saw little relevance for the idea of 'truth', seeing it, as Schopenhauer had done, as mere mystification. As there is no knowable external reality to which people can compare their knowledge, there can be no truth. The most that can be achieved is the production of a broader worldview through the combining together of the different partial perspectives that various individuals derive from the diverse spheres of life in which they are involved. Just as an individual can bring some order to the chaos of perspectives that he or she passes through during the course of a single lifetime, so it may be possible to achieve an even broader frame of knowledge by comparing and collating the divergent perspectives and worldviews of different individuals:

> there is *only* a perspective seeing, only a perspective 'knowing'; and the *more* effects we allow to speak about one thing, the *more* eyes, different eyes, we use to observe one thing, the more complete will our 'concept' of this thing, our 'object' be. (Nietzsche 1887: III, Section 12)

This 'completeness', it must be emphasised, is not judged in relation to a thing in itself, as Nietzsche followed Kant's rejection of the epistemological relevance of noumena. Perspective knowledge is not knowledge of an external, noumenal world. Nietzsche rejected the very idea of acquiring knowledge of the thing in itself or of the associated ideas of cause, necessity and coercion. All such ideas are concepts that we have invented in order to describe our perspectival experiences (Nietzsche 1887: 21). Completeness results from the fact that all perspectives have an equivalent status. There is no way of judging one as better than another: all perspectives are partial, in the sense that they reflect standpoints and interests, and they are all equally valid. A richer and fuller view can be obtained, therefore, only by combining them together. For example, those in different physical locations will see a chair in different ways and each description is, in principle, 'true', given the location of the observer. There is no possibility of describing *the* chair 'as it really is', independently of any particular perspective. There is no anonymous standpoint from which it is possible to arbitrate between bodies of knowledge. The combination and synthesis of perspectives, then, does not produce a more 'accurate' representation of something existing outside knowledge. It produces a richer and more comprehensive view precisely because it retains and articulates the separate descriptions produced from various perspectives.

This argument is linked to Nietzsche's radical decentring of knowledge. Although I have, for convenience, discussed his views in relation to individuals, he does not treat the individual ego, in Cartesian manner, as an absolutely certain starting point. Though we may intuitively say 'I think' or 'I will', there is no way that it is possible to establish that there is an 'I' that thinks or wills. All that can truly be said is that 'there is thinking', 'there is willing', or 'there is feeling' (Nietzsche 1886: 17). Knowledge is a kaleidoscopic concatenation produced from the thinking, feeling and acting that takes place. A totality of tessellated knowledges can be posited as a necessary consequence of the existence of a plurality of knowledges, but this can neither be grasped nor analysed as a totality. The complex totality within which we live exists and can be inferred, but it cannot be grasped as a single picture within an individual mind. It is as illusory as it is real, and the very distinction between illusion and reality become meaningless.

Their relativist position was implied, though not stated, by Howard Becker (1967), who asked 'whose side are we on?'. He argued that all of social life is a matter of values and so it is not possible to regard one view as correct and another as false: they are simply different definitions of a contested reality. Sociologists must, inevitably, side with one point of view or the other: 'We must always look at the matter from someone's point of view' (1967: 131). The crucial question is simply that of *whose side* to take in this contest to define reality, and this choice is dictated by our own value preferences. Becker's own preference was to look at things from the standpoint of the subordinates, the 'underdogs', whose voices tend to be otherwise ignored by the powerful. More radically, Marxist, feminist, and post-colonial writers have emphasised that the existence of divergent definitions is not simply a matter of values but of the actual social location of a group: people cannot avoid seeing the world from a particular standpoint that is beyond their direct control and derives from their location within specific social relations.

These arguments of Nietzsche have also informed the work of Michel Foucault (1971), who has had a major influence on contemporary ideas of the relativity of knowledge. Foucault took up the ideas of Roland Barthes and Jacques Derrida on discourse, but gave these a social dimension that related discourse to the exercise of power. Barthes and Derrida stressed discourse as a textual phenomenon, to be analysed in purely internal and logical terms through, for example, the linguistic and literary rules that allow particular statements to be formed. Foucault's social concept of discourse directed attention to the historical conditions that allow one statement rather than another to actually appear in texts. Where Barthes and Derrida were mainly concerned with discursive *competence*, Foucault turned his attention to discursive *performance*. Thus, a corpus of statements, such as those conventionally labelled as 'medicine', 'economics', or 'sociology' may seem to be only loosely integrated, composed of numerous incompatible elements: they exist as 'systems of dispersion'. The task of an 'archaeology of knowledge' is to uncover whatever regularity or order might exist in these statements, and whenever such regularities can be uncovered, Foucault defined the corpus as a 'discursive formation' or, simply a discourse. To describe a corpus of statements as a discursive formation is to say that it exhibits an underlying order that reflects the perspective or 'gaze' adopted by those who produced it. Discursive formations, then, are aggregations of texts and social institutions that articulate the power relations of those involved in the institutions (Foucault 1982).

Lyotard (1979) extended these ideas to build the basis of contemporary postmodernism. He argued that the plurality and diversity that is apparent in scientific knowledge reflects the entry of contemporary societies into a postmodern condition in which all thought can, finally, be recognised as relative, partial and limited. In pre-modern societies, he argues, certainty and truth were sustained by tradition and custom: people simply accepted, without question, all that they inherited from the past. Modern societies initiated a break with tradition and opened up all matters to reflexive criticism. The postmodern condition is marked by the final abandonment of the search for absolute certainty: the 'grand narratives' of 'truth', 'objectivity' and 'science' lose their credibility as reflexive scepticism comes to pervade the whole of human life. From this point of view, people are able to express only their own views and perceptions with any certainty. The worlds that we describe and in which we act are constructions made by embodied, located observers and there can be no question of assessing these constructions against an external reality. All perspectives are equally valid as possible worlds. No individual can claim a privileged status for his or her views; nor can they effectively challenge the views of others. We simply have to accept that we live in a world of complex and contradictory intellectual 'simulations' (Baudrillard 1977).

Discussion

————Gayle ————————————————————————————

JOHN'S ACCOUNT OF THE FOUNDATIONS of the claims for an objective social science and the counter-claims and challenges that followed reminds me of my own struggles in taking an epistemological position. I accept that knowledge is always specific to time and place and we always collect and analyse data from our own political, personal and intellectual perspective. As a feminist sociologist, I attempt to create social and political change and I am aware that this affects my approach while at the same time acknowledging that it is me who does the final edit, who makes the final decision about what my respondents 'really meant'. With this in mind, I am sensitive to issues of power and control throughout the whole research process and have always tried to highlight my role in the choice of research questions and methods and the selection and interpretation of respondents' narratives and accounts when presenting research 'findings'. As I argue in Chapter 5, I agree with others who have argued that everyone theorises about their own place in the social world, but as researchers we further categorise, and analyse and eventually reach conclusions based on our interpretation of the data and the academic and political theories and understandings to which we have access.

I start from an epistemological position that rejects both a simplistic foundationalist standpoint position and a position of complete relativism. I do not believe that I am able to generate the 'true story' of the social world, but by asking different sorts of questions of under-researched groups and about less studied issues I believe that my research highlights complexities of differences of experience that have previously been overlooked or ignored. I acknowledge the impossibility of full representation, but an approach which may possibly involve a less than complete representation of the other is better than no representation at all. Thus, I believe that 'my story' can stand as a challenge to, in opposition to and as a criticism of 'other stories'. I also believe that in order for our work to be valuable and accountable our research choices and practices must be transparent. Thus, an explicit account of the knowing/doing relationship is essential for the knowledge we produce to be open to critique by others and to have any meaning or status at all.

————Malcolm ————————————————————————————

I TOO WRESTLED WITH THE problem of foundationalism versus relativism. If I were forced to choose one over the other as the lesser evil (though I'd rather not), it would be foundationalism. I say this because like the foundations of a building, epistemological foundations do not go to infinite depth. Science proposes and the empirical world disposes. Flawed research programmes can continue to exist for a long time – in the social sciences too – but if they are contradictory or not fruitful in terms of results, they get abandoned. The noumenal world notwithstanding, truth will be partly visible through error. We may not be able to prove conclusively X is the case, but sometimes we can prove that it is not. Science at its most positivist and 'foundationalist', from around 1860 to 1960, gave us the discoveries of Einstein, Bohr, Crick and Watson, and in social science the work of Rowntree and Booth, the Lynds and Keynes, and it also produced many intellectual blind alleys and errors. This is not to defend it, because I think there are better models of science, but simply to say that even the most dogmatic foundationalism won't save a bad theory in the long run.

There is something rather hypocritical about epistemological relativity, at least of the Nietzchean or Lyotard kind. A denial of the concept of truth becomes a performative contradiction in an everyday life that requires us to believe that aeroplanes can fly, food nourishes and mostly people are not lying to us. A denial of the possibility of truth conflates different ways of using the term 'true' or 'truth'. What is almost certainly the case is that complete truth, or even the complete truth about a particular thing, is not knowable principally because we would not know that we knew! But this is not the same as saying 'I know that Gayle lives in Plymouth', a statement that is empirically verifiable and is either true or not true. We absolutely require a truth with practical adequacy to exist in the world. Similarly, the search for truth that will reveal practical knowledge seems to me to be a worthwhile enterprise and a pillar of objectivity.

━━━John

MY PHILOSOPHICAL DISCUSSION HAS, I see, marked a fruitful starting point for our journey through the debates on objectivity and truth. Both Gayle and Malcolm have recognised that the Scylla of foundationalism and the Charybdis of relativism are the dangers that, like Odysseus in his navigation through the Mediterranean and Adriatic, we must seek to avoid. Gayle rejects foundationalism, though she does not wish to embrace relativism. Malcolm chooses, albeit reluctantly, foundationalism. When Odysseus took the advice of Circe and sailed closer to Scylla than to Charybdis, six of his crew were devoured. Malcolm may be in danger of having some of his comfortable beliefs devoured if he remains too close to foundationalism.

There is, in fact, a third way between foundationalism and relativism. This is a position that recognises the power and importance of each pole in the dilemma but seeks to reconcile these and to defuse their ravenous energy to destroy rational scientific enterprise. This third way is explored in the next chapter, which suggests that a proper starting point for knowledge can be found through recognising but transcending the relativity of knowledge.

THREE

Relationism and Dynamic Synthesis

The relativistic arguments reviewed in Chapter 2 claimed that our knowledge of the world depends upon the position that we occupy in it. In this chapter we turn to various arguments that have been put forward to ground this perspectival or standpoint approach to knowledge and we present a first step towards overcoming their relativistic implications.

──John's argument ────────────────────────────────────

A BASIS FOR UNDERSTANDING PERSPECTIVAL approaches was explored by Karl Mannheim in the sociology of knowledge that he built during the 1920s and 1930s. Mannheim allied the historically informed arguments of Hegel and Dilthey with Nietzsche's perspectivism in order to reconstruct Marx's claims about the relationship between human consciousness and mental activity (Mannheim 1922, 1923, 1924).[1] He saw the sociology of knowledge as a way of providing a firmer foundation for Weber's claims for the objectivity of science and the role of scientific method in achieving this.

Mannheim's argument was that people's social locations consist of their social relations with others and, through these, their relations to their history and the natural environment. This 'existential embeddedness' in a communal lifeworld shapes life chances, interests and opportunities for action. Those who occupy a similar social location will tend to have a similar range of experiences and opportunities and so will be enabled and constrained in similar ways in their actions. Social locations provide the standpoints from which subjective value preferences are formed and from which perspectives on knowledge derive. They are, therefore, the social and personal bases from which objects of knowledge can be constructed. While Weber had said little about the origins of values, seeing them simply as arbitrary and irrational conditions for practical actions, Mannheim traced them back to the whole way of life followed by a

─────────────

[1]For Mannheim's comments on the importance of Nietzsche, alongside Marx, to the sociology of knowledge see his 'The problem of the sociology of knowledge' (1931: 278). See also Antonio (1995).

person or social group. Shared values are social facts that must be understood in relation to a person's social location (Mannheim 1929b, 1931).

This led Mannheim to the conclusion that a diversity of perspectives is an inescapable consequence of the social character of human existence. It is impossible for people to escape the interests, values and general concepts that are reproduced and transformed in their historically-situated actions, and the diversity of historical action is the basis of a diversity of historical experience and perception. Individuals select and interpret the objects of their knowledge from the particular standpoints that they occupy, and the world of objects that they construct is, therefore, relative to their social location. It is their location that determines how and in what respect reality is accessible to a person and how this can be conceptualised (Remmling 1975). Mannheim argued that:

> the world is known through many different orientations because there are many simultaneous and mutually contradictory trends of thought … struggling against one another with their different interpretations of 'common' experience. (Mannheim 1931: 241)

These arguments rest on the Nietzschean view that all social systems are organised around a fundamental power division between the 'master' ('noble' or 'overman') position of the principal actors and the 'slave' (or 'last man') position of subaltern underdogs. Social locations are power relations between principals – the dominant group or social category – and the subordinate subalterns (Scott 2001: Chapter 1). The standpoint of the principals is integrally linked to the pattern of domination from which they benefit and is the basis of knowledge that accords with and legitimates their position, while the standpoint of the subalterns is the basis of knowledge that embodies an experience of subjection and oppression and that may, therefore, be explicitly critical of the dominant viewpoint. Dominant ideas, Mannheim argued, are often formulated as claims to universality, to objectivity and impartial knowledge. Such universality is, however, a false consciousness, an 'ideology': what is expressed as the impartial and anonymous view from nowhere (or the view of God) is nothing more than the authentic or inauthentic expression of the interests and concerns of the principals. The perspective of the subaltern, on the other hand, reflects its own oppression and implies a critique of the power of the principals. Their ideas may, then, be formulated as utopian and emancipatory claims of liberation from oppression.

Mannheim followed György Lukács and the Marxist tradition in taking class positions as the crucial social locations shaping perspectives on knowledge, but he also recognised generational differences as sources of shared experiences and interests (Mannheim 1927). Other 'bases of collective existence' that he identified as shaping perspectives and knowledge include situations of competition (Mannheim 1929a), professional or scholastic education, status distinctions, religious sectarianism and occupational groups (Mannheim 1931). As a Hungarian Jew working in Germany and exiled to Britain, he is also, no doubt, likely to have seen ethnic differences as a further source of perspectival differentiation. The important point that he made, however, was that the empirical question of *which* locations are important in particular cases should not be prejudged. It was important to recognise that *any* social location must have such an effect. Mannheim recognised, also, that the various sources of social differentiation cross-cut and intersect – much as Nietzsche had argued – and that any individual knowing subject can be seen as the 'condensation' of the particular combination of social positions that he or she occupies. Behind these cross-cutting divisions he recognised class divisions as basic, as all other social divisions, he felt, are dependent on the structure of production and domination.

These same ideas have been elaborated in a variety of standpoint theories. The class standpoint theories of Marxism were the earliest and, until recently, the most influential. According to this position, class divisions are the fundamental social divisions and all variations in knowledge can be reduced to the class location of the observer. The rise of second-wave feminism from the 1970s involved a number of writers who stressed gender divisions and the consequent male and female standpoints from which experiences necessarily inform knowledge construction. Most recently, post-colonial studies have reinforced arguments that concern the centrality of racial and ethnic divisions and the consequent differentiation of the coloniser and the colonised standpoints on knowledge.

Within each of these approaches, a complete relativism has been avoided by an implicit or explicit epistemological privileging of the consciousness associated with one standpoint over all others. Specifically, subaltern groups – the disadvantaged and the oppressed – are seen as having the possibility for a greater insight into the nature of the world by virtue of their subordination. Marxists stress the superiority of proletarian consciousness over bourgeois illusions; feminists stress the superiority of women's perspectives in the face of 'malestream' knowledge, and post-colonial theorists stress the superiority of the viewpoint of the colonised. In each case, there has also been a recognition that social scientists and others engaged in intellectual activity play a key role in giving voice to the subaltern standpoint and in mediating its relations with other forms of consciousness. These arguments are explored in the following sections, and the argument then returns to Mannheim's arguments to see whether a more secure avoidance of relativism is possible.

Class standpoints in the Marxian tradition

Karl Marx saw all forms of consciousness as reflections of what he called 'social being' (Marx 1844b; Marx and Engels 1846). The way in which humans live their lives with one another is the basis on which they develop a consciousness of the human condition. In actual societies, however, there is no single 'human' standpoint, as Feuerbach (1841) had believed, because social conditions vary considerably. Human standpoints vary with the historical conditions and material circumstances in which people find themselves. Consciousness varies with social conditions and so forms of consciousness must be recognised as necessarily being merely partial views of the world. They may, nevertheless, be taken as valid and authentic guides to how particular people do, as a matter of fact, see the world and construct their actions.

The particular social circumstances emphasised by Marx were the historically formed class relations, rooted in property and lack of property, and the material interests that these generate (Marx and Engels 1848). Historically formed property relations structure material production and distribution by defining employment conditions and work relations – they define the position occupied in a technical division of labour, subjection to authority and surveillance, and socially organised conditions of work. Class relations are the bases of all life chances available, or unavailable, to workers and employers and those with whom they live in their families and neighbourhoods. In this way, they condition particular and shared social experiences.

The particular circumstances of a class or class fraction set horizons of possibility for class members and sustain a definite consciousness that dominant classes, such as the capitalist bourgeoisie, foster ideas that express and articulate the material relations from which they derive their advantages; and subordinate classes, such as the proletariat, foster ideas that express their alienation and oppression by the dominant class and the structure of class relations that it sustains. Actually, existing consciousness draws on ideas inherited from the past and reflects their current experiences, concerns and aspirations, and may differ from the potential consciousness inherent in their class position. Marx adds that control over the means of production gives control over the means of communication and education, ensuring that the ideas of the ruling class become the ruling ideas of their society. Forms of consciousness are narrowly 'ideological' when they are presented as universal views that are true for all, regardless of circumstances. The ideas that they originate are disseminated across the whole society and become its dominant ideology (Marx and Engels 1846: 64). The dominant ideology is the basis of a 'false consciousness' in the subordinate class, a consciousness that misunderstands or misrepresents its own partiality. In ideology, things as they appear from particular historical and material circumstances are, falsely, taken to be things as they really are: 'appearances' or 'illusions' are misrepresented as 'essences'.

When the dominant ideas become a part of the consciousness of the subordinate class, the latter has what Gramsci (1929–35) called 'dual consciousness': they develop a consciousness rooted in their own immediate experiences of material oppression, but this may remain latent as they also take over the ideas they acquire through their exposure to the dominant ideas. Because the consciousness of a subordinate class is complex and contradictory, it may be an inauthentic guide to the realities of their situation. Referring to the proletariat in capitalist society, Marx and Engels held that:

> It is not a question of what this or that proletarian, or even the whole prole-
> tariat, at the moment *regards* as its aim. It is a question of *what the proletariat
> is*, and what, in accordance with this *being*, it will historically be compelled
> to do. Its aim and historical action is visibly and irrevocably foreshadowed in
> its own life situation as well as in the whole organisation of bourgeois society
> today. (Marx and Engels 1845: 47)

What this means is that the true consciousness of the proletariat follows from
its social location, from the social relations within which its activities must take
place. As these conditions are alienating and oppressive, they produce experiences from which proletarians can learn and can come to realise the need to
change their social relations. At any one time, however, their dual consciousness may prevent them from achieving this insight and understanding.

It is on this basis that Marx developed his account of the role of intellectuals
in class struggle. A key task for intellectuals, he held, is to engage with ideolo-
gies through a critique that grasps the partiality of all appearances and makes
people aware of their social circumstances and the consequent limitations on
their viewpoint. Partiality may be unavoidable, but people can become reflexively aware of the partiality of their own knowledge (Lichtheim 1965: 20). For
Marx, then, objective or true consciousness is that which is critically aware of
its own social determination.

Marx did assume, nevertheless, that a truth could be discovered, even if real,
historically located individuals could not attain it. This true representation of
the historical process is one that is valid for all people and is, therefore, the
only valid guide for practical action aimed at emancipating people from their
alienation, exploitation and oppression. In his early work, he saw this truth as
rooted in a universal 'species being' that is masked by historically specific forms
of alienation (Marx 1844a). This species being comprises the 'nature' of people
as human beings and the creative potentials of existence they possess by virtue
of this. The underlying unity of humankind provides a standpoint from which
all other knowledge can be judged, if only this standpoint could be attained
under real historical conditions. Marx saw his own intellectual work as an
attempt to engage with the ideas of the bourgeoisie and the proletariat in order
to move proletarian consciousness closer to this underlying true consciousness.

This position is difficult to sustain without a resort to the positivist arguments that became the dominant tendency in later Marxist orthodoxy. Both
Engels (1886) and Lenin (1909) tended to see scientific consciousness as a direct
reflection of reality and so held that Marxism, as a scientific social theory, provided a true knowledge that transcends all limited class standpoints. Lukács
rejected this positivist position, seeing science itself as a bourgeois illusion.
Instead, he sought a different basis for a 'standpoint of totality' from which
truth could be grasped. His solution was to make a Romantic wager on the

proletariat as capable, in the long term, of attaining this standpoint. He therefore placed his faith in the creative potential of the collective action of the
historically most oppressed social class, much as the Russian populists had
placed their faith in the peasantry. The proletariat, Lukács held, is the 'identical
subject–object' of history. The extent of its alienation is such that it is the 'condensation' of all oppressions and so can be considered as the 'universal class'.
As the final and most extreme sufferers from the alienation induced by class
relations, it is the historical embodiment of humankind's species being and the
drive to emancipate itself from alienation (Lukács, 1967).

This led Lukács to reinterpret the role of intellectuals. In practical politics, it
is necessary for the proletariat to develop from its actual, partial consciousness
to the truly universal 'revolutionary' consciousness of which it is capable. This
latter consciousness, 'imputed' to it by Marxist theory, is brought to it by the
Marxist intellectuals who join with its members in socialist and communist
parties. The intellectuals in the party – those who have made the wager on the
proletariat – must put their skills in its service and, by engaging with proletarians in practical struggles, guide them towards the universal consciousness that
will allow them to achieve their own liberation.

Gendered standpoints and feminist theory

The first wave of feminist thought at the end of the nineteenth century and in
the first decades of the twentieth century raised issues about gender divisions that
had rarely been broached before (but see Wollstonecraft 1792). While some male
sociologists had, indeed, contrasted the social positions of men and women, they
had largely seen these in terms of conventional domestic roles. Olive Schreiner
(1899) and Charlotte Gilman (1911) were the leading thinkers to develop a radical understanding of male oppression of women. These insights did not enter
the mainstream of social theory until the emergence of so-called second-wave
feminism in the 1970s. Central to these feminist arguments is the idea that the
distinctive position that women occupy *vis-à-vis* men is the source of quite distinct perceptions and experiences of the world. Women's thinking and knowledge
are consequences of their distinct social position, which they explored through
a distinction between biologically given 'sex' and culturally defined 'gender'
(Friedan 1962). Radical feminists held that existing bodies of social theory were
structured around male views of the world and they challenged this 'malestream'
knowledge with views that they held to be rooted in the distinctive position and
standpoint of women. Far from seeing biological sex as justifying 'natural' and
obvious gender differences, however, the radical feminists saw gender as mal-
leable and variable, as reflecting and contributing to socially established power
differences between men and women. They recognised that, in modern societies

at least, there are strong links between sex and gender in systems of 'patriarchy', and this led them to re-evaluate the part played by biology in the social construction of gender. Their work on sexuality, the intimate and reproduction saw these 'private' relations as the focus of women's specific experiences and perspectives on the 'public' world (Rubin 1975; Rich 1980).

These arguments underpinned the more comprehensive accounts of women's experiences that came to be known as 'feminist standpoint' theorists. Nancy Hartsock (1983a, 1983b) rejected the Enlightenment model of science for its male bias and argued for an epistemology built around an explicit awareness of the gendered character of all human activity. Hartsock turned Lukács's position against itself, arguing that it is not the lived experiences of social classes but those of men and women that are the bases of differences in social knowledge. Bourgeois science was masculine science, and the proletarian standpoint merely reproduces many of its key masculine features. The successor science to bourgeois science, therefore, must be a feminist science, as only the woman's standpoint adequately breaks with the male experience.

Hartsock saw men and women as having different lived realities. Women's activity is largely confined to the family, the home and the domestic sphere, while men have been able to participate actively in the public sphere of economic and political activity. These differential forms of participation, grounded in a sexual division of labour, involve them in experiences and concerns that differ radically and are the basis of a distinctive standpoint and perspective on the world in which they live. The social position of women is defined by its focus on the female body, kinship, sexuality, intimacy and care. Women are closely engaged in the process of human reproduction through child bearing and child raising, and are centrally involved in the nurturing and subsistence of labour of all kinds. This leads women, Hartsock argues, to construct knowledge that is more contextual and reflexive than that of men (see also Chodorow 1978; Haraway 1991).

As formulated by Sandra Harding (1986), the feminist standpoint position involves the view that the oppression of women in their everyday lives gives them a different standpoint from men. They see and therefore know differently the relations through which they are subordinated to men. Male accounts of reality provide a false objectivity, an assumed 'God's eye view'. Feminist accounts, on the other hand, embody self-reflective, situated knowledge that is rooted in women's immediate experience and their situated intimate concerns. Women's experiences of oppression and social exclusion, and their practical struggles against these, gives them a standpoint from which they can challenge their domination by men. The woman's standpoint is one from which the 'real relations' of domination are visible, as women are compelled to understand both their own position and that of those who oppress them. Hartsock terms this a *feminist* standpoint, rather than simply a 'woman's' standpoint, because she sees it as containing an emancipatory potential that requires particular forms of politics:

> I use the term 'feminist' rather than 'female' ... to indicate both the achieved character of a standpoint and that a standpoint by definition carries liberatory potential. (Hartsock 1983a: 289)

The most forceful and sophisticated formulation of this argument in relation to sociology has been provided by Dorothy Smith in a series of important publications (1987, 1990, 1999).[2] Her central idea is that discourses are mediated through texts – including those written by sociologists – that are integral to the 'relations of ruling'. Sociology and other social sciences, as currently practised, are embedded within the institutional framework of the university system and so embody the power relations that organise it. Thus, 'social science knowledge represents the world from a standpoint in the ruling relations, not from the standpoint of those who are ruled' (Smith 1999: 16). These ruling relations, at their most general, are those of class, gender and racial power, and Smith gives particular attention to their gendered character.

The gendered relations of rule are those of patriarchy: the institutionalised barriers and exclusions that limit women's participation in rule. Patriarchy confines many women to a mode of experience that is organised around giving birth to, caring for, and servicing other people in domestic contexts. Women involved in paid work, on the other hand, have a 'dual consciousness', part deriving from their involvement in patriarchal relations and part from their location in relations of ruling. Men, who depend on the domestic care provided by women, have no need to focus their attention on their own bodily needs and experiences to the same extent as women. Work relations are organised around the presumption that these needs are provided for in the domestic sphere and so will not interfere with participation in the public world of work and politics. The particular patterns of rule and exclusion change over time, and hence the distinctive characteristics of the gendered standpoints also change.

Central to this change is the developing consciousness of the participants and their active concern for emancipatory social change through critique and collective action. Smith sees the production of knowledge within universities as playing a key role in sustaining or subverting the relations of rule and, hence, in blocking or promoting emancipatory change. The patriarchal structures of the universities within which sociological knowledge is produced have reflected the world from a male standpoint. Women who enter academic sociology have

---

[2]Smith (1999) consists of essays written at various points during the 1990s. Smith (1990) is also a collection of essays, one of which on 'The ideological practice of sociology' was a pioneering statement from 1974.

been constrained to think through their experiences in terms of the dominant discourse and so will tend to be alienated from the authenticity of their own experiences. A critique of power is possible only when the relations of ruling and the texts that sustain them are criticised, and such a critique became possible, so far as gender is concerned, when women challenged the dominant discourse for its neglect of their specific experiences. Female academics were able to successfully challenge and, incompletely, transform male-dominated discourse because of their base in the women's movements. It was their activism in movements oriented to resistance and opposition that sustained their challenges to the ruling relations as they appear in the universities. Central to this challenge was the placing of women's experiences in a central position, so allowing the construction of knowledge from a 'woman's standpoint'. This did not simply involve adding an extra set of special topics to existing sociology, but required its complete recasting:

> It is not enough to supplement an established sociology by addressing ourselves to what has been left out or overlooked, or by making women's issues into sociological issues. That does not change the standpoint built into existing sociological procedures, but merely makes the sociology of women an addendum to the body of objectified knowledge. (Smith 1990: 12–13)

Smith holds that sociology has to abandon the pretence of detached, objective knowledge, which rests on what she calls 'the methodology of the positionless account' (1999: 51). The real experiences of people are the ultimate test of the validity of sociological knowledge. What we know of others is conditioned by our own location, and this conditioning of knowledge must be recognised. The development of knowledge is not a matter of truth but of authenticity. This means that all observers and theorists must recognise the authenticity of knowledge produced from other standpoints. There can, therefore, be no privileged standpoint with superior rights to speak and write or to impose 'our' reality on others. Where Hartsock sees the feminist standpoint as superior to and, in principle, seeking to replace malestream knowledge, Smith recognises that both male and female standpoints have a legitimate part to play in sociology. The divergent standpoints must be reconciled by recognising a 'larger socio-economic order' of which they are a part. Neither viewpoint is to be subordinated to the other, and the legitimacy of each is to be recognised within the academic practices of sociology and other social science disciplines.

Smith's position began from a recognition of the importance of class and race alongside gender, and her developed position modifies the stark standpoint theory of Hartsock to recognise the multiplicity of standpoints from which knowledge is constructed. She points out that women differ from one another according to their class, race and other social characteristics, and so sociology must reconcile itself 'to multiple narratives revealing varied and many-sided versions of the world from multiple and fragmented discursively constituted positions' (Smith 1999: 101). Harding (1993) recognised this, but aimed to incorporate it into a modified standpoint theory, holding that a 'less partial and distorted' account than any of the more fragmentary perspectives can be provided by a multifaceted feminist standpoint that contains plurality within a recognition of what it is that unites women.

This position was developed in more radical directions by Black feminists and feminist poststructuralists who held that the diversity of women's experiences is such that an oversimplified view of a single and essential 'female' standpoint had to be abandoned. Thus, bell hooks (1981) and Hill-Collins (1990) pointed to racial and ethnic differences among women and the consequent multiplicity of perspectives. Judith Butler (1990) pushed the debate back into the area of sexuality and Rosi Braidotti (1991) cast this argument in a more generalised form in relation to theories of self and identity.[3]

Colonised standpoints and post-colonial studies

Many of the formative sociologists explored ethnic conflicts and their political consequences for racial stratification, state formation and the building of imperial structures. The implications of such power structures for knowledge construction have long been recognised by anthropologists and were aptly summarised by Paul Bohannan:

> The essence of colonialism is that there are always two, often opposed, ways of looking at the power system and at the world in general: one is of the colonizing power and the other represents the views of the colonized people. The two viewpoints grow naturally and silently out of different cultural viewpoints and goals. The colonizers and the colonized, even when they are as generally similar as Africans and Europeans, have many cultural disparities. Thus, one group reacts to any given situation in a way quite at odds with the reaction of the other group. (Bohannan 1961: 22)

Each group in the colonial encounter develops a particular and distinctive view of the situation: 'There were two sides and neither totally knew the "codes" – the connotations of word and deed – in which the other group perceived the situation, valued it, communicated about it, and acted' (ibid.: 24). The colonial confrontation between, say, Europeans and Africans, however, is not simply a matter of the confrontation between European and African cultures. The

[3]See also the edited collections produced by Nicholson (1990), Alcoff and Potter (1993) and Lennon and Whitford (1994).

differences in ideas and attitudes between Africans and Europeans are rooted in colonial power structures, and not in innate racial differences or free-floating cultural differences. Variations in perspective and the associated knowledge derive from power differentials between the colonial masters and those who are, often literally, their slaves. The principles and practices followed in the exercise of colonial power are reflected in an imperial discourse that expresses the attitude of the dominant class in the home society and their need to establish and maintain power over indigenous peoples in the colonies. Similarly, the view of the world taken by colonised peoples is built on their indigenous culture but transforms it on the basis of their subjection and resistance to the power of the colonisers.

This fundamental feature of the colonial encounter is the starting point for those who have developed post-colonial theorising. This approach had its origins in the work of the Subaltern Studies Group and their explorations into Indian history.[4] Most of the members of this group were based in Britain, and some were not ethnically of the Indian sub-continent, yet they were united by the view that intellectuals necessarily speak on behalf of particular social groups. They took their inspiration from the attempts of the British Marxists to construct a 'history from below' and saw their own task as articulating a view of colonial India from the standpoint of the colonised subaltern. History, they argued, had largely been written from the standpoint of the dominant groups in the colonial encounter, and it was important to redress the balance by making heard the hitherto unheard voices. Thus, Partha Chatterjee (1986; see also 1993; Guha 1983) held that the nationalist thought of Nehru and the Congress Party had taken over much of the discourse of the imperial West and had been tainted by this. It was necessary, he argued, for there to be a return to the indigenous discourse of the masses, as Gandhi had advocated. The voice of the masses had to be heard, as they stood in the subaltern standpoint.

This giving of voice was not simply a matter of espousing the actual consciousness of subordinate, indigenous peoples, as this is both confused and contradictory. The masses are conscious of their own immediate concerns and experiences, but they are also influenced by an imperial discourse embodied in the dominant institutions and the nationalist movement. This 'dualistic consciousness' ties them into a dualistic political practice that is inimical to their own liberation (Guha 1982). The intellectuals must put their intellectual skills and capacities in the service of the colonial peasantry so as to help them to break with the imperial discourse and to articulate the indigenous voices in more

---

[4]The Subaltern Studies Group includes Partha Chatterjee, Ranajit Guha and Dipesh Chakrabarty. Their work was published in a series of volumes published from 1982, and much of this has been selected in Guha and Spivak (1988).

autonomous, rational and systematic ways. Indigenous consciousness had to be developed and articulated by intellectuals into a worldview that goes beyond the philosophical parameters of colonialism. The masses in the developing countries had to break with the thought patterns of the West and its associated concepts of nation, democracy, citizenship and socialism. Post-colonial theory is precisely this rational, imputed consciousness of the subalterns that goes beyond the conventional nationalism that had dominated liberation struggles.

Important sources for this post-colonial perspective were Franz Fanon on Africa and Edward Said on the Middle East. In an influential work, Fanon (1963) set out Marxist-inspired views of colonialism similar to the earlier work of Amilcar Cabral and, in the 1930s, of Cyril James (1938). Fanon saw the colonial system as one in which 'settlers' create 'natives' through political, economic and cultural practices that lead each to occupy a distinct social and physical 'zone' of the colonial territory. Settlers and natives were defined by their relation to each other. The settlers organise themselves as administrators, soldiers and police, and they live and work in bright, clean housing. The indigenous population, on the other hand, is restricted to low-paid work and to the poor and dirty towns, villages, districts and reservations. The frontier between the settler and native zones is marked and monitored by army barracks and police stations. The most extreme form of this separation was that of the apartheid regime in South Africa. The physical, economic and social separation of settler and native, Fanon argued, is based on a prior 'racial' differentiation of the conquerors and the conquered, each defining their counterpart as 'other':

> It is neither the act of owning factories, nor estates, nor a bank balance which distinguishes the governing classes. The governing race is first and foremost those who come from elsewhere, those who are unlike the original inhabitants, 'the others'. (Fanon 1963: 33)

This social separation is the basis of both the native experience and of the ways in which natives are seen by the colonisers. The native is perceived as 'the other' in his or her own land. The customs, traditions and myths of the indigenous population are seen by the colonisers as signs of their 'poverty of spirit' and their 'depravity' (ibid.: 34). The native is perceived as 'evil', as dehumanised and lacking in values and is, therefore, seen as needing to be controlled and regulated, often through force. Justified in terms of the 'civilising' mission of the settler, this system of control inculcates in the native mind the idea that, without the presence of the settlers, he or she 'would at once fall back into barbarism, degradation and bestiality' (ibid.: 170). Submissiveness and dependence are encouraged in the mind of the native, shaping their perspective on the colonial situation.

Fanon held, however, that the colonised were not mere passive recipients of the dominant ideas. They had their own insight into the colonial situation and could be active agents in their liberation from colonial power. A key part in developing native resistance to colonialism is played by native intellectuals, by the writers and politicians that Fanon saw forging new identities that go beyond those enshrined in the imperial discourse. In sub-Saharan Africa, intellectuals rejected national labels that were the creations of the colonists, such as 'Angola' or 'Dahomey', and they attempted to forge a wider 'African' identity. In Arab territories, this assertion of a broader culture took the form of a promotion of Islam and a renewal of Arab culture (ibid.: 171). The colonial identities established were seen as the key to understanding how decolonisation will transform identities. Transnational ethnic solidarities of a pan-African or pan-Arab character are important means for overcoming European colonisation and were a basis for understanding the colonial processes through which people had been forged into 'nations' with specific experiences in common (ibid.: 188). This was particularly characteristic of African and Arab nationalism.

Fanon also held that there are fundamental similarities in the position not only of African and Arab, but of 'negroes' in the United States and the negroes and indigenous peoples of Latin America. All are racialised others whose crucial formative experiences are the results of the oppression exercised, generation after generation, by their white masters. Thus, black nationalism in the United States develops interdependently with other forms of colonial nationalism. Such views of the 'essential black subject' (Hall 1992) aligned Fanon with the earlier claims of William Du Bois (1903).

Said (1978) traced a discourse of 'orientalism' in the literary, political, historical and other texts of Western intellectuals studying Eastern societies. It was highly influential in western theories of 'civilisation', from Herder to Spengler, and its assumptions permeated much of western thought. The object of this discourse – 'the Orient' – is depicted as a specific geographical area with distinct characteristics, though Said claimed it to be a construction that was produced from a Western standpoint and reflects its specific will to power. It is a form of discourse that is integrally linked with western power over the Middle and Far East. European exploration and trade in the eighteenth century, he argued, established relations of power over extensive territories in the east, stretching from the Mediterranean to China. These territories were the objects of power relations and were constructed as objects of knowledge geared to advancing this power. These theoretical objects, then, reinforced the new power relations of colonialism (see also Prakash 1990). Although it embodied enlightenment ideals of rational, objective knowledge, it was constructed from a dominant, hegemonic standpoint. It was both negative and stereotypical, focusing on the despotism and cruelty of oriental regimes and the 'backwardness' of oriental culture. Oriental subject races were seen as incapable of logic and rationality, embodying Lévy-Bruhl's (1921) 'primitive thought', and these ideas of inferiority were often associated with assumptions about biological racial differences. The contrast was drawn between the rational, peaceful, liberal and logical westerners and the irrational, bellicose, despotic and illogical orientals (Said 1978: 49):

> Orientalism was ultimately a political vision of reality whose structure promoted the difference between the familiar (Europe, the West, 'us') and the strange (the Orient, the East, 'them'). (Said 1978: 43)

It was the confrontation of hegemonic imperial power and subaltern resistance that led to particular forms of decolonisation and nationalist movements, including the Palestinian *intifada*, and this was the context from which Said saw contemporary post-colonialism developing. The image of orientals as 'other' was discrepant with the knowledge and consciousness of the 'orientals' themselves, and Said held that the self-representations of the colonised and formerly colonised peoples, as found in indigenous histories and other colonial sources, can be reclaimed from within an emancipatory post-colonial discourse. In the same way as Fanon, Said saw intellectuals as transforming the actual consciousness of subalterns into a more emancipatory form, and he saw his work as contributing to the building of a subaltern counter-discourse (Said 1993). The construction of this counter-discourse, however, is not straightforward. Third World intellectuals can give voice to these forms of resistance, but they may, equally, contribute to the hegemonic discourse, as happened in many nationalist movements. Said saw the key role in the emergence of post-colonial discourse as played by those who have cultural power both *within* and *outside* their own culture – and he gave particular importance to those 'exiles' who identify with the subaltern standpoint (Said 1994).

Post-colonial ideas were further developed by Giyatri Spivak and Homi Bhabha in their critiques of Guha and Chatterjee of the Subaltern Studies Group. The Subaltern writers had argued that the official documents of the colonial period could provide evidence for the views of the normally silent and unrepresented subalterns and the resistance they exercised against colonialism. This required a critical reading of the sources, and the task of the intellectual is to capture peasant consciousness through its effects on colonial structures and the reflections of the colonial authorities on this. Spivak, however, argued that the subalterns do not speak through the colonial texts (Spivak 1985). She argues that it is only ever possible to approach the subaltern perspective through a dialogue based in a standpoint outside the subaltern position itself. In this 'transaction of positionality', intellectuals do not speak 'on behalf' of the subalterns, but only ever 'about' them. Western-educated colonial intellectuals – who are *in* the West but not *of* it – can enter into dialogue and construct a post-colonial discourse from indigenous, native viewpoints without simply endorsing that viewpoint (Spivak 1990: 57). The strictly 'indigenist' concerns of traditional village communities, manifest in fundamentalism and irrationalism, can be transcended through this dialogue. Spivak sees this also in the way in which the gendered character of post-colonial subalterns can be recognised through engagement with feminist politics and theory. Bhabha develops a similar argument, exploring the relationship between 'traditional' indigenous views and the ideas of the intellectuals through his concept of 'hybridity' (Bhabha 1994).[5] Following Said, Bhabha sees 'subject peoples' as the ideological constructs of a colonial discourse (see also Spivak (1988) on the 'colonial object'), and Bhabha aims at articulating the more autonomous identities of the subject peoples themselves. Whereas an indigenist standpoint would merely embrace the fundamentalism and irrationalism that is found in actually existing native village societies, a post-colonial discourse emerges from the synthetic articulation and reconstruction of this from the standpoint of Western-educated and resident intellectuals. The intellectual, drawn from but also separate from the subject people, gives post-colonial discourse its hybrid character.

Relationism, dynamic synthesis and realism

I have shown that Marxist, feminist, and post-colonial theories have each set out a standpoint theory according to which knowledge reflects the social location of embodied agents. Each approach has also grappled with the question of the conditions under which perspectival knowledge can be said to have a truth or objectivity that transcends the experiences and interests of particular classes, genders and ethnic groups.[6] In accordance with the general approach to the sociology of knowledge taken by Mannheim, they have each seen intellectuals playing a key part in the formulation of trans-locational knowledge through their engagement in research and in practical political actions. In the remainder of this chapter we will show that Mannheim's arguments point towards an initial solution to the problem of objectivity and of overcoming the opposition between the assumption of absolute knowledge and the embrace of total relativism.

In recognising the social location of knowledge, Mannheim aimed not to justify relativism but to move beyond simple assertions of a 'correspondence' between knowledge and an external reality by re-establishing a new and more satisfactory basis for certainty and objectivity. He held that the arguments of Kant and Nietzsche had made it possible to avoid falling into an epistemological chasm between absolutism and relativism. He would not settle for a solution that privileged a particular material standpoint, be it that of the proletariat,

---

[5]This book consists of essays first published in the 1980s.

[6]The following section draws on an earlier argument in J. Scott (1998).

women or racialised minorities. True knowledge transcends social locations and it is not possible to establish 'objective' knowledge by arbitrarily privileging a particular 'subjective' standpoint. What is needed, he held, is a recognition that various perspectival knowledges – each with their own subjectively valued truth or authenticity – may be part of a larger and more comprehensive, but still not absolute, picture. He called his alternative historical epistemology 'relationism'.

The basic problem of relativism, according to its critics, is that it allows each person to regard their way of seeing the world as correct and meaningful but to see all others as illusory or biased. This undermines any trans-situational view of truth and seems to leave nothing but illusion and falsity. Relationism, too, takes seriously the variety of socially situated claims to knowledge and truth, holding that all knowledge can be regarded as 'true' in so far as it is an authentic expression of particular concerns and interests: socially situated knowledge may have a relational truth in so far as it is derived in technically reliable ways from a particular standpoint. Relational truths are partial and limited. They are restricted by the features of the social location and perspectives from which they are constructed. Mannheim's relationism sees the various relational truths as essential elements in more comprehensive 'synthetic' accounts of the world.

Mannheim developed his argument by considering, first, the possibility of acquiring objective knowledge of the physical world. His argument can be understood by analogy with the pictorial representation of physical reality in art. No single person located in a room full of objects can see the room in all its complexity. However, combining the various images apparent from a multiplicity of locations within the room provides a better grasp of the overall structure of the room, even though the combined picture cannot be said to 'correspond' to reality. This was the principal implication of Einstein's explorations into the questions of relativity that arise when observers change their location and their speed of movement. The variant observations and measurements that are made, Einstein argued, can be reconciled only by seeing them in relation to a more general theory of relativity that demonstrates their partiality.[7] A similar strategy was attempted by the Cubist movement in art. Following the example of Cézanne, artists such as Picasso and Braque sought to combine multiple perceptions of an object from several points of view in order to synthesise them into a single aesthetic representation. This representation is completely detached from any idea of correspondence with a real object, but it serves as an aesthetically

---

[7]Mannheim himself says relatively little about natural science, but a very brief discussion of the arguments of Heisenberg and Einstein suggests that a fully relational view could be extended to the natural world (1931: 275).

plausible simulation of that object.[8] Mannheim's epistemology follows a similar strategy. The noumenal world may be ultimately unknowable, but our conceptual grasp on this world may be more or less adequate to the extent that we are able to transcend our own perspective without distorting or misrepresenting the truths produced from other perspectives. The way in which the adequacy of any particular view of the world can be improved is through the combination of a multiplicity of perspectives:

> The problem is not how we might arrive at a non-perspectivistic picture but how, by juxtaposing the various points of view, each perspective may be recognised as such and thereby a new level of objectivity attained. (Mannheim 1931: 266)

Social reality, however, is more complex than physical reality. Social phenomena are meaningful, in the sense that they are constituted by and can be understood only through ideas and values (Mannheim 1931: 264). The social world includes the symbolic meanings from which it is constructed, among which are the situated meanings of its participants. Social structures, then, do not exist independently of the humans who construct them, and all observations are made from within the very social world that is under observation. Thus, 'what is intelligible in history can be formulated only with reference to problems and conceptual constructions which themselves arise in the flux of historical experience' (Mannheim 1929b: 71). Social reality is the outcome of the practical acts of synthesis produced in the dialogue, negotiation and conflict that occurs when groups coexist. Historical situations result from practical actions based on the knowledge of participants, and rooted in their varying perspectives. The varying knowledges of the participants enter into the constitution of the historical situations that they attempt to understand. Indeed, Mannheim explicitly accepted the pragmatist dictum that when people define situations in particular ways, their definitions have real consequences for the development of that situation.

Social science does not, of course, simply reproduce the situated meanings of participants. It aims to understand these meanings in relation to the social location of the participants and their relations to each other. Mannheim argues that social scientists do not adjudicate between different viewpoints but assess their relational truths and attempt to reconcile them within a larger picture through

---

[8]The Cubists sought a philosophical basis for their aesthetic ideas. Cézanne's ideas on art have been linked to Bergson's philosophy of mind. Bergson held that human beings accumulate information about different aspects of objects and then synthesise these into a conceptual knowledge of the object itself (Fry 1966). Picasso linked his own work with Husserl's views on comprehending the essence of an object. Many Cubists allied themselves with the work of mathematicians aimed at a 'fourth dimension' vantage point for grasping the diversity of three-dimensional perspectives (Henderson 1983).

an intellectual synthesis. Synthesis is a movement of mediation that involves an accommodation and incorporation of opposites. Rival views are not completely superseded in a new totality but are retained as moments of that totality (Kettler and Meja 1995: 54). An act of synthesis involves 'crystallizing structures of thinking out of a sea of opinion, mapping them, then linking them in a coherent design' (ibid.: 66).

A more comprehensive truth can be achieved by transcending the relational truths and synthesising them into a broader historical representation:

> All points of view in politics are but partial points of view because historical totality is always too comprehensive to be grasped by any one of the individual points of view which emerge out of it. Since, however, all these points of view emerge out of the same social and historical current, and since their partiality exists in the matrix of an emerging whole, it is possible to see them in juxtaposition, and their synthesis becomes a problem which must continually be reformulated and resolved. (Mannheim 1929b: 134)

This synthesis involves an 'assimilation and transcendence of the limitations of particular points of view', allowing 'the broadest possible extension of our horizon of vision' (Mannheim 1929b: 94, 95). A synthesis of these partial views gives a more comprehensive view of the historical reality than does any one of them on its own.

The act of synthesis is especially complex because the social worlds studied by sociologists are constantly changing. Following the Hegelian historicisation of the Kantian position that he found in Dilthey, Mannheim recognised that no form of historical understanding can ever be absolute and final. Any intellectual synthesis in the social sciences is simply a tentative and precarious reconciliation of diverse, contradictory and constantly shifting historical perspectives. As social reality is constantly changing as a result of the practical actions of the participants, there can only ever be a 'dynamic' synthesis that is itself subject to constant reformulation:

> since ... all these points of view emerge out of the same social and historical current, and since their partiality exists in the matrix of an emerging whole, it is possible to see them in juxtaposition, and their synthesis becomes a problem which must continually be reformulated and resolved. (Mannheim 1929b: 134)

Gunther Remmling suggested that 'successive attempts at the interpretation of the historical and social world form a meaningful context in as much as they are all directed toward the distant goal of a comprehensive world interpretation incorporating all partial perspectives' (Remmling 1975: 70). This 'distant goal', however, recedes as fast as it is approached. Each new synthesis is a part of the historical process and transforms the reality to which it relates, making further attempts at synthesis necessary. Intellectual synthesis is a never-ending task.

Mannheim's claim is not that objectivity is a result of avoiding the extremes of two polarised perspectives and finding a middle way between them. This argument had already been repudiated by Weber, who held that an academic publication for which he had editorial responsibility 'will struggle relentlessly against the self-deception which asserts that through the synthesis of several party points of view ... practical norms of scientific validity can be arrived at' (Weber 1904: 58). Weber was here opposing the naïve idea that simply because policy positions differ from each other, a 'mid-point' synthesis that steers a line among them is somehow more objective and less partisan. Weber rightly showed that this procedure cannot yield valid normative or factual judgements. Nor is Mannheim's claim that a more comprehensive truth is produced simply by adding up the various partial truths and forging them into a consensus. This would run quite counter to his argument. The dynamic synthesis that Mannheim advocated can be achieved only if the relativity of the partial truths is recognised, appreciated and incorporated into the kind of more comprehensive account that Einstein sought in physics and the Cubists in art.

Mannheim saw it as important to retain the idea that some bodies of knowledge may be 'false'. While relational truths are authentic to the experiences and concerns of those who produce them, they may fail a test of practical adequacy. Everyday statements connect with the noumenal world through attempts to intervene in it or to alter it in relation to practical goals, and they may involve explicit or implicit claims about the world that do not allow the formulation of successful action plans. Knowledge, Mannheim argued, has to be seen as 'an instrument for dealing with life-situations at the disposal of a certain kind of vital being under certain conditions of life' (1931: 268). That is, knowledge has the practical function of assisting people in their actions. If their knowledge proves to be an inappropriate guide to successful action – if their actions fail in their intentions – then the knowledge can be seen as false. It may remain an authentic expression of group interests and concerns – a 'true' expression of their worldview – but it does not allow them to successfully realise their interests and so it is, in practical terms, false. A false consciousness fails to comprehend the 'dynamic reality' that results from the interplay of the meanings and actions of social groups (Mannheim 1929b: 84–5).

The dynamic synthesis produced by the sociologist must also face the test of practical adequacy. Mannheim pointed to parallels between his ideas on practical action and the pragmatism of Charles Peirce, though he did not develop this claim in any detail. Peirce (1877, 1878) held that all thinking takes place within practical situations and so must be seen as shaped by the particular location of the thinker and the specific perceptual and motivational context that this involves. Thinking originates in attempts to solve practical problems through trial and error. Successful responses are likely to be repeated and so become habits of thought and action. From this, Peirce drew the conclusion that the meaning of a concept is given simply by the habits of thought and action with which it is associated. Its meaning is specified by the use that actors intend to make of it. Our conception of an object is simply the set of beliefs that we hold about the practical implications that it has in relation to our actions. The concept of 'hardness', for example, means that an object to which the concept is applied is not likely to be scratched by other objects, that it will offer resistance if pushed, that it makes a noise if struck, and so on. There is nothing more to the concept of hardness than these particular effects. A hard object is one that habitually responds to specified actions in characteristic ways.

For pragmatists, all knowledge is related to the particular concepts involved in its construction, and relativism is avoided by their emphasis on practical adequacy. Knowledge is 'true' if it works in practical contexts. True beliefs are those that provide us with expectations and lead us to actions that are effective in bringing about cognitive satisfaction. Knowledge has such consequences if, at some level, it grasps something of the noumenal reality to which it refers. It is only because objects of knowledge have certain intransitive characteristics that it makes any sense to attempt to compare alternative descriptions with each other.

The intellectuals and synthesis

Our discussion of Mannheim's argument has so far been concerned with the nature of the intellectual understanding of social phenomena that can be achieved in social science. Mannheim also attended to the question of *how* this can be achieved. He saw social scientists as members of the larger social category that he termed 'intellectuals' and, like the standpoint theorists, he saw intellectuals as the agents capable of transforming practical, everyday consciousness into more systematic theoretical knowledge. Mannheim was concerned to show that a dynamic synthesis with a high degree of practical adequacy can be achieved only if intellectuals oriented to its production are appropriately motivated and organised. He saw a sociology of intellectuals as an essential addition to his sociology of knowledge if epistemology is to be reconstructed in such a way as to make objective, truthful knowledge possible.

The intellectuals are those with a high level of education and who are active participants in the production of systematically organised culture. Mannheim's central claim was that the sought-for synthesis in knowledge could be brought about only by those intellectuals who have established a degree of 'detachment' from their social location. Following Alfred Weber, he described these as the 'relatively unattached' intellectuals (Mannheim 1932–33b; see also Mannheim

1932–33c).[9] The term that Mannheim used to describe them was '*relativ fre-ischwebende Intelligenz*'. The best translation of this is not the widely-used phrase 'free floating intellectuals', though this is certainly one of its literal translations. A much better translation of '*freischwebende*' is 'freely-balanced' or 'impartial', the whole phrase translating as the 'relatively impartial intellectuals'. These are intellectuals recruited from a variety of classes and social groups and so forming 'a relatively classless stratum which is not too firmly situated in the social order' (Mannheim 1929b: 136).

The emergence of such a group in the modern world was made possible by the breaking of the ecclesiastical monopoly over education and communication. No longer a politico-religious caste, the intellectuals developed with a focus on institutions and organisations that could provide an arena for voicing the views of various strata and so demonstrating that there can be no single, absolute truth (Mannheim 1936: 10–11). They may not be entirely free from social liaisons, but they do have cross-cutting social attachments and a detachment from full-time political participation that gives them a considerable autonomy from the immediate clash of interests (Mannheim 1932–33b: 105–6). As a result, they are better able to synthesise the rival social perspectives that they encounter.

Relatively impartial intellectuals, then, are an 'interstitial' category that exists 'between' the major social groups. Their solidarity derives *solely* from their intellectual interests and concerns and not from any pre-existing class, gender, ethnic, or other social interests. They do not, therefore, align themselves collectively with any particular party or political programme. This relative lack of direct involvement in partisan causes means that they do not react to practical issues in the same way as those who are directly involved in the material struggles of everyday life. Their relative detachment enables them to take a broader outlook and make a more considered and better-thought-out response that takes account of a wide range of viewpoints. They are peculiarly well placed to consider matters from several perspectives. The claim is, then, that 'certain types of intellectuals have a maximum opportunity to test and employ the socially available vistas and to experience their inconsistencies' (Mannheim 1932–33b: 106):

> His [*sic.*] acquired equipment makes him potentially more labile than others. He can more easily change his point of view and he is less rigidly committed to one side of the contest, for he is capable of experiencing concomitantly several conflicting approaches to the same thing. (Mannheim 1932–33b: 105)

---

[9]Mannheim's key essays on the intellectuals were written in 1932–33, but were not published until some years after his death. Some of the terminology in the essays seems to have been altered by his editor and translator, and the originals are no longer available. But see his 'The sociology of the intellectuals' (1932).

Mannheim recognises that intellectuals can give voice to partial viewpoints, acting as apologists or what Gramsci (1929–35) called 'organic' intellectuals, but the relatively unattached do so in a frame of mind that is open to modification in the light of evidence and the views of others. As a result, they are oriented towards the attainment of perspective-free representations of the noumenal world and its structures. This is possible only if they are aware of their potential and of themselves as a social group. They must have a reflexively grounded conception of themselves *as* intellectuals with a particular will towards the synthesis of rival viewpoints. In seeking to maximise their social detachment, they create the conditions under which the perspective that they themselves adopt is a synthesis of more partial perspectives and so comes as close as is humanly possible to perspective-free knowledge.

Complete detachment is, of course, impossible. Sociologists must constantly enter the social world of partisan attachments if they are to acquire the data and the raw materials for any understanding of that world. A complex balance must be maintained between involvement and detachment (Elias 1983). The achievement of a high level of detachment is very unusual and depends on quite specific social conditions. These conditions are particularly characteristic of the 'contemporary intellectual', who is a member of a formally open and secular social group that is committed to the 'intellectual process' rather than to specific political programmes. The 'vocation' or calling of the contemporary intellectual, Mannheim argued, is to synthesise, from his or her own current social position, as many partial perspectives as possible (see the related view in Weber 1919). They are, in Bauman's (1987) words, not the authoritative *legislators* but the *interpreters* of culture. Mannheim (1927) saw the post-1880 generation of intellectuals who produced classical sociology – a generation of which, of course, he was a part – as having been the first to move forward the prospects of a scientific investigation of social affairs. The contemporary intellectual is aware that there can no longer be any talk of absolute truth, and that partial truths must be recognised and synthesised:

> The modern intellectual ... does not intend to reconcile or to ignore the alternative views which are potential in the order of things around him, but he seeks out the tensions and participates in the polarities of his society. (Mannheim 1932–33b: 117)

The intellectual who is capable of achieving a dynamic synthesis, then, is one whose commitment is to the life of the mind and the autonomy of science, rather than to specific, practical interests and programmes. The relatively impartial intellectual is one who participates in a diverse intellectual community where the competition of those with differing partisan commitments and interests regulates debate and prevents the unchallenged expression of particular points of view. Such intellectuals struggle to establish and maintain the intellectual autonomy and the multifaceted hybridity that allows them to compare and to synthesise the perspectives of those who participate in the practical struggles that they study.

It is within such an intellectual community that it is possible to establish what Mannheim referred to as 'genuine discussion' (Mannheim 1932–33a). An intellectual community must be formed, he held, in which 'genuine discussion' is the principal concern of all involved. Such discussion is the *process* through which scientific truth can be established. In these circumstances, cultural matters are pursued in a 'democratic mode', reflecting the fact that scientific truth does not depend upon the authority or power of a particular theorist, but on the exercise of reason alone:

> The essential feature of genuine discussion is that no argument from authority and no dogmatic assertion based upon mere intuition is admitted. (Mannheim 1932–33b: 192)

'Truth' is that 'which can be ascertained by everybody in ordinary experience', or 'which can be cogently proved by steps that everybody can reproduce' (Mannheim 1932–33a: 185). Thus, 'all initial positions have some right to be considered' (ibid.: 192) and 'all participants are equally and jointly responsible for the conclusion reached' (ibid.: 194).

Mannheim's view of the character of an intellectual community founded in genuine discussion was echoed by Popper (1945) in his discussion of the 'open society' and by Habermas (1970, 1981) in his description of the 'ideal speech situation'. An open society is one in which there is a free interchange of ideas, without any resort to force, coercion or manipulation. An ideal speech situation is one in which pure communication, free from any distortion by power and interests, is able to bring about an untrammelled rational discourse. A dynamic synthesis is possible to the extent that the conditions under which intellectuals operate correspond to these. Science is a *collective* process involving individuals committed to truth and objectivity and who are able to participate in free rational discussion through an intellectual division of labour that synthesises a concatenation of viewpoints. Intellectual synthesis is a collective product of a 'free market' of conjecture and refutation in which selective processes ensure the production of true knowledge (Toulmin 1972: 139–41).

These conditions are not easily achievable, and social factors may limit their realisation. The question of gender differences is the least considered part of his own work. As his own language makes clear, Mannheim did not seem to be aware of the implications of the fact that the contemporary intellectuals about which he wrote were almost exclusively male. As has been made clear by feminist writers in recent decades, the prospects for scientific truth and objectivity are undermined by the exclusion of women from science, the patriarchal structure of universities, and the consequent failure to incorporate the authentic truths of women's experiences into the framework of genuine discussion. A proper recognition of female standpoints – alongside class, ethnic, generational and other standpoints – and the full inclusion of women in the intellectual community must be central to a relational epistemology and the possibility of dynamic synthesis.

Mannheim's position might appear to be hopelessly idealistic. The difficulties of establishing 'genuine discussion' in our universities, let alone in the political sphere, are immense. This should not, however, be a reason for rejecting his aspiration for the genuinely free and open discussion of scientific differences. Mannheim's advocacy of genuine discussion is a call for sociologists and other social scientists to be involved in the maintenance and enhancement of the conditions of academic freedom and intellectual autonomy. It is only by striving to protect what genuine discussion there is and by trying to expand its reach that the irrationalism of the present chaos of relativism can be avoided. Mannheim points out the only way in which we can truly know the social world.

Discussion

————Malcolm ————

JOHN'S DISCUSSION OF MANNHEIM AND Marx led me to realise how much they have shaped the debate about the social situatedness of knowledge. It seems hard to disagree with the initial premise of both, that our social position shapes what we come to know, but also, by implication, what we choose to privilege and pass on.

However, the tensions in this position are nicely sharpened by the later feminist standpoint positions, and somewhat later modified, if not abandoned, by Sandra Harding in 'strong objectivity'. There are three tensions: first, our gender or class (or any other position for that matter) does not wholly determine what we know. It may determine some of what we know, but not all of it. This leads to a paradox because if we assert that all knowledge is from a standpoint, then any challenge to that particular statement is heretical. Thus standpoint theory becomes a meta-orthodoxy about where knowledge comes from and gets passed on.

The second tension lies in what counts as a standpoint. Is it a claim that a standpoint presumes epistemological privilege in all things that can be known? I don't think anyone would claim this, so if it is not, what are the particular things about our social locatedness that constitute a 'standpoint'? Being a 'woman' is too broad because, as so many feminists have pointed out, there is very little that unites the knowledge base of a figure such as Margaret Thatcher and a working-class woman. Class is likewise too broad because cultural and occupational stratification is highly nuanced even in particular societies, yet alone in societies across place and time.

The third tension lies in what might be called 'the fact of the matter'. Just because many people believe X is the case, does not make X the case. Any form of argument from the position of social locatedness runs the risk of conflating an 'ought' with an 'is'. While I would agree that my social locatedness influences my views on homelessness (views which I believe to be correct), they make no difference to the reality of how many people are homeless and the conditions they experience.

Dorothy Smith's position, in respect of sociology, is altogether more sophisticated. Yet reading it now in the second decade of the twenty-first century, when many women have reached positions of seniority in the discipline and the demographics of junior faculty indicate that in around 20 years the discipline will be very much more feminised, one wonders how that change can happen? It was certainly not an overthrow of the gendered divisions she speaks of (they are still there), but maybe a series of minor changes in practices, but also a changing awareness of those divisions by women sociologists (indeed, partially brought about by Smith's own writings), that created the possibilities for change. Social locatedness certainly shapes, but does not determine, what we know or how we act. By extension, it shapes much of what we privilege as topic or method in social science, but it does not determine these things.

——Gayle

FOR ME, THE VALUE OF standpoint positions is that they provide a way of naming oppression and highlighting the experience of groups that have traditionally been defined as different, as 'other' to the adult, male, white, middle-class, able-bodied norm. Standpoint epistemologies have also provided a challenge to mainstream theories and approaches within the academy. Although some researchers and theorists argue that there is still some way to go, there is no denying that feminism, gender and women's studies, gay, lesbian and queer studies, disability studies, and so on have had a significant transformative impact on dominant ideas and methodological approaches, not least within the social sciences. Yet, because, as John and Malcolm both point out, standpoint positions are both relational (constituted by politics and theory) and limited in that they imply simplistic unity rather than allow for difference and diversity, any argument for a superior successor science based on a standpoint position is similarly limiting. Postmodernism highlights the significance of difference, but, with its focus on meaning and language, denies any reality outside the discursive and accepts no narrative as automatically superior. From this perspective, a multitude of standpoints is possible and neither is superior to any other.

Once we acknowledge the existence of difference within a standpoint or different standpoints or competing discursive positions, we acknowledge alternative knowledge claims which of course have implications for any claims for objectivity. Yet, an approach which recognises this and which acknowledges ontological separations as well as similarities offers a critique of 'fake' accounts and gets us closer to a fuller, 'truer' understanding of the social world (see Stanley and Wise 1990; bell hooks 1996; and Letherby 2003c for further discussion).

———John———

THERE ARE A NUMBER OF misunderstandings in what Malcolm and Gayle have argued. Both imply that standpoint theories require the identification of a single and all-embracing standpoint: that of 'woman', 'working-class', 'colonised', etc. However, this applies only to some formulations of standpoint theory by early feminists and some Marxists. There is nothing in the idea of standpoint *per se* that requires this. I use the term as equivalent to 'perspective' and explicitly recognise that any perspective (or standpoint) is necessarily pluralistic and nuanced: we all occupy a multiplicity of diverse positions and so our perspectives on the world are both subtle and fractured. This was something that I specifically raised in my discussion of Nietzsche. I never see the world simply as, for example, a man, but always as a specific classed and racialised man with specific bodily characteristics of age, sexuality, disability, etc., and with specific historically grounded life experiences. It is, therefore, incorrect to hold that standpoint arguments cannot recognise difference: the idea of difference is central to the very idea of perspectives or standpoints on knowledge.

It is also important to note that, contrary to what Malcolm says, my position does not elide the distinction between our image of the world and the world as it really is. I made this clear in Chapter 2. The mere fact that people *believe* something to be the case does not *make* it the case: to argue this would be absurd. My argument is that a standpoint (diverse and fractured as it is) provides us with 'authentic' knowledge – knowledge that is 'true' to our perspective – so long as it is pursued rigorously and systematically. However, there is no simple correspondence between our image of the world and its reality. This is why, following Mannheim, I took up the idea of synthesis as a way of overcoming the relativism of the postmodern critique of knowledge. A synthesis of a large diversity of perspectives provides a better view of the world than does a view from any one perspective alone. However, even this synthesis does not provide us with a perfect and complete picture of the world as it really is. In order to try to bridge the gap between such a synthesis and the noumenal world, something more is required. The argument I set out in this chapter is the first step in a journey to objectivity; it is not the terminal point of that journey. We will be pursuing that journey in the remaining chapters of the book.

FOUR
Situated Objectivity in Sociology

In recent decades sociology and social research more generally, have had an uneasy relationship with the question of objectivity. Mostly sociologists no longer discuss the issue, though a few still defend what can be broadly characterised as a value-free position, or its opposite, that of a denial of the possibility or desirability of objectivity (Kincaid 1996 or Taylor 1994 respectively). Middle positions are often pragmatic yet problematic fudges, confected to resolve the apparent contradictions between qualitative and quantitative approaches to sociological research. Thus, some will claim that objectivity is possible in quantitative research, but not qualitative research (e.g. Sarantakos 2005: 92–3), which does beg the question of the status of objectivity in mixed methods research?

While subjectivity is a necessary feature of good sociology, it is not a sufficient condition. Subjectivity, though it may itself be the subject of reflection or examination (as Gayle will argue in Chapter 5), by definition must relativise knowledge to the individual and this makes generalisable knowledge claims beyond that individual logically unsustainable.[1] The individual must remain the arbiter of any reflexive insight. Equally, value freedom is a logical and performative contradiction, because value freedom, however construed, is itself a value. To make the statement that 'my sociology is conducted without values' is to hold at least one value. A hybrid of the value freedom – subjectivity positions – is equally untenable. Value freedom can brook no compromise; once one concedes to the presence of some values, the argument for the freedom from others becomes itself subject to a contextual value judgement (Williams 2005a). Subjectivities can be shared by individuals and are shared knowledge, but even the weakest intersubjective validation likewise invokes the need for some kind of rules to say which knowledge can be agreed and why. While value freedom is a flawed doctrine, its opposite, that there can only be subjectivity, is also problematic.

---

[1]Though as Gayle argues, a theorised subjectivity is a necessary starting point for objectivity.

The need for a principle of objectivity remains, and, indeed, it is one that is not logically opposed to subjectivity.

The problem with value freedom is not its aim – that of objectivity – but the means by which it attempts to achieve that aim. Value freedom is the means to objectivity, but it then follows that if objectivity is a state which is desired, then it is one which is valued – it has value.

————Malcolm's argument ————————————————————

THE ARGUMENT IN THIS CHAPTER is that objectivity is a value, a desirable value and socially situated one. Objectivity is a *situated* value because it is nested within other values, each of which has a cultural specificity. Nevertheless, objectivity, while it has cultural specificity, has characteristics and knowledge outcomes which can likewise transcend particular cultures.

Situated objectivity is achievable and can be achieved in all investigative disciplines. Though this chapter is primarily concerned with the issue of objectivity in sociology, the argument I make could be made for other social sciences, the natural sciences, criminal investigation and some humanistic disciplines, such as history. The first section of the chapter is concerned with the characteristics objectivity must have in any circumstances, though it is important to note that objectivity is not a characteristic of every society, nor is it (or should it be) present everywhere in our own.

Objectivity is a social characteristic and many writers have prefigured key elements of my argument, in both sociology (and other social sciences) and in the natural sciences. In the second section I will review some of these positions: the 'classic' argument for value freedom from Max Weber and Alvin Gouldner's response; Howard Becker's (apparent) call for partisanship in sociology; and finally an explicit call for objectivity to be seen as social, from Helen Longino. In the final section of the chapter I will show how objectivity is situated within sociology.

The necessary characteristics of objectivity

Values in any sphere of activity can be thought of as nested. Another way of putting this is that every value is comprised of other values and will itself underlie values. The term 'value' is used in a number of ways. For example:

- Numeric values indicating a quantity, or point on a scale, e.g. 20° Celsius or £120.
- Something that is valued, e.g. jewellery or good grammar.
- Moral values, e.g. honesty.

A moment's thought shows that these shade into each other. Which rituals embody moral values and which are simply valued? Is politeness a moral or social value and is there any difference? When does numeric value take on an evaluative characteristic? While numeric values may have concrete referents and may be translatable one into another (Celsius to Fahrenheit or Kelvin), they are all minimally social values.[2] That is, they are all subject to social agreement. For example, in the United States, temperature is commonly measured in Fahrenheit whereas in most of the rest of the world Celsius is used.

Parsons used the term 'value' to indicate something that is valued (Parsons and Shils 1951: 395). This is less glib than it appears. While we use the term 'value' in many different ways, as I indicate above, they are also valued in that they have utility. A numeric value 100 degrees Celsius has utility as the measurement of the boiling point of water, just as a moral value may produce the utility of social solidarity. My argument here is that objectivity contains three necessary values, that is, for objectivity to be present, they too must be present. Though they must each be present, the content of two of them is not fixed. These are:

- Purpose
- Differentiation
- Truth

The first two, purpose and differentiation, are pretty much the content of agency[3] and it is trivially true that we pursue purposes, and to make sense of the world we must differentiate one thing from another. But in the context of objectivity these take on a special meaning.

Purpose is investigation. Investigation, in an informal sense, is equally indispensible in any society. We informally 'investigate' the whole time – train times, a recipe for a dish, a person's name, etc., but in post-Renaissance society investigative purpose has become formalised in a number of spheres, such as criminal investigation, historical investigation, natural science and social science. Each of these is driven by particular purposes and agreed practices, often peculiar to our society and a reflection of the values of our society. Now, within these values, there is huge variation and disagreement, and purposes (even within the activities I mention) will be different.

It is possible to be neutral in respect of specific purpose, but not all purpose. For example, the Medical Research Council (National Institutes of Health in the USA) spends millions each year on research into cancer. Few would disagree that

---

[2]This does not preclude individual values, though one may argue that these too must have social antecedents. Indeed, a reflexive examination of one's subjectivity is likely to make reference to values beyond the individual.

[3]This is captured in a fundamental point made by Parsons and Shils (1951) when they speak of a theory of action that must begin from the orientation of action as motivated towards objects of orientation. The actor may be individual or collective and 'object' is used in much the same way as I use it in Chapter 6.

cancer is an evil, though more may argue that the money might be better spent on improving diet, eliminating smoking, etc. Similarly, the latest child of sociology is criminology and what a robust child it has become! Though the reasons why are perhaps complex, a fascination with the criminal milieu and mind by the public and government alike, increased surveillance, heightened awareness of risk, etc., have provided the impetus and resources for a growth in both university students and research.

It might be thought from the foregoing that purpose was always ideological, even narrowly so. It is true that much purpose in investigation does derive from political or economic goals. The exploration of the polar regions of the earth may produce good science, but much of its motivation is to investigate and map the presence of mineral resources. But even relatively 'blue sky' investigations have social antecedents. As Steve Fuller (1997: 141) remarks, governments vie to do 'big science' as a mark of national prestige. The motivation and purpose for big science is not just about neutral scientific investigation.

Investigative activity will be for a purpose and its purpose will shape the activity. Nevertheless, the social values that shape that purpose may be themselves assessed objectively (I will return to this below) but once that purpose is established, then objectivity must be assessed in relation to it.

Similarly, there is need for differentiation. By differentiation I mean the willingness to differentiate between one thing and another. A weak version of this is more or less just that, a willingness to accept that a particular thing/event has certain characteristics and not others. This is something we take for granted in western society, but is by no means universal in other societies. A willingness to differentiate may just produce observational or logical categories. A stronger version of differentiation is that these categories refer to real things, what I shall describe as 'objects' in Chapter 6. But for the moment, my argument depends only on a willingness to embrace the weak version of differentiation.

Differentiation, like purpose, gives rise to particular categories (themselves values) in investigation. A mathematician, using base 10, will agree on particular decimal conventions, a social scientist may agree on differentiation between levels of measurement. These differentiations, like purposes, reflect a particular kind of activity, in this chapter specifically the differentiations used in sociology.

Finally, there is truth. Truth and differentiation shade into each other in day-to-day activity when we accept that one thing is not another, for example, the statement 'John wrote that book' is a differentiation and a truth claim (which of course may be disputed). However, in investigative activity we seek to make such truth claims, but investigation is also driven by the value of truth-seeking. The postmodern, or humanistic, 'turn' in sociology has led some to say that 'there are many truths' or that 'a truth cannot be found' (see Norris 1996 for a critical discussion). Both are correct, in a sense, that there are many truth *claims* that cannot be verified, or will depend on different starting premises. Equally, 'the truth' may not be capable of verification, that is, even if we found it we may not know we have. However, I will say two things (and will return to this matter in Chapter 6). First, what we find out, or are capable of finding out, will have different epistemological statuses. It is perfectly possible to discover the demographic composition of urban–rural migration, but the truth of individual motivation is very much harder to establish. Sometimes we can find 'truth' through the elimination of error, that is, we hypothesise that something is X, but it turns out not to be the case. Indeed, this way of going about investigation, attempting to falsify hypotheses, has a long history in natural science and, to a lesser extent, social science (see, for example, Outhwaite 1983; Williams 2000). Secondly, and most importantly, to seek truth is a value, a good thing to do, but in seeking it there is no necessity that we will find it.

Each of these values is necessary in the pursuance of objectivity, itself a value and one peculiar to our society. Of these three, only truth-seeking has a fixed content. While each of the others must be present, their content will depend on social context.

The social context of objectivity

While there are those who argue for a limited defence of value freedom in social science (for example, Nagel 1961; Hammersley 2000), these are usually attempts to separate social or moral values from the investigative values of scientific enquiry. I do not believe that this can be done successfully, because investigation itself is a social value and the nature of particular investigations will depend on particular social values. I maintain that we must begin from a position of values, specifically that must we hold the value of truth-seeking as a regulatory ideal, that we must establish some form of differentiation that provides utility for our purpose, and, indeed, that we must have a purpose.

There have been many variations on what might be called 'value-led inquiry'. These range from the wholly partisan, where enquiry is seen only or primarily as a tool to advance the social position of a particular group, to those which acknowledge the starting point of social values in enquiry, but aim to transcend it through method. In their 'strong' form, the former include emancipatory enquiry (Brown 2001) and some forms of Marxist or feminist standpoints (see Gayle's discussion in Chapter 5). Other approaches have openly acknowledged the role of 'partisanship' and I will describe two of them here, the work of Howard Becker (1967) and Helen Longino (1990). However, before doing this I will briefly refer to one of the earliest sociological statements about objectivity, that of Max Weber.

Max Weber's concept of 'value-free sociology' has been often misunderstood or misrepresented. Indeed, his account centrally locates the importance and neces-sity of values and in some respects prefigures contemporary calls for 'reflexivity'.

Weber maintained that if it is the case that the concepts of the social world were subjectively constructed by agents, it must follow that the moral and political views and regimes will differ between times and places (Weber 1974: 64). According to Weber, all concepts are known through human subjectivities and because then there were no concepts to discover that are free of human subjectivities, social laws have no 'scientific justification in the cultural sci-ences'. However, Weber (1904) did not embrace the epistemological relativism this would seem to imply. He was concerned to show how, under these cir-cumstances, a scientific sociology was possible. His starting point can be sum-marised as saying that in matters of policy there will always be a debate about 'ends', about what should be achieved and therefore what investigation should be pursued. Investigation is value-driven and in sociology the subject matter of investigation *is* values. However, he claimed that it does not follow from this that the moral and political values of commitment should bias investigation.

The social scientist should not be indifferent to policy issues. Indeed, the desire and need to investigate arises directly from commitment. However, in investigating the issues that arise from such commitment, the social scientist should examine his/her value positions for their logical coherence and their relationship to other concepts and principles. Indeed, Weber proposes two levels of analysis (1974: 77): the first, that of the cultural significance of a phenomenon; and the second, an investigation of the causal factors that lead to the mass significance of such a phenomena. The existence of the money economy (his example) is a concrete historical fact, thus (he implies) existing outside any given subjectivity, but nevertheless a product of subjectivities.

What is often described as Weber's 'value-free sociology' was not a sociology without values, but rather a sociology that began with values, yet was neutral in the conduct and means of its subsequent investigation. Within it can be found a kind of 'proto' reflexivity in respect of examining the starting values, but a key characteristic of Weber's argument is that prior context is not relevant once investigation is under way.

Weber had considerable influence on US sociology, though via the translations and work of Parsons. For many, this Weberian–Parsonian legacy produced a very normative, even conservative, sociology where objectivity or 'value freedom' was preserved within methodological approaches – a narrow reading of Weber. This state of affairs was criticised by Alvin Gouldner (1962). Though he was concerned with what had happened to US sociology in the 1950s, he blamed Weber, arguing that his view of a 'value-free sociology' had produced a group myth that sociol-ogy was value free. The myth had become an excuse for complacency among US sociologists, a self-serving narrow professionalism that did not contribute to the public interest (Gouldner 1968: 109). His alternative to this, of 'objective partisanship', is that objectivity should be directed to particular goals, some of which are universal, for example the alleviation of suffering.

This question was posed in a 1967 paper of the same name by Howard Becker. In this he seems to go further than Gouldner, suggesting that sociologists take sides and cannot help but do so. As Gouldner (1968) notes, though he skirts around the question, he never fully answers it and his meaning, or what it should mean, has been the subject of debate since.

Both Gouldner and, much later, Martyn Hammersley (2000) have questioned whether Becker intended that we should take a side and that the side we should take is that of the underdog. Nevertheless, Becker's question and its common interpretation, that sociologists should take the side of the underdog, has been influential in sociology. Even though Becker has been differently interpreted, the core of his argument is quite simple.

His question is: should sociologists be value neutral or should they express a commitment to a particular cause? His answer is not unlike the position I have set out in respect of purpose:

> For it [value freedom] to exist, one would have to assume, as some apparently do, that it is indeed possible to do research that is uncontaminated by personal and political sympathies ... the question is not whether we should take sides, since we inevitably will, but rather whose side we are on. (Becker 1967: 239)

Becker goes on to say that whatever perspective one takes in sociological investigation, it will always be one that is from the standpoint of 'superordinates' or 'subordinates'. The 'complacent' US sociology which Gouldner complained of is in the first category. Yet by the time Becker was writing, in 1967, this criticism was less true and he, Becker, had become a leading sociologist of deviance (see Becker 1963). But sociologists of deviance, presumably because they must try to understand or empathise with the deviant(s), are accused of bias by superordinates. Superordinates are the voices, the power, of official and approved morality. They may be, for example, the officials of institutions such as asylums. The subordinate parties are those who, it is alleged, have violated that morality and may be the inmates of institutions such as asylums.

Becker maintained that there is a hierarchy of credibility where the superordinates determine and legitimate definitions, practices, etc. The further up the superordinate hierarchy, the greater the credibility. If researchers conduct their research within the terms of these normative definitions and practices, etc., then they will not be accused of bias by superordinates, though their standpoint will have been that of the normative position. Conversely, if they adopt the definitions, or investigate (say) the complaints or situations of subordinates, they will be accused of bias by those higher up the hierarchy of credibility.

His conclusion is that sociologists are usually politically liberal and

> usually take the side of the underdog; we are for Negroes [sic] and against Fascists. We do not think anyone biased who does research designed to prove that the former are not as bad as people think or that the latter are worse. (Becker 1967: 244)

However, while sociologists might not accuse each other of bias, parties who are offended by the research or findings will, and they will focus on deficiencies in conceptualisation or research focus. Becker's conclusion from all of this is that 'there is no position from which sociological research can be done that is not biased in one way or another' (1967: 245).

In Becker there is a recognition of the value-laden nature of enquiry and the role of power and rhetoric, but there is also some justification in Gouldner's criticism of this position as replacing the myth of value-free social science by a 'new but no less glib rejection of it' (Gouldner 1968: 103).

If we are to take Becker at his (apparent) word, there is no redemption in respect of objectivity. The sociologist must simply decide whose side she is on and conduct her research from that 'side'. Does it then follow that she only accepts or even seeks evidence that is convenient to her 'side'? As Becker notes, she will certainly face accusations of bias, but how will she deal with the specific content of those accusations that may concern the nature of the research question, methods adopted, sampling, analysis, etc.?

Becker is entirely correct in his analysis that sociologists will bring values to enquiry and that these lend perspective. But he makes two, in my view wrong, assumptions: that all of these values must belong to the motivating ideology of the 'side' – that they have no generalisable content beyond that 'side'; and, secondly, that a value position somehow translates into advocacy for that position, either in the eyes of the critic or the researcher. I do accept that later interpretations do cast doubt on the extent to which Becker holds the latter position, but that a lot of sociology takes it in practice is enough that it is a position held and to be criticised.

Helen Longino, though she does not share the 'standpoint' epistemology of many other feminist philosophers of science, does begin from the position that science is inherently social; and the social process and content of science preserves masculine values. The feminist standpoint epistemologies emphasise the androcentricity of scientific values, but Longino's position differs from them by introducing a distinction in the kinds of values that exist in science. Indeed, one might say that Longino brings 'method' back into a social epistemology of science.

Longino (1990) uses the terms *constitutive* values to describe the internal values of science, such as accuracy, explanation, etc., what might be broadly characterised as methodological values, and *contextual* values, which approximate to individual or social values. She draws two conclusions from this. The first is that science must adopt constitutive values, though these may be subject to methodological dispute, for example, a current dispute is whether randomised control trials can lead to valid causal claims (Byrne 2002: 62–3). The second is that contextual values will underlie and influence constitutive ones. They do not always do this, but that they often do is unavoidable and, moreover, necessary. If it were not, science would be an impossible project. Scientists, then, must embrace a set of values in order to do science. Indeed, we can interpret Longino as saying that science must have 'purpose' and this is unavoidable. Longino's position on values in science is similar to the one I set out above as an argument against the possibility of value freedom.

This, taken no further, simply reinforces the kind of position Becker has been taken to hold, that we take a side, we must take a side, and having done so our investigations are cast in the values of that side. This is not where Longino wants to go, and having acknowledged the role of values and the social basis of science, she tries to demonstrate how it is that a scientific community can come to do good science. First, she sets out a number of criteria that would produce a critical science based upon intersubjectively agreed standards – what she terms the 'transformative interrogation by the scientific community' (Longino 1990: 216). She calls for scientists to be aware and to make other scientists aware of the background assumptions held. Thus:

> Values are not incompatible with objectivity, but objectivity is analyzed as a function of community practices rather than an attitude of individual researchers toward their material. (ibid.: 216)

Observation, for instance, is an interactive, not passive, process and will be directed by a theory. Therefore, '[w]hat is observational and what is theoretical changes depending on what can be contested or what can be taken for granted' (ibid.: 220). Science is essentially social knowledge and she criticises the tendency in Anglo-American philosophy of science to reduce knowledge of a particular thing to individual knowledge. Rather, how we know something and how we validate that knowledge should be a social activity. Longino is therefore less concerned with how the individual comes to see her value orientation, but with how those values can be examined communally.

Although she accepts a causal connection between non-scientific and scientific values, Longino prioritises the value of objectivity construed as a transformative interrogation by the scientific (and extra-scientific) community as the way to good science.

Once one denies the possibility of bracketing off social values from the practice of science, it becomes hard (presumably Longino would say impossible) to believe there can be a non-social guarantor of objectivity and an alternative social 'guarantee' must be substituted. In using the device of the transformative interrogation by the scientific community, objectivity becomes redefined as intersubjective agreement. What is objective becomes the consensus of that community:

> That theory which is the product of the most inclusive scientific community is better, other things being equal, than that which is the product of the most exclusive. It is better not as measured against some independently accessible reality but better as measured against the cognitive needs of a genuinely democratic community. (Longino 1990: 214)

The core of Longino's philosophy is that knowledge is social, yet existing science retains in its commitment to value freedom a Cartesian separation between the individual knower and the object of knowledge. Her argument, in respect of values, is substantially compatible with my own except in the important respect of the 'transformative interrogation'.

Although this latter leaves open the possibility that science will discover the truth of the matter, the fact that contextual values can and should influence the way science is done means that at some point the scientist, or scientists, must make decisions that are based on the non-methodological values they hold. There is widespread acceptance, especially in social science, that more than one theory may be logically consistent with the data, and indeed various strategies have been proposed by philosophers to deal with this problem of theory choice, from falsification to Bayesian probability (Couvalis 1997). However, such attempts are predicated on the assumption that the deadlock can be broken eventually, but what if it can't? Longino discusses a case study of rival behavioural research programmes, the selectionist and linear hormonal programme. Both programmes, she maintains, are grounded in assumptions about sex and gender and the results of neither can be determined on the basis of constitutional values alone. As a feminist she is specifically critical of the linear hormonal programme for its androcentric and deterministic assumptions and 'the limitations on human capacity imposed by [its] explanatory model' (1990: 190), but also because of the deleterious effects its findings, if they were to be accepted by the policy community, would have on women's lives. Conversely, the selectionist programme, while it too is not free of contextual values, nevertheless better offers the possibility to understand ourselves and others.

Longino is not simply saying here are two theories, neither of which can be corroborated or falsified, but one is androcentric so we should choose the other. She seems to be saying that she has good reason to believe that androcentric theories inadequately describe the world, and an outcome of this mis-description is the sexist bias that is already written into the assumptions of secondary theories, which finally get translated into the policy outcomes of the science conducted. We might add that this in turn sets the agenda for the selection of future projects. Therefore, on the basis of good science, we should reject those theories seen to be androcentric, the pay-off being better theories and better outcomes. However, it does not follow that even when theory choice is less difficult or there is clear corroboration of a theory through findings, the assumptions behind such a theory are invulnerable. When these assumptions are themselves falsified, the theory is shown to be wrong. To choose theory A over theory B because the underlying value assumptions of B are known to lead to bad science is not to give a clean bill of health (in this respect) to A (Popper 1979: 14).

Nevertheless, Longino could argue that if the scientific community, through its transformative interrogation, can demonstrate that the value antecedents of a theory are based on 'bad science', then surely there is a duty to reject that theory, even if the value provenance of its rival is unknown. However, this assumes that the present transformative interrogation is correct in its judgement, but this must be taken to mean that the correctness or truth of the matter may well be dependent on utility decisions made socially. Truth itself becomes both consensual[4] and pragmatic. One must also assume that once such truth is ascertained by the community then any alternative account would be epistemologically deviant to that community.

Toward situated objectivity in sociology

We can find elements of what I term 'situated objectivity in each of the foregoing accounts and something can be taken from each.

Weber acknowledges and even advocates that social investigation will begin from a perspective that it will be more than simply scientific curiosity. However, his belief is, and was shown to be wrong, that the social position underpinning the investigation can be left behind when investigation begins. Every research methods primer will tell us that our research is driven by the research question, that it makes a difference not just in what is asked but how we do it. Gouldner recognised this in US sociology and called for an objectivity that went beyond the narrowness of objectivity of method and existed outside it, but his prescriptions were vague.

One can say that the corollary of admitting values is that value-led enquiry is all we can do, and this was Becker's view, but rather like siding with one football team or another, we apparently must buy into the totality of values of that side.

---

[4]This assumes consensus can be reached. Couvalis (1997: 161) maintains that she fails to show how such an ideal community can come to agree on the choice of one theory over another.

Despite his later protests, objectivity in any form must disappear if this position is taken to its logical conclusion. Nevertheless, Becker was half right: sociology will always be conducted from a perspective (though I do not believe this is the same as taking sides).

Helen Longino, although concerned with natural science, offers a more sophisticated position than the previous ones, though to an extent she returns to Weber by acknowledging that methodological practice can produce results which can challenge or advance knowledge. She quite rightly sees a transference between methodological values and other values. However, her conclusions are essentially pragmatist. That the community will be the arbiter of good scientific practice and ultimately knowledge decisions will be those that benefit that community, all things being equal.

Each of these accounts emphasises the role of values and each attributes purpose, which produces specific differentiations. Implicit in Weber is the belief that method will lead us to truth. In Becker there is either a denial truth can be found or, worse, an implicit relativism. Longino does preserve the notion of truth and that it can be revealed as a result of social process, but this seems almost secondary to the particular social conditions she advocates for truth-seeking. In Longino, the pursuance of truth is not explicitly a value which drives enquiry.

Situated objectivity emphasises truth-seeking as the immutable value present in objectivity. Purpose will be different in every context and the differentiations made will depend on purpose. Yet, let us concede to Becker that the particular purpose will make a difference to the pursuit of truth.

From this it does not follow that, first, the purpose itself is overtly ideological or limiting in its knowledge objectives. Furthermore, the purpose itself may bring with it knowledge and practices that will correct for 'bias'. Indeed 'bias' and 'purpose' are not the same thing (though they can be sometimes). Secondly, even though the investigation will be towards a purpose, the investigation itself is capable of changing that purpose, or producing unexpected or more widely generalisable results. A good example of the latter was Stouffer's work. Samuel Stouffer conducted extensive research in the Second World War for the US War Department (Stouffer 1949). As John Madge (1963: 288[5]) notes, that this could happen indicated the growing respectability of social science. But the military were not conducting research purely for its scientific value, but rather with the aim of military efficiency, for example, through a better understanding of soldiers' morale, or which army companies would best perform in combat. Yet his and his colleagues' work contributed significantly to sociological knowledge, especially

---

[5]The discussion in Madge (1963: Chapter 9) is partially an account of Stouffer's research relationship with the military and serves as a good example of how sociologists conduct research in partisan settings yet are able to maintain critical distance and produce findings that can transcend those settings.

that of the concept of relative deprivation. A well-known finding was that those soldiers in units where promotion was uncommon looked more favourably upon promotion opportunities than those in units that enjoyed greater promotion opportunities (Madge 1963: 329). This in itself was a finding that had transferability to many other organisational settings.

A helpful heuristic device that is a nod in the direction of Gouldner (who maintained that objectivity should exist not just in method) is to think of objectivity operating along two axes. The first of these might be seen as that of the discipline's relation to wider society (rather similar to Longino's contextual values). Let us call this the vertical axis. In sociology, at the top, we would find the historic and national social context for the discipline, assuming that it exists at all. Soviet era societies, though they conducted some sociological investigation, nevertheless did not acknowledge the existence of the discipline. Contrast this with the United States in the period 1918 to 1990.

Indeed, the golden age[6] of social science was probably in the United States between the 1930s and the 1960s. This was also 'positivist' social science at its zenith. Indeed, the age of positivism coincided with the growth of American economic and cultural dominance more generally, and particularly in sociology. The latter was motivated by the tremendous advances in science and engineering in that country in the first quarter of the twentieth century. There were criticisms, especially from Robert Lynd and C. Wright Mills, but these fell on deaf ears in a profession 'trained in statistical methods, with mutually reinforcing motivations to win promotion and produce the "facts" needed by mayors, presidents and corporations' (Manicas 1987: 226). Jennifer Platt's excellent *A History of Sociological Research Methods in America 1920–1960* (1996) charts this golden age and the relationship of method and methodology to societal imperatives and concerns, and can be seen as an historical example *par excellence* of the relationships on the vertical axis. It was the nature of this policy relationship, whereby sociology was alleged to be simply the tool of government and the status quo, which motivated Gouldner's complaint. But if one takes the long view, this was a golden age not just because of the status and activity of the discipline, but also because of its contribution to methodological development and because it was the basis for a later, more catholic sociology (see Abbott 2001).

Lower down the axis comes the problematic: the funding regimes and the links between public sociology and wider society. Here sociology will be shaped by national priorities and funding availability, but it can also influence society itself. Giddens' 'third way' (1998, 2000) or Etzioni's 'communitarianism' (1993) were both said to have been influential to the New Labour government in the

---

[6] I qualify this comment in that it was a period that combined growing credibility of social science in the public mind with increasing methodological sophistication.

UK in the 1990s and 2000s. A little lower down the vertical axis come the disciplinary organisation and ethos. These are, for example, very different in the USA and the UK. The American Sociological Association has much more power and influence (though probably less than they would like and possibly less than they had) than its UK counterpart. The disciplinary ethos is different and stems, at least in part, from the very different nature of research and teaching in each country. While US sociology is big enough to support a flourishing intellectual market in qualitative and quantitative methods (and indeed a powerful constituency for mixed methods), in the UK there has never been an equivalent quantitative sociology, in either size or prestige (Williams and Vogt 2011: 9–11).

Finally, despite these contrasts, it is not the case that national sociologies exist in a vacuum, and this is increasingly less the case as a result of the ease of international travel and the internationalisation of publishing.

These things are much more than simply contextual values; they are overlapping and intermeshing cultures that have active agency in promoting values up and down the axis. One of these values is, of course, objectivity. Not methodological objectivity, but objectivity about the purpose and role of sociology.

The horizontal axis is somewhat simpler and consists of the cultures, methodologies and methods of a discipline. Nevertheless, these too have historic and geographic variation and will exist within the national ethos of the discipline, which I locate on the vertical axis. The horizontal axis has its methodological hierarchies and power struggles (e.g. the 'anti-positivist' movement of the 1960s onwards, or the current battle over the efficacy or otherwise of randomised control trials). Nevertheless those who invent, decide or adopt particular methods or methodologies will exist within a professional cadre (often in the academy) and will share many norms, values and practices. These, for example, career structures or gendered divisions of labour, are rarely amenable to individual or small group influence (others may say decisions to adopt one or other sampling method are). There are enormous differences in methods in national sociologies,[7] but crucially, there are wide areas of methodological agreement, once particular methods are adopted. For example, there is pretty much consensus about which tests of significance can be used with parametric and non-parametric data respectively, circumstances under which a null hypothesis can be rejected, agreement on appropriate sampling strategies, etc. Though qualitative research is, by its nature, less rule-bound, there are good and bad practices and experienced qualitative researchers come to know the difference. I have written elsewhere of Herrnstein and Murray's (1994) 'Bell Curve' work and David Drew et al.'s (1995) statistical

---

[7]For example, Francophone researchers have pioneered Time Location Sampling (TLS) to sample hard-to-research populations, whereas in Anglophone countries Respondent Driven Sampling (RDS) is more prevalent and TLS is not well known (Marpsat and Razafindratsima 2010).

critique of it (Williams 2000: 118–19). In this case, the neo-racist claims of their research were effectively refuted through a critique of the weakness of their operational constructs and the statistical failings of their models.

My specification of the horizontal axis is not a return to Weber, because the interrelationship between the axes is not one way. Method cannot overcome purpose that seeks only a given answer, though it is possible for this to happen. Purpose itself is scrutinised on the vertical axis and, once adopted by the researcher, will set bounds for the pursuance of truth. A society may decide to invest heavily in the investigation of types of criminality so that criminal justice solutions may be found. The researcher will seek to pursue truth within these purposes, but the purpose itself may not have been objective and should perhaps have been an investigation of the social basis of criminality in poverty and social exclusion.

Objectivity, like any values, will always be situated. It is not a binary variable – one is not simply objective or not objective. Just as we assess historical actors in their context, so we must assess objectivity in its context.

While the general features of a society will certainly shape disciplinary concerns, sociology will often identify particular issues for attention. For example, in the last few decades, US and British sociology has shifted a research focus from traditional concerns, such as stratification, the family, community, etc., towards an eclectic range of topics – as John Scott put it, a 'fragmentation of the discipline' (Scott 2005). For example, surveillance, citizenship, human rights, consumerism, the body, emotions and risk. While each of these can in principle be researched objectively, the choice of topic to research will likely be determined by particular interests, and while that too is perfectly reasonable, a more general question might be how the endeavours of research in these areas might contribute more generally to sociological knowledge? In other words, is an abandonment of a concern with traditional areas (and the subsequent fragmentation Scott complains of) a collective abandonment of objectivity towards the discipline? If this is the case, then the lack of objectivity at the second level is transferred upwards to the first.

A lack of objectivity within the pursuance of a particular area is perhaps more common and more tangible. The sociology of risk provides such an example. Iain Wilkinson has reviewed research and writing in the area of the sociology of risk (Wilkinson 2001). In the last few years 'risk' has become an important topic for sociology and has achieved prominence through the writings of Ulrich Beck (1992, 1995) and Mary Douglas (1992). As Wilkinson (2001: 2) notes, the prominence of these two sociologists rests on quite different foci on risk. For Beck, the critical rationality that emerges from risk consciousness has transformative political potential, whereas for Douglas the aim is to advance a structural-functionalist interpretation of risk. Wilkinson maintains, in choosing one approach over the other, that there is an inevitable political commitment and that the incommen-surability of such positioning cannot be resolved through objective evidence because '[o]ur knowledge of technological risks and their associated health and environmental hazards consists in processes of discourse which are always open to debate and subject to change' (Wilkinson 2001: 2).

Nevertheless, Beck, as a sociologist, is quite openly using his work to promote an agenda and, as a political activity, this may be laudable. Indeed his analyses of the antecedents of 'risk society' may in the long run prove valuable, but his work (and that of Douglas) does not take into consideration 'the vast amount of research conducted into the social perceptions of risk over the last 20 years' (Wilkinson 2001: 2). Indeed, the 'sociology of risk', more generally, virtually ignores the literature of actuarial and psychological research of probabilities of risk and individual perceptions of these probabilities, see, for example, Renn (1992), Slovic (1992) and Gigerenzer (2002). Wilkinson's own view that the positions on risk are incommensurable assumes that the contentions that Beck and Douglas made were untestable. Indeed, as he describes, the findings of sociological studies of risk perceptions are confused and inconsistent, but does it follow from this that these inconsistencies and the incorporation of empiri-cal studies from outside sociology would not yield to further analysis? In other sciences, inconsistency and lack of incorporation would be seen as a challenge rather than a doctrine of despair or the acceptance of the inevitability of a retreat into prior ideological positions. The sociology of risk certainly has pur-pose, but its differentiation and search for truth seems to be mortgaged to prior ideological assumptions and either wilfully or carelessly ignores research from outside sociology. The subjectivism underlying much of sociological writing on risk perhaps makes this inevitable.

Conclusion: Finding objectivity

Objective/not objective are not dichotomous states, neither is objectivity some-thing one can have a bit of or a lot of. Ultimately, as Longino correctly diag-noses, it is a social category both in its content and in that we value it in our investigative activities. It must have purpose, but that purpose is not immune to an objectivity test. That test lies in the pursuance of truth, with the caveat that truth itself will be pursued from a perspective. Sometimes we must take the historic long view. In the natural sciences, discovery and theory adjudication rarely takes place at one time, through one deciding experiment. Sociology is a relatively young discipline, but already we are able to reassess our verdict on his-torical periods, their problematic and their methods. The message is that while objectivity is a necessary ingredient to good investigation and we should strive towards it, even with the best will in the individual and the community we may not achieve it.

Finally, there remains one unfinished piece of business. Earlier in the chapter I maintained that for the argument I make to succeed, one needs only to take the weak position on differentiation. However, the weak position on differentiation leaves the situated objectivity argument open to charges of epistemological relativism, that is, the differentiation of our categories is arbitrary, or just a matter of contemporary social agreement. As Becker observed, sociologists are mostly of liberal persuasion, though we have been tested, through the temptations of Project Camelot in the 1960s and, more recently, through the Minerva Consortium (Gusterson 2009). In each case the US government has tried to recruit social scientists to a narrow militarily inspired research agenda, much narrower and more constrained than the one Stouffer found in the 1940s.[8] This certainly has purpose and differentiation and, within its confines, truth may be sought. But we are back to Gouldner's complaint and worse.

My argument for situated objectivity must rely not just on its epistemology, but also on some firmer ontological assumptions about the nature of social 'objects'. The ontological argument does not remove the moral imperative, but may make it easier to make decisions about differentiation. I will develop this argument in Chapter 6.

Discussion

———John———————————————————————————

MALCOLM HAS BEGUN TO MOVE us away from the subjectivity – or intersubjectivity – of the perspectives on knowledge that we must necessarily adopt. He moves us towards an awareness that the knowledge constructed from a particular standpoint can be

---

[8]Project Camelot was research to investigate the causes of and means to avoid 'internal war' in other countries and in reality was at least partly intended to recruit sociologists (and other social scientists) into counter-insurgency efforts (Horowitz 1967). The sociological community was mostly opposed to this, though as Earl Babbie (1995) asks, what might have happened had Project Camelot 'been proposed to a steadfastly conservative and anti-communist social research community?' The Minerva Consortium similarly sought to recruit anthropologists for military purposes at a time when the USA was increasingly intervening militarily in Third World countries, such as Somalia and Afghanistan.

There is a historic point to make here. In the 1940s there was a virtual national consensus in the USA that Germany and Japan must be defeated through war, whereas such a consensus did not exist at the time of Project Camelot or Minerva, and indeed the focus of the latter was not military efficiency but rather to use anthropological knowledge as a tool in more covert military activity.

regarded as 'objective' only if, in some sense, its descriptions are in conformity with its 'object'. This is what justifies us in claiming that the knowledge is 'true' and that it avoids any suggestion of 'bias'.

This conformity to the object has typically been seen in terms of a 'correspondence' between knowledge and reality. I argued in Chapter 2, however, that the idea of correspondence or conformity is highly problematic. It is simply not possible to treat phenomenal knowledge and noumenal objects as similar things that correspond to each other in a one-to-one way. The noumena, as they are in themselves, are completely unknowable and we can have no rational grounds for believing that they are constituted of the same stuff and have the same structures as the mental representations by which humans must live their lives.

The question left unanswered by Malcolm's argument is how conformity with the object is to be understood. For all that he breaks with the value judgements that are the source of bias, seeing objectivity 'in context' does not yet get us beyond subjectivity to an appreciation of what might be meant by producing knowledge that is in conformity with reality.

———Gayle ————————————————————————————————

I AGREE WITH MALCOLM ON a lot of issues. I agree that objectivity is value-laden and as values are always situated, objectivity is situated. I agree that there is not a binary divide between objectivity and subjectivity, that one is not simply objective or not objective and that objectivity is something that we should strive towards but also something that we may not (maybe cannot) achieve. All of this seems obvious and sensible to me and so I am frustrated when social scientists argue simplistically (and naïvely) for objectivity. If I had a pound for every time a student – often at final-year undergraduate or even postgraduate level – used the terms 'bias' (in my mind, the four-letter word of social research: mis-used and over-used just like many a swear word), 'value freedom' and 'objectivity' inappropriately, I'd be quite a bit better off than I am. For me, at least, the worst of all epistemological crimes is to define quantitative methods (however well or badly used) with objectivity, and qualitative methods (however well or badly used) with subjectivity. This, as Malcolm notes, not only hinders a full epistemological understanding of quantitative and qualitative research, but has implications for mixed methods research also.

In thinking about my own value-laden approach to social research, I have always started from a different position; from the position of myself as a situated individual, not least in terms of my gender and my class and family origins and subsequent opportunities and challenges. Thus, I begin by reflecting on my inevitably subjective position and the implications of this for the work I do and the choices I make. My argument, then, is for theorised subjectivity, rather than situated objectivity, as a more appropriate starting point when working towards objectivity.

——Malcolm ————————————————————————————

JOHN IS CORRECT IN SAYING that in seeking truth I believe we should seek correspondence with reality. As a logical point, that is correct. But there are two things to say and they are related. First, we run the risk of reifying the idea of the 'noumena' as somehow having a fixed content that is unknowable. One can concede the logical point, but also know that in many areas of investigation (particularly science) what was once noumenal becomes phenomenal. In Chapter 6 I will argue that realism is a viable strategy in the pursuit of truth and objectivity. The second point is a reiteration that we pursue truth, but with no guarantees that we will find it, though along the way we will certainly uncover things we did not know previously.

I have argued that objectivity is situated, but mostly I have not talked about the individual. Gayle's starting point is different from mine, though I believe there is compatibility. She argues that it is inevitable that we must begin from the fact of our own situatedness and thus our subjectivity. In the next chapter she develops this argument to say that our research requires a theorisation of our own subjective position.

FIVE
Theorised Subjectivity

Having established in Chapters 2 and 3 that knowledge is situated and contextual, the discussion in Chapter 4 made a claim for objectivity as a situated value. In this chapter debates and discussion surrounding subjectivity are brought to the fore, challenging the view that subjectivity is inevitably problematic, and instead arguing for the need for the careful consideration of the significance of subjectivity as part of the pursuit for objectivity.

———Gayle's argument————————————————————————

MY AIM IS TO MAKE the case for theorised subjectivity, to begin from the position of the subjective when reflecting on the relationship between objectivity and subjectivity. In almost all of the articles and books, including this one, that focus on objectivity and subjectivity, the initial and, often, primary focus is on objectivity: what is it?, can we ensure it?, if we can't, what can we do instead? and so on. From this perspective, subjectivity as a position is always considered not only in relation to objectivity but as secondary, subservient to it. Not surprisingly given the historical privileging of the 'scientific method', through 'peer review, publications and conferences, shaping and directing the common understanding of … research [and epistemological approaches] within the field', with reference to historical debates on objectivity and subjectivity the social sciences have operated as an 'epistemic community … building a normatively science-based or research-question-based joint understanding of the relevant kind of knowledge' (Poutanen and Kovalainen 2010: 2.1).

   Subjectivity is more often than not defined as inevitably problematic and as something to be avoided or controlled. I accept that objectivity too is often problematised but this problematisation generally includes discussion of why we still need objectivity and how to defend it. As Martyn Hammersley (2011) notes, while most social scientists have never completely accepted or adhered to objectivity, much methodological and epistemological thinking and research practice has been strongly affected by it. Objectivity, then, is always the elephant in the room and continues to have influence 'especially among quantitative researchers and in the context of research methods training courses' Hammersley (2011: 30–1). Qualitative researchers too, I think, are concerned with similar issues, not least because they have to defend their work from accusations of bias more often than quantitative researchers. Furthermore, there is the influence of the so-called 'paradigm wars', with objectivity being unproblematically associated with quantitative methods and subjectivity with all things qualitative. Sometimes this argument has been extended/ connected to arguments that link the quantitative to objectivity to masculinity, and the qualitative to subjectivity to femininity (Oakley 1998; Westmarland 2001). Indeed, many qualitative researchers have been part of this debate and some have 'attacked, or abandoned, the concept of objectivity itself, while others have sought to fundamentally reconstruct it' (Hammersley 2011: 30–1).

My aim here is to defend both objectivity *and* subjectivity and to start from a different position from most thinkers and writers in this area; from the position of *theorised subjectivity*. All social research involves individuals – both researchers and respondents – who have subjectivities, who make subjectivities. Theorised subjectivity acknowledges that research is a subjective, power-laden, emotional, embodied experience but does not see this as a disadvantage, just as how it is. Starting with subjectivity, though, does not mean that we shrug our epistemological shoulders and give in to the subjective, indulging in our subjectivities. Rather it requires the constant, critical interrogation of our personhood – both intellectual and personal – within the knowledge production process.

This position, then, not only turns the debate on its head but rescues subjectivity from its secondary sideline. My thinking in this area owes much to both auto/ biographical sociology and to feminist theory and my starting point is always Charles Wright Mills. Mills (1959: 204) reminded us that the social scientist is part of society and not an externally located observer: 'The social scientist is not some autonomous being standing outside society, the question is where he [*sic*] stands within it.' From this perspective, then, the acknowledgement and use of the personal in intellectual work is as asset and not a burden:

> … learn to use your life experience in your intellectual work; continually to examine it and interpret it. In this sense craftsmanship [*sic*] is the centre of yourself and you are personally involved in every intellectual product in which you work. (Mills 1959: 216)

There are links there too with the work of Karl Mannheim, who argued that all knowledge is 'socially rooted' and that '[t]he proper theme of [the sociology of knowledge] is to observe how and in what form intellectual life at a given historical moment is related to the existing social and political forces' (Mannheim 1936: 60).

Following on from this auto/biographical sociological (social scientific) study – either focusing on one, several or many lives – highlights the need to liberate the individual from individualism; to demonstrate how individuals are social selves – which is important because a focus on the individual can contribute to the understanding of the general (Mills 1959; Okley 1992; Stanley 1992; Evans 1997; Erben 1998). In addition, auto/biographical work highlights the relationship(s) and similarities and differences between the self and other within the research and writing process. Thus, as David Morgan (1998: 655) notes:

> [auto/biography is not] ... simply a shorthand representation of autobiography and/or biography but also [a] recognition of the inter-dependence of the two enterprises. ... In writing another's life we also write or rewrite our own lives; in writing about ourselves we also construct ourselves as some body different from the person who routinely and unproblematically inhabits and moves through social space and time.

It has become commonplace for the researcher to locate her/himself within the research process and produce 'first-person' accounts. This involves a recognition that, as researchers, we need to appreciate that our research activities tell us things about ourselves as well as about those we are researching (Steier 1991). Further, there is recognition among social scientists that we need to consider how the researcher as author is positioned in relation to the research process, not least with reference to the choice and design of the research fieldwork and analysis, editorship and presentation (Iles 1992; Sparkes 1998; Letherby 2003c).

There are resonances with these views in feminist work but feminists often go further in terms of an explicit recognition of the researcher's self. Feminist researchers argue that we need to consider how the researcher as author is positioned in relation to the research process, and to ignore the personal involvement of the researcher within research is to downgrade the personal. Thus, feminists are concerned with the relationship between the process and the product. This includes concerns over who has the right to know, the nature and value of knowledge and feminist knowledge within this, the relationship between the methods chosen, how they are used and the 'knowledge' produced. Within this there is also an acknowledgement that there is 'no technique or methodological logic that can neutralize the social nature of interpretation' (Holland and Ramazanoglu, cited by Morley 1996: 142), which results in a value-explicit if not value-free approach. For me, this is theorised subjectivity.

In what follows I demonstrate how my work links to that of others working in this area and reflect further on the advantages and problems of theorised subjectivity – a concept I first proposed in 2003 (Letherby 2003b 2003c). As I have already suggested and continue to argue below, theorised subjectivity relies on a recognition that, while there is a 'reality' 'out there', the political complexities of subjectivities, and their inevitable involvement in the research/theorising process, make a definitive/final traditionally defined objective statement difficult or impracticable. Furthermore, I suggest that theorised subjectivity recognises the values – both positive and negative – of the subjective BUT should not be automatically equated with involvement. Reference to the similarities and differences between *theorised* subjectivity and *situated objectivity, good enough objectivity, corroborative objectivity, strong objectivity* and *feminist fractured foundationalism* are made.

Objectivity, bias and other epistemological starting points

Martyn Hammersley views objectivity as an essential epistemological virtue:

> I suggest that we see objectivity as one, among several, epistemic virtues that are essential to research. Other epistemic virtues include a commitment to truth and truthfulness (Williams 2002), intellectual sobriety (a determination to follow a middle way between over-cautious or excessive enthusiasm for any particular knowledge claim, form of evidence, or method) and intellectual courage (a willingness to resist fear of the consequences of pursing inquiry wherever it leads, including personal costs relating to life, livelihood or reputation) (Montmarquet, 1993: 23). Like objectivity these other epistemic virtues relate to distinctive sorts of threat to the rational pursuit of inquiry, and the need to resist them. (Hammersley 2011: 39)

For Hammersley, then, anything other than objectivity is bias and a 'threat to the rational pursuit of inquiry', but this denies both the complexity of the research process and the complexity of the concepts at issue. I agree with Malcolm (Williams) who notes that 'value freedom' is itself a value, and if value freedom is a value, so is objectivity (Williams 2005a: 108; and see Chapter 4 this volume). He argues for the existence of a value continuum and adds:

> To be objective in science commits us to values of law. Objectivity, then, is not an homogeneous value and its context will determine its relationship to other values (and therefore what it is in context). This is a key point, because when we talk about objectivity in science we are talking about something different to objectivity in other spheres. But, if my argument about the value continuum is right, then the meaning of objectivity in any discipline will relate to its internal use *and* its use in the relationship of that discipline to the rest of the social world. (ibid.: 108, original emphasis)

So for Malcolm (see Chapter 4 this volume), 'objectivity is a value, a desirable value and a socially situated one'. Richard Jenkins (2002: 8) argues similarly for everyday realism, or what he credits David Silverman as calling 'cautious positivism'. He suggests that objectivity along with theory and systematic enquiry are together the three legs of the sociological stool and what distinguishes sociology from common sense. For Jenkins:

> Everyday realism carries with it a responsibility to document the observable realities of the human world as accurately as we can. Objectivity is one of the key issues in this respect. If we are to make any plausible claim at all to understand the human world, and if the understanding that we offer is to stand any chance of being accepted as non-partisan or unbiased, then it is vital that we make at least some attempt to be objective... (ibid.)

Jenkins (ibid.) continues with a consideration of the relationship between political/emancipatory social science and objectivity and argues against 'disinterested value-free sociology', while at the same time insisting that a political and ethical approach to our work should not prevent us from striving towards objectivity. What we need to do, Jenkins (2002: 10) suggests, is keep our 'hard won critical distance'; when we are researching in order to 'facilitate the clearest, most complete view possible'. We need to do this in order to find out 'as *much* as we can, as *honestly* as we can, and as *systematically* as we can' (ibid., original emphasis). Jenkins (2002: 38) adds:

> Necessarily, and from whatever perspective it is done, sociological research – *in* the human world as well as *into* it – cannot be anything other than an ethically sensitive activity. ...
>
> [T]he human world is an observable reality – or, to be perhaps more precise, is composed of observable realities – only the best, and the most honest, observations are good enough. As I have already argued, this doesn't mean that we can make sense of the world of humans without pre-existing conceptual frameworks for doing so. Nor does it mean that our methods are innocent, neutral techniques. (original emphasis)

Here we see an argument that supports the view that value-free objectivity is not possible or desirable, but we need to work hard and aim for epistemological objectivity which is important and necessary for our work to be taken seriously by those outside the discipline. However, this effort, Jenkins (2002: 12) suggests, is likely to result only in 'good enough objectivity'. Similarly, Tim May with Beth Perry (2011) draw on the work of Pierre Bourdieu to point out some of the things that social researchers can miss:

> Interactions between a medic, an intern and a nurse ... are undergirded by hierarchical relations of power that are not always visible during the directly observable interaction. (Bourdieu, in Bourdieu and Wacquant 1992: 73)

With this (and work by others who similarly problematise the practice of research) in mind, May with Perry (2011: 61) see connections with 'radical contructivism which does not deny ontological reality as such' but insists that the 'best one can hope for is a "corroborative objectivity" that is rooted within the subjective experiences of the particularity of lifeworlds'.

Situated objectivity (Williams 2005a and Chapter 4, this volume), good enough objectivity (Jenkins 2002) and corroborative objectivity (see May with Perry 2011) all challenge traditional claims that research can be free from all values, interests and assumptions. Another such critique of objectivity comes from feminism. An early feminist critique of traditional 'male-centred scientific' epistemology (that research is not only undertaken mostly by men but centres on male perspectives and focuses on male interests) was feminist empiricism. Feminist empiricism leaves intact much of the traditional 'scientific' understandings of the principles of adequate enquiry but feminist empiricists seek to use 'traditional' methods and approaches more 'appropriately', challenging the way that methods are used rather than challenging the methods themselves. For example, Magrit Eichler (1988) insists on non-sexist research and the elimination of sexism in titles; sexism in language; sexist concepts; sexism in research designs; sexism in methods; and sexism in policy evaluation. Feminist empiricism, then, challenges the 'value-free' aims and claims of traditional approaches but does not challenge the objective scientific goals (Stanley and Wise 1993; Letherby 2003c; Abbott et al. 2005).

Feminist standpoint epistemology, like feminist empiricism, begins from the view that so-called 'masculine' science is bad science because it excluded women's experience. As John argues in Chapter 3, feminist standpoint epistemologists advocate the development of a 'successor science' to existing dominant social science paradigms. They argue that the 'personal is political' and, drawing on Marxist ideas, suggest that women are an oppressed class and as such have the ability not only to understand their own experiences of oppression but to see their oppressors' viewpoint. The view here is that research based on women's experience provides a more valid basis for knowledge because 'it gives access to a wider conception of truth via the insight into the oppressor' (Millen 1997: 7.2). It is not just that the oppressed see more – their own experience and that of the privileged – but also that their knowledge emerges through the struggle against oppression: in this instance the struggle against men. Advocates of feminist standpoint epistemology argue that objectivity *is* possible, but that the critical scrutiny of all aspects of the research process is necessary to achieve objectivity. This presents a challenge to traditional notions of objectivity which Harding (1993) argues are weak because the researchers' own values, assumptions and so on are hidden. The standpoint approach is not the preserve of those concerned with researching women's experience. For example, some researchers working in the areas of disability, 'race' and ethnicity, and childhood argue for a standpoint approach. For example, when searching for an epistemology based on the experience of African-American women, the values and ideas that African writers identify as being characteristically 'black' are often very similar to those claimed by white feminist scholars as being characteristically female. This suggests that the material conditions of oppression can vary dramatically and yet generate some uniformity in the epistemologies of subordinate groups (Hill-Collins 1989). Similarly, researchers working in the area of childhood have argued that as both women and children are subject to patriarchy, those in power regard both groups as social problems and both groups find it hard to have their points of view heard and respected (Mayall 2002). Returning to feminist standpoint epistemology and feminist epistemological claims, for Sandra Harding feminist objectivity acknowledges that *'knowledge and truth are partial, situated, subjective, power imbued, and relational.* [and] The denial of values, biases, and politics is seen as unrealistic and undesirable' (Hesse-Biber 2007b: 9, original emphasis). For me at least, although Malcolm might disagree with me, there are similarities between situated objectivity (Williams) and strong objectivity (Harding).

Epistemologically, there are some problems with taking a standpoint position. Focusing on the standpoint of one particular group can imply that their perspective is more real, more accurate and better than that of others. Also, if we accept a position which implies that there is only one (real, accurate, best) experience, this can only be built upon the suppression of less powerful voices. The view that more oppressed or more disadvantaged groups have the greatest potential for knowledge also implies that the greater the oppression the broader or more inclusive one's potential knowledge. This leads to an unproductive discussion about hierarchies of oppression: that is, those who are more oppressed (if this is possible to measure) are potentially more knowledgeable. Even if we find the most oppressed group of all, how do we know that their way of seeing is the 'most true'? In addition, a specific problem with feminist standpoint epistemology is the focus (of some supporters) on biology and traditional values given to women and womanhood, which positively redefines 'female' characteristics but in doing so reinforces feminine stereotypes (for examples see Griffin 1983; Ruddick 1990; and for critique, Wajcman 1991; Letherby 1994). Any standpoint position brings with it the danger of viewing a group of people as all the same and, as noted above, women are not a homogeneous group. Writing about researching gay and lesbian communities, Didi Herman (1994: 12) tells us:

> I am more persuaded by standpoint critics who argue that identity standpoints, while perhaps being a necessary stance within some forms of political campaigning, do not reveal true or better interpretations of social phenomena

within academic research. Furthermore, such standpoints impose a homogeneity upon the category being claimed which cannot reflect or represent the diversity within it.

I agree, and once we acknowledge the existence of several standpoints it becomes impossible to talk about 'independent truth' and 'objectivity' as a means of establishing superior or 'better knowledge' because there will always be alternative knowledge claims arising from contextually grounded knowledge of different standpoints (Letherby 2003c).

Feminist postmodernism provides a radical critique of both traditional (masculine) approaches and feminist empiricism and feminist standpoint epistemology. Feminist postmodernism completely rejects the possibility of the objective collection of facts, and from this perspective there are no universal theories and any attempt to establish a theory, a truth, is oppressive, whether from the perspective of male or female experience. Thus, feminist postmodernism (like other forms of postmodernism) rejects any claim to knowledge which makes an explicit appeal to the creation of a THEORY/a TRUTH. Feminist postmodernism, then, takes issue with the whole notion of a standpoint (Millen 1997). For postmodernists, there is not one truth but many truths, none of which is privileged (Flax 1987; Ramazanoglu with Holland 2002; Abbott et al. 2005). The emphasis on difference and the empowerment/emancipation of the other connects well with the concerns of feminists (e.g. Maynard 1994; Letherby 2003c; Hesse-Biber et al. 2004), but there are problems here too; for if all explanations are equal, feminist readings of female oppression are no more valid than any other perspective on women's experience (e.g. Jackson 1992; Hesse-Biber et al. 1999).

There have been attempts to bring the strengths of feminist standpoint epistemology and feminist postmodernism together, and feminists argue that we should acknowledge that there are material conditions that women share and yet recognise the importance of difference and the significance of each of the multiple identities that individuals occupy (e.g. Di Stephano 1990; Stanley and Wise 1993; Letherby 2003c; Naples 2003). By doing this we acknowledge that gender is a 'difference that makes a difference', even it if is not the only difference, or even the defining feature of a person's life (Di Stephano 1990: 78).

Stanley and Wise's (1993, 2005) feminist fractured foundationalism (FFF) is a methodological approach which 'recognises both that there is a materially grounded social world that is real in its consequences (foundationalism), and insists that differently-situated groups develop often different views of the realities involved (fractured)' (Stanley and Wise 2005: 1.6). This position does not dispute the existence of truth and a material reality but acknowledges that judgements about them are always relative to the context (situated) in which such knowledge is produced. Further, this is an approach which aims for a transparent

feminist research process and also challenges the view that researchers (in relation to their respondents) hold a position of 'epistemic privilege' (Stanley and
Wise 2005: 1.4). I return to this below in relation to my own argument for theorised subjectivity.

Making a case for theorised subjectivity

> ... [W]hat we do and how we do it affects what we get. Another way to put
> this is to say that who we are affects what we think we know. One important
> conclusion of this is that social scientists have a responsibility to ensure that
> when they speak about other people, they do so on the basis of warrantable
> knowledge. The audit trail through research question, methods, data collec-
> tion, analysis and interpretation needs to be clear, systematic and explicit.
> (Oakley 2004: 191)

In my own work, I have attempted to work towards a position that recognises
both the personhood of the researcher and the complexity of the researcher/
respondent relationship and yet allows for useful things to be said. Given the
association of objectivity with masculinity and 'masculine knowledge' (see
above), many feminists, as noted above (see Hammersley 2011), reject the pursuit of objectivity and instead argue that 'bias' (itself an overused and misused
word) is inevitable. Others, again as noted above, have attempted to redefine
objectivity. For example, 'strong objectivity', which:

> ... combines the goal of conventional objectivity – to conduct research com-
> pletely free of social influence and or personal beliefs – with the reality that
> no one can achieve this goal ... and recognizes that objectivity can only oper-
> ate within the limitations of the scientists' personal beliefs and experiences.
> (Hesse-Biber et al. 2004: 13; see also Harding 1993)

Rather than attempt to redefine objectivity, I have instead been concerned (and
have concerns) with 'the pursuit for objectivity' as the starting point of any discussion of objectivity and subjectivity and in the epistemological labour process.
I have argued that if instead we start by accepting our subjective position – the
significance of our personhood (intellectual and personal) within the research
process – and really try to understand the complexities and the influence of
these, these 'biased sources' can themselves result in useful data' (Letherby
2003c: 71). I have also argued that ironically, 'this acknowledgement of subjectivity by feminists and the associated 'super-sensitivity' to the relevance of the
personhood of the researcher can feasibly lead to the conclusion that our work
is more objective, in that our work, if not value-free, is value-explicit' (Letherby
2003c: 71). Yet, given that, for me and for others, the word 'objectivity' has so

many connotations with the traditional, authorised masculine approach, I have felt more comfortable referring to this approach, which acknowledges both the inevitability of bias and the usefulness of reflection on it, as 'theorised subjectivity' (Letherby 2003a, 2003c, 2011b).

In a critique of my argument, Sue Wise and Liz Stanley (2003: 1.37) suggest that:

> ...'theorised subjectivity' helps resist slipping back into conventional malestream notions of objectivity, which position the academic researcher/theorizer as different in kind from those she does research 'on' but retains, indeed is even predicated upon, an objectivity/subjectivity binary.

Stanley and Wise (2005) argue for the need to rethink the binary divide between objectivity and subjectivity. They see their development of feminist fractured foundationalism (FFF) as an attempt to do this by tackling the epistemological division head-on while being as concerned with grounded research practice as with theoretical conceptualisations:

> ... FFF was formulated to recognise both the materiality of social life and reality and its socially interpreted and culturally constructed aspects, as well as an epistemological position which rejects the tired old realism/idealism binary as a misconceived simplification. (Stanley and Wise 2005: 1.5)

Feminist fractured foundationalism, then, necessitates producing feminist knowledge in an open, accountable and defensible way. This relates to earlier arguments by Stanley (1993), who advocated a focus on the intellectual auto/biography of the researcher and the analytical reflexivity necessary in order to produce 'accountable knowledge':

> ...auto-slash-biography ... disputes the conventional genre distinction between biography and autobiography as well as the divisions between self/other, public/private, and immediacy/memory. (Stanley 1993: 42)

> Through the notion of 'intellectual autobiography', I have tried to put such precepts concerning reflexivity ... into analytical practice, in particular by focusing on the processes by which evaluations, interpretations and conclusions have been reached from whatever 'data' I have worked on. (Stanley 1993: 45)

Important here is the research labour process and feminist fractured foundationalism focuses on analytical processes concerning knowledge production and associated knowledge claims. I agree with this, as I wrote in 2002 about my PhD research:

> I am conscious that I 'took away their words' and then analysed the data from my own political, personal and intellectual perspective. As Fine (1994) argues, research involves 'carving out pieces of narrative evidence that we select, edit and deploy to border our arguments' (p. 22). Thus, I am aware that my voice is the loudest. With this in mind I attempted to be sensitive to issues of power and control throughout the whole research process. When writing up my data I highlighted my role in the selection and interpretation of respondents' narratives and in terms of presentation of 'findings'. In interviews and letters, I asked respondents to reflect on issues that they had spoken or written of previously and incorporated (some) individual changes into my analysis and writing. (Letherby 2002b: 3.7)

Thus, I accept the importance of analytical reflexivity, of acknowledging and detailing the significance of the intellectual auto/biography of the researcher/ writer. But what I think feminist fractured foundationalism lacks is a similar acknowledgment of the significance of the personal auto/biography of the researcher/writer. Not only do many researchers begin their research with an interest in what they are studying (e.g. see Katz-Rothman 1996; Wilkinson and Kitzinger 1996) and/or have views on what they might find, but respondents too are political beings and all this and the researcher/respondent relationship itself impacts on the research process and product. For example, as I argued with Pamela Cotterill:

> As feminist [and other] researchers researching women's [and men's and children's] lives, we take their autobiographies and become their biographers, whilst recognizing that the autobiographies that we are given are influenced by the research relationship. In other words respondents have their own views of what the researcher might like to hear. Moreover we draw on our own experiences to help us understand those of our respondents. Thus their lives are filtered through us and the filtered stories of our lives are present (whether we admit it or not) in our written accounts. (Cotterill and Letherby 1993: 74))

Developing this, I suggest that 'theorised subjectivity' relies on a recognition that there is a 'reality' 'out there' but the political complexities of subjectivities are always part of the research process and impact on the research product. Thus, we always need to acknowledge the relationship between *knowing* and *doing* (Letherby 2004). All of this, I have previously argued, makes a definitive/final statement (objectivity) impracticable. In 2003 I suggested that what was practicable, desirable and necessary was the theorisation of the subjective (which includes the researcher's motivation and research practice and the respondent's expectations and behaviour) and its significance to knowledge production (Letherby 2003c). I wonder now if this could be interpreted as a rejection of objectivity as a goal. It is not. Rather, theorised subjectivity starts by recognising the value as in worth (rather than moral value) – both positive and negative – of the subjective.

Theorised subjectivity is a reflexive approach that acknowledges the significance of both intellectual and personal auto/biography of researchers and of respondents. And while I agree with Stanley and Wise (1993, 2005) that as researchers we are not intellectually superior to our respondents, I do think it is important that we acknowledge our intellectual privileges and the implications of these. I agree that we all 'observe, categorize, analyse, reach conclusions' and thus that 'people theorize their own experience ... and so researchers of the social are faced with an already "first order" theorized material social reality' (Stanley 1991: 208). So I believe that respondents as well as researchers are reflexive, theorising individuals. Reflexivity – both descriptive (the description of one's reflection) and analytical (involving comparison and evaluation) – are essential parts of the research process and both researchers and respondents engage in it. But as researchers we are in a privileged position, not only in terms of access to multiple accounts, but also in terms of discipline training which enables us to engage in 'second order theorising' which involves 'interpretation', not just 'description' of respondents' as well as the researchers' analytical processes (Letherby, 2002b).

Furthermore, I, like other (feminist) researchers, do make strong knowledge claims and argue that my research is 'broader', 'fuller' than what has gone before. So, I am arguing that my research is in some ways 'superior', and stands as a successor to what has gone before:

> At many places in my writing I have presented several sides of an argument but accept that I evaluated these in terms of MY feminist and sociological standpoints. So I have the final say. I am not only claiming a privilege here but also a 'superiority': a right to be regarded as a knower in a way that respondents do not have. This may involve some misrepresentation of their words but a final decision is necessary if (feminist) research is to say anything at all, have any effect at all, and not be concerned solely with issues of representation rather than 'reality' itself. (Kelly et al. 1994; Letherby 2003c: 4.4)

Hammersley (2011: 31) would likely classify my position as an abandonment of objectivity, a 'sceptical approach' that:

> ... denies that it is possible for us to escape the influence of our social identities and locations, or that it is desirable for us to try to do this; *and it insists that this undermines any possibility of knowledge.* Closely related to the argument that any claim to objectivity is naïve or deceitful, that the idea of gaining knowledge of a world that is independent of our beliefs about it is an illusion. ...

As I hope I have made clear, I am not arguing against objectivity as an epistemological value, nor do I see reflexivity as a substitute for objectivity (Hammersely
2011). What I do suggest is that we need to recognise subjectivity as an inevitable part of the pursuit of objectivity for if we do not, we are likely to miss (more
of) the things that impact on our ability to speak as knowledge producers. I
start from an epistemological position that rejects a simplistic foundationalist/
standpoint position. I do not believe that I am in a position to generate the 'true
story' of any experience I research but I do believe that 'my story' can stand
in opposition to and as a criticism of 'other stories' (both feminist and non-
feminist, academic and lay). Thus, 'doing (feminist) methodology' highlights
for me the problems in taking an epistemological position. In all of my work I
have found myself arguing for an epistemological position somewhere between
'epistemic privilege' and 'postmodernism'/relativism. I do not claim to have ever
found 'the answer' but by starting to ask different questions of different/under-
researched groups I believe that my research highlights complexities of differences of experience that have previously not been considered. I do not claim
that my work is, by definition, superior to other knowledge claims, and indeed
I accept that it should be subject to critical enquiry (Stanley and Wise 1993).
Thus, I have sympathy with Millen who, reflecting on her own research, writes:

> Whilst I do not believe that there is some sort of final, complete reality,
> and I am aware that my own subjectivity as a female feminist scientist has
> affected the outcome of my research. I do believe in a compromise between
> a completely subjective, unique and creative account of experience and a
> partly reproducible, objective and contextualised understanding in which
> my subjectivity has been critiqued. (Millen 1997: 8.5)

Am I arguing for good enough objectivity then? Yes probably. Do I agree with
the claims of and for situated objectivity, of corroborative objectivity? Yes I do.
But, as I have already stressed, I see an advantage in starting with the concept
that is often demonised and linked with bias and error. An example:

> In order to make any progress in reconceptualising objectivity, we probably
> need to differentiate among the ways in which error arising from 'subjec-
> tivity' can arise, and treat it as designed to counter just one of these. I pro-
> pose that it is treated as being concerned solely with error resulting from
> preferences, and the preconceptions associated with them, deriving from
> substantive commitments that are external to the pursuit of knowledge. In
> these terms objectivity amounts to continually being one's guard against
> errors caused by preferences and preconceptions coming from this source.
> (Hammersley 2011: 37–8)

I am not the first feminist to argue for the reclaiming of the subjective as others have suggested that 'conscious subjectivity' should replace the 'value-free

objective' of traditional research (e.g. Duelli Klein, cited by Wilkinson 1986: 14; Katz-Rothman 1996; Morley 1996). But this does not mean, at least I don't think it does, that we should embrace subjectivity and deny objectivity. For me, objectivity and subjectivity are intertwined in that when we make an objective claim subjectivity is always involved. 'Good enough objectivity', then, is not about standing back as far as we can and maintaining a critical distance, but involves us in constantly and continually interrogating our subjectivities. This means an acceptance of subjectivity as inevitable and a willingness to accept this inevitability as something we can work with. If we don't understand the significance of subjectivity/ies in research, we are stuck. If our aim is to get any-where near an objective truth, we need to see subjectivity not as a hindrance but as a resource in this endeavour.

Thinking cautiously about theorised subjectivity

In her early reflections on the status of knowledge Barbara Katz-Rothman (1996: 51) went so far as to suggest that there had been a fundamental shift in methodo-logical thinking, where an 'ethic of involvement had replaced an ethic of objectiv-ity'. From this perspective, writing from personal experience rather than from a position of 'detached objectivity' is likely to give the writer 'credentials'. She adds:

> In the circles I travel in now, if you see an article by a colleague on breast cancer you write to see how she is, wonder when she was diagnosed. If you see an article on Alzheimer's you assume someone's got a parent or in-law to help. I can track my colleagues' progression through the life cycle, through crises and passages, by article and book titles. (Katz-Rothman 1996: 51)

Similarly, Michael Hemmingson (2009: 139–40), in making his case for auto/ ethnography (see below for some definitions), argues for an 'eight moment' of qualitative enquiry which can be defined as 'an era of complete rejection of all previous rules, theories, and restrictions, where the proceeding "experts" step aside and make room for the new ... voices'.[1] In the eight moment, then,

---

[1]N.K. Denzin and Y.S. Lincoln (1994) write of five, possibly six, moments in qualitative research. The first moment they identify as an objectivist and positivistic programme where research-ers 'were concerned with offering valid, reliable and objective interpretations in their writings' (ibid.: 7) through to the sixth, which is characterised by 'reflexive, experiential texts which are "messy, subjective, open ended, conflictual and feminist influenced"' (ibid.: 559). Later, Lincoln and Denzin (2000: 1048) identify the seventh moment as a period of 'ferment and explosion, that is 'defined by breaks from the past, a focus on previously silent voices, and a concern with moral discourse, with critical conversations about democracy, race, gender, class, nation, freedom, and community'.

there is no 'right' or 'wrong' method and 'It is time for the "professors" and "teachers" … to step down from the lectern and discontinue imposing dusty limitations' (Hemmingson 2009: 143).

It seems to me that Hemmingson (2009) is arguing for methodological free-for-all; for researchers to be able to do just anything they like. This is not what I mean by theorised subjectivity. If we do just what we like with no fear of critique or sanction, how can we claim that our work is accountable? Furthermore, although intellectual, emotional, sometimes even sexual connections are made between respondents and researchers within the research process and personal experience is sometimes the motivation for research and critical writing, it is not always desirable or possible to research issues close to us (Wilkinson and Kitzinger 1996). Furthermore, identification – either prior to or during the research process – should not be seen as a prerequisite to 'good' research and it is inaccurate to assume that *all* research is grounded in the auto/biography of researchers. In addition, researchers do not always identify with respondents and vice versa, even when they share an experience and/ or identity (Letherby and Zdrodowski 1995; Jewkes and Letherby 2001). Thus, researchers do not have to draw on their own life experiences to do *good* work but, as noted above, our life experiences/identity are present at some level in all that we do and it is important to acknowledge this (Cotterill and Letherby 1993; Fine 1994; Letherby 2003c; Katz-Rothman 2007). With this in mind, I feel much more comfortable with Katz-Rothman's later reflections on the production of 'accountable' knowledge (see also Stanley 1999; Letherby 2003c):

> Whether the stories we use are our own, or those of our informants, or those we cull from tables of statistically organized data, we remain story-tellers, narrators, making sense of the world as best we can. … We owe something … to our readers and to the larger community to which we offer our work. Among the many things we owe them is an honesty about ourselves: who we are as characters in our own stories and as actors in our own research. (Katz-Rothman 2007: unpaginated)

Any discussion of accountable knowledge relates to discussions of power within the research process and an acknowledgment that power imbalances are always present through choice of topic, through fieldwork relationships to representation of findings. Feminists, for example, have argued for, among other things, the importance of developing approaches that privilege rather than subsume the respondent's voice (Roberts 1981; Ribbens and Edwards 1997; Ramazanoglu and Holland 2002; Letherby 2003c). Yet, it is important not to over-passify respondents by always defining them as vulnerable for the power balance in the respondent/ researcher relationship is often dynamic (Cotterill 1992; Letherby 2002, 2003c). Several writers – feminists and others – have also argued that emotion is an integral part of the research process (e.g. Ramsay 1996; Young and Lee 1996; Coffey 1999; Hesse-Biber 2007b; Sampson et al. 2008). Traditionally, women researchers across the social sciences have been portrayed as 'more accessible and less threatening than men', which, coupled with their 'superior' communicative abilities, has thought to make the interactions of fieldwork generally easier (Warren 1988: 45). This supports more general stereotypical expectations of women as primarily responsible for 'working with emotions' (e.g. see Hochschild 1983; James 1989; Ramsay 1996) and belittles the emotion work that female and male researchers do. Clearly, displays of emotion can be difficult and even dangerous for both the researcher and the researched, and female and male researchers have written about this (see, for example, Karen Ramsay 1996; Peter Collins 1998). Helen Sampson and colleagues (2008: 929) suggest though that emotional risk is gendered:

> The feminist agenda has arguably shifted the paradigm for qualitative research and women and feminists are not exclusively affected by this, just as the paradigm is not only influenced by feminist researchers. However, whilst there are male researchers who conduct research with concern for participant and researcher relationships, the evidence ... suggests that it is female researchers who suffer greater exposure to emotional risk as the result of their attachment to feminist methods. Male researchers' preoccupations appear to be more related to physical risk and their concerns revolve around physical violence and fear of such violence, of putting their 'bodies on the line' when doing research.

Reflecting on the place of emotion in the research process, Stanley and Wise (2005: 3.4) distinguish between the necessary 'analytical dimensions of emotion' and what they see as 'wallowing or describing emotion for the sake of moral credentialism':

> It has been put to us that we present this research as an intellectual/moral/ political endeavour, while it ought to be presented as an intellectual/moral/ emotional/political one and that we should reflect on our emotional engagement with the research process and the relationship between this engagement and the product of the research. Certainly we have no objections to and much support for doing this where relevant and appropriate. Indeed, we first argued this about emotion as a component of all social research over twenty-five years ago (Stanley & Wise 1979) and have consistently supported this position ever since. However, the key words are 'where relevant and appropriate', and we do not accept that either apply with regard to this specific research at this particular stage in what has been a long engagement with the South African War for one of us (Liz) and a much longer engagement with unnecessary child deaths for the other (Sue). That is, close familiarity, and also time and its passing, both take the edge off

what would be for newcomers and in relation to present-day child deaths a much more emotional experience. Under such circumstances, the analytical dimensions of emotion certainly should be included within research writing when putting FFF [Feminist Fractured Foundationalism] into practice – but we must stress analytical dimensions here, not just wallowing or describing emotion for the sake of moral credentialism. This is not to say that neither of us had no emotional responses to the specific details of what we were researching; but it is to emphasise that these were very much background to the analytic tasks in hand, and this account of the research is concerned with presenting the process and product of these.

I am not suggesting that as researchers we should 'wallow' in emotion and I am also critical of writings that appear to be claiming any moral superiority for engaging with 'sensitive' issues. (With a colleague I am currently engaged in a project in which we are attempting to unpick terms such as *vulnerable*, *hard-to-reach*, *sensitive*, *hidden*, which we argue are often over/mis-used, sometimes with a claim to, what we call, 'academic heroism' (Coomber and Letherby 2011).) But I think that emotion *is* integral to methodological processes, not least because 'emotion' is central to communications and relationships with others, as well as a 'means by which we continually learn and relearn about a just-now-changed, back-and-forth relation between self and world' (Hochschild 2008: 5). Thus, emotion is an inevitable part of our individual and social life; emotional expression within the research process is often data in itself (e.g. Hochschild 1983; Young and Lee 1996; Lee-Treweek and Linkogle 2000; Gray 2008) and involvement in research often involves emotion work for both researcher and respondent (see above). Research, then, is inevitably a power-laden, emotional, embodied experience.

I noted earlier that my argument for a theorised subjectivity owes much to auto/biographical sociology. Despite an increased focus on auto/biography in sociology and elsewhere, those who write auto/biographically (including myself; see Letherby 2000 for detail of this) have been criticised for self-indulgence and weak intellectual work (e.g. Katz-Rothman 1996; S. Scott 1998; Letherby 2000; Sparkes 2002) (see Probyn 1993 for a critique of what she calls 'the me generation'). But as Bogusia Temple (1997: 5.3) suggests, this is because auto/biographical work challenges the academic orthodoxy, which suggests that not only is there one correct way to write about research but that there is only one audience – a (traditional) academic audience – that knows how to read 'correctly' (Mykhalovskiy 1996; Temple 1997; see also Sparkes 2002 on the challenges of and to new forms of academic writing). Sara Delamont (2009) differentiates between work that she identifies as autobiographical ethnography and autobiographical reflexivity. For Delamont, the latter is beneficial, even essential, whereas the former is 'the narcissistic substation of autoethnography for research': 'we are not paid generous salaries to sit in our offices obsessing about ourselves' (Delamont 2007: 3). Similarly, William Housley and Robin Smith (2010: 4.4) suggest that autoethnography 'may promise phenomeno-logical insight but, if left in isolation' misses 'the *social* character of the catego-ries of experience that are reported upon'. They cite Denzin (2003: 268) who argues:

> The autoethnographer functions as a universal singular, a single instance of more universal social experiences. This subject is 'summed up and for this reason universalized by his [her] epoch, he [she] resumes it by reproducing him [her] self in it as a singularity' (Sartre, 1963, p. ix). Every person is like every other person, but like no other person. The autoethnographer inscribes the experiences of a historical moment, universalizing these experiences in their singular effects on a particular life.

And add:

> In the case of autoethnography, as defined in the aphoristic quote above, we observe a simultaneous reduction and conceptual inflation. The experience of the individual (and not just any individual but the generalised ethnogra-pher) is reified to the highest degree while the organisational and distribu-tive contingencies, framings and stratifications at play are sidelined. In our view, the link between social actors (the part) and society (the whole) is not revealed by simply extrapolating self as a form of analytical lens but, rather, through a sustained incorporation of matters of situated process, organi-sation and emergent social formations (Atkinson, Delamont and Housley, 2008). (Housley and Smith 2010: 4.4–4.5)

Speaking for autoethnography, Michael Hemmingson (2009) writes:

> In a peer-review of a book manuscript to mine ... a reviewer/reader presented an explanation of a/e that I feel is succinct and on the mark:

> ... When the procedure features the personal lives of the author framed by a cultural context the methodology is increasingly being referred to as 'autoethnography'. Influenced by the postmodern challenge to the represen-tation of a cohesive view of the world and conceptualizations of university truths, this approach favours a constructionist epistemological perspective making both a methodological and theoretical deployment of performance-driven strategies as the researcher becomes the subject of study for data collection, representation, and the interpretation of embodied and intersub-jective knowledge. This lends a highly introspective and personal orienta-tion to autoethnography that reveals multiple aspects of consciousness and self-consciousness that are personally and/or politically emancipatory. Not

surprisingly, authoethnography interrogates issues of power and authority across the entire spectrum of the research process, including the conceptual-ization of the research project, its implementation, and textual production. (Hemmingson 2009: 129–30)

For me, the problem with autoethnography is the suggested lack of attention to the 'other'. I am not saying here that autoethnographers pay no attention to con-text and to others within that context, for they do, but as Tessa Muncey (2010) and Carolyn Ellis and Arthur P. Bochner (2000) respectively note:

> Autoethnography is a research approach that privileges the individual. It is an artistically constructed piece of prose, poetry, music or piece of art work that attempts to portray an individual experience in a way that evokes the imagination of the reader, viewer or listener. (Muncey 2010: 2)

> ...[autoethnography is] an autobiographical genre of writing and research that displays multiple layers of consciousness, connecting the personal to the cultural. ... Autoethnographers vary in their emphasis on the research process (graphy), on culture (ethnos), and on self (auto). (Ellis and Bochner 2000: 739–40)

Thus, autoethnography implies focus on the one whereas auto/biography – whether the focus is on the auto or the biography – necessitates close attention to the relationship between the self and other (see also Fine 1996; Wilkinson and Kitzinger 1996; Letherby 2011a) and requires constant reflection on our status as 'insiders' or 'outsiders' (we can of course be both and our position can change) to the issue under study. Theorised subjectivity acknowledges the ever presence of auto/biography in research, which might or might not include reference to the researcher's personal experience in the research writings, which might or might not include the researcher as respondent in the research. It is of course possible to do bad auto/biography, but self-awareness and a critical scrutiny of the self is quite different from self-adoration and self-indulgence (Okley 1992) and critical auto/biography explicitly acknowledges that 'knowledge is contextual, situational and specific, and that it will differ systematically according to the social location (as a gendered, racial, classed, sexualized person) of the particular knowledge-producer' (Stanley 1993: 49–50). For me, then, all our work is auto/biographical and this is what theorised subjectivity acknowledges BUT this DOES NOT (as noted above) necessarily equate with involvement:

> Conscious of this at the start of my research, I was concerned to 'make myself vulnerable' (Stanley and Wise 1993) within the research process, in terms of situating myself personally, politically and intellectually both with respondents

and in my writing. I was aware of the danger of positioning my experience as the norm, against which others would be judged, and agree with Temple (1997) that 'It is by listening and learning from other people's experiences that the researcher can learn that "the truth" is not the same for everyone'. (Letherby 2002b: 5.2)

And so:

> ... self conscious auto/biographical writing acknowledges the social location of the writer thus making clear the author's role in constructing rather than discovering the story/the knowledge' (Letherby 2000: 90).

Finishing thoughts

Rather than advocating objectivity as an obtainable epistemological virtue or 'struggling' to find a way to justify the use of the term (by acknowledging that our attempts are situated, good enough and/or corroborative), I have argued here that we would do better by beginning from a position that acknowledges what reflecting on subjectivity can do for the research process and the resulting knowledge. Thus, as highlighted in this chapter, theorised subjectivity involves us in thinking and talking differently about objectivity and subjectivity. In presenting these ideas at conferences and seminars it has been suggested to me that the 'epistemological community' of social researchers might find this too challenging, too subversive. Honestly, I do not see why. For me, subjectivity is not something we can wish or theorise away but is inevitable in all our endeavours and, as such, is something we should – we must – engage with. Why not do this up front?

Discussion

———Malcolm ——————————————————————————

IN BRINGING SUBJECTIVITY 'BACK IN' Gayle's starting point is to deny that subjectivity and objectivity are dichotomous or fundamentally opposite. In this I am fully in agreement, and to see theorised subjectivity and situated objectivity as different perspectives on the same set of issues is a view I find attractive. But willing this to be so is not enough and although I think Gayle and I want to arrive at the same place, I think our journeys may be different.

In some ways our biographies are similar. We are both from working-class backgrounds and both of us (to borrow Barbara Katz-Rothman's phrase) began from an 'ethic of involvement'. But, since those beginnings our research biographies have been different. Gayle's has been largely ethnographic and brought great insight and empathic understanding into researching personal and sensitive issues. My research background has been primarily quantitative, the analysis of Census data, the derivation of measurement instruments and a theoretical interest in probability. Yet we are both, in our different ways, followers of C. Wright Mills in believing investigation is socially rooted. Where we may differ, and where I may be closer to Martyn Hammersley, is that I agree with him that objectivity is an epistemic virtue (like truth or reliability), but only in so far as one should try to be virtuous! He calls its absence bias, but this is a narrow view and supposes that the matter is individual and, like sin, can be vanquished. Objectivity is contextually situated, but within context is achievable. This achievement, however, may be easier in some contexts than others and indeed its pursuit may be more vigorous in some contexts than others. It is in this where Gayle's and my background differences show.

Let us take the issue of homelessness. We would probably both agree that homelessness (however we define it) is a bad thing. Some of the only qualitative work I have done has been in the exploration of housing pathways in young people's biographies. This was sensitive work and it was not always desirable (or possible) to remain detached if one wished to understand how these young people had ended up in their often very difficult circumstances. I would like to think that I did begin from an understanding of my own subjective position and an acknowledgement of my involvement, but whether I did or not, I fully agree with Gayle that a later 'objective' understanding would have been facilitated by an earlier knowing engagement with my own subjective starting point. But contrast this with the majority of the homelessness work I have done, which has been to develop and implement reliable instruments to measure the number of homeless people in locations, over time. A starting point here was much more Weberian, in that I acknowledged that I and our clients (local authorities) saw homelessness as a social problem. Philosophically, one can imagine a view where it is not seen as such, so in that sense we began with an intersubjective value agreement, but from then onwards our sole aim was to devise reliable measures and implement them. I would be the first to admit (and have written about this) that we did not always achieve levels of reliability we'd have liked, but this was much more of a technical issue than a failure of objectivity. Later, other issues arose where my engagement was much more political and involved criticism of (what I believed) were *biased* methods of measurement favoured by certain governments for political reasons. Gayle is right about the connectivity of subjectivity and objectivity, but the kind of research, or moment in that research, will (or perhaps should!) cause us to emphasise its subjective or objective aspects.

This leads me to two other connected issues that are themes in Gayle's chapter. First, can an acknowledgement of our subjectivity make us more objective? Here I would respond with a cautious 'yes'. Such an audit will doubtless reveal things about ourselves that are previously unacknowledged and this must be a good thing, but it relies on a kind of psychological induction that amasses more data about oneself, but without ever knowing whether the important bits have been gathered. More mundanely, it risks complacency.

Second, can we escape our social locatedness? This must depend on how we think about 'locatedness', but if we mean 'can we imagine other places or scenarios (challenging our own preconceptions) and act upon these things?', then yes! Why else would we go to the trouble of challenging our subjectivity? However, this too has its limits. I, for one, have always been sceptical about the veracity of Geertz's Balinese cockfight. Geertz did not speak the language and was reliant on translation and observation. If he did get it right, then he did transcend his social location, but I suspect he just got some of it right. We only have his word for it!

──── John ────

MALCOLM ARGUES SOCIAL LOCATION PROVIDES the basis for all research and illustrates this by arguing that the cognitive underpinning for his investigation of homelessness came from his own working-class background. Putting it simply, a working-class background of relative disadvantage gives the basis for an empathy with and understanding of the homeless and so provides a crucial and insightful starting point for the exploration of homelessness as a social condition.

I'm not sure that this is what Gayle's position implies. Her emphasis on the necessary involvement of the personal subjectivity of the researcher in what is being researched seems to invoke moral and political concerns rather more than the merely cognitive concerns highlighted by Malcolm. This can be illustrated from my research on the powerful and the upper classes. I come from a first-generation middle-class background and not from a dominant class position, and so do not have any experience of exercising the kind of power that I study. My interest in power reflects, rather, my exclusion from power and my recognition of the effects of power on myself and on others. My research is subjectively oriented not by a personal *similarity* with my objects of study but by a *difference* from them.

In short, I am in a similar position to Geertz in relation to Balinese society, and I would see this as a fairly typical position for the sociologist to occupy. We are invariably in the position of the outsider looking at the unfamiliar, but motivated by a subjectively felt awareness of the consequences of the actions of our subjects for others like us. Unless we recognise this, we would have to conclude that social scientists can only ever study people who are like themselves: women could only be studied by other women, the working class by other workers, criminals by other criminals, the mentally ill by the insane, and so on. This, I would argue, is an absurd and unnecessary claim that would totally undermine any idea of objectivity. I'd like to know how Gayle stands in relation to these contrasting views that Malcolm and I have put forward.

——Gayle ————————————————————————

ALTHOUGH WHEN I RESEARCHED WOMEN'S and men's experiences of infertility and involuntary childlessness I fit the medical definition of 'infertility' and was at that time 'involuntary childless', I have never experienced teenage pregnancy/young motherhood, a topic I have spend the last 10 years researching and writing about. Interestingly, although I clearly shared an identity with the respondents in the former of these areas of work, there were many occasions when their experiences, perspectives and beliefs were different from mine. Thus, the insider/outsider dimensions of research are complex. I believe that a consideration of our subjective position is relevant within all social research, not least because of the need to constantly reflect on the relationships between the self and 'other' within research and because things are often not as they seem. I note Malcolm's warning about not acknowledging the gaps in our analysis and, again, complacency; all the more reason, I'd say, for a constant, critical interrogation of the self – for theorised subjectivity.

SIX

Social Objects and Realism

In Chapter 4 it was argued that a necessary condition for objectivity is that of differentiation, that is, a willingness to accept that a particular thing or event has certain characteristics and not others. On one level that does not rule out a provisional differentiation of one thing from another on the basis of a sense perception or an idea,[1] but it might also be said that the adjective 'objective' implies the noun 'object'. If we allow that objectivity does indeed imply objects, then we must ask what is meant by an object? In the physical world such a question might invite philosophical debate, but, at least from the pragmatic or methodological perspective of a physicist, a minimum criterion is that a physical object should have mass and spin. In the social world, the task for the social scientist in defining an object that we may be objective about is harder.

——Malcolm's argument

SITUATED OBJECTIVITY IS SOCIAL PROCESS. The questions social scientists ask and the process of asking those questions takes place in a social context. The claim, in Chapter 4, was, despite the contextual nature of the questions we ask and the way we ask them, there are objective features of investigation (truth and differentiation) that transcend context. They are the enduring values of science. They are epistemological values.

But this presents a philosophical problem. If investigation of the social world is in social context, how can we have knowledge that goes beyond that context? Truth and differentiation may transcend as values, but how can we know that particular truth claims about the objects we differentiate transcend the context? The physical world has properties that transcend context. Scientists do not always know what they are, they are often wrong, but at least they know that there are things to

---

[1] Such a view would be compatible with empiricism, whereby sensory identification serves as a 'placeholder'.

know beyond a given time or place. There are many things not known about the fundamental laws of time and space, but we can be reasonably confident that they exist and will carry on existing. In the physical world we can specify a few, but very important, laws (e.g. gravity, thermodynamics) that operate in all circumstances humans find themselves in; moreover, lower level laws and regularities are reducible to these fundamental laws.

We can't say that of the social world. Social structure is different over time in the same place and different between places. It is not just the context of investigation that changes (this is true for the natural sciences), but the context of existence too. It is not that the physical world does not change, but there is invariance in the physical world. Invariance implies that there are objects and relations between those objects[2] and that these things remain relatively unchanging over time and space. There is also plenty of variance, but that can often be captured within higher level invariance. Biological systems, for example, can be subject to stochastic change, but the nature of that change is captured within a higher level and simpler set of transformation rules to that higher level (Nozick 2001). Invariance itself does not mean stasis, it is always relative, but the relativity can be captured by some transformation rules, such as in any system S subject to transformation T, there will be a set of rules that describe T. Is there invariance in the social world and are there objects and relatively enduring relations between those objects? The claim of invariance is an ontological one; it is saying that the world is a particular way, whatever we may believe or wish it to be. It is, then, a position diametrically opposed to the relativism John described in Chapter 2.

In this chapter I will argue that there are objects and there is invariance, but the invariance is found in conceptual necessity rather than the kind of natural necessity that underwrites the physical world. I will set out the idea that the social world contains 'objects', that is, those things we direct 'objectivity' towards. Social objects, I maintain, are caused and have causal properties. Because this is an argument from a realist perspective, I will begin the chapter with a brief overview of some features of realism in social science. It is only fair to say that this is a somewhat selective overview, with which many social science realists will take issue.[3] However, my purpose is to sketch out a version of realism that embraces contingency as its central property, because this is key to my subsequent argument for social objects.

Secondly, I will show how objectivity relates to those objects, that is, how we might discover invariance in the social world and come to formulate strategies that can reveal social objects and their mechanisms over relatively long periods.

---

[2]Talk of objects and relations between them only makes sense at an atomic level. At a sub-atomic level phenomenon simultaneously take on the characteristic of wave and particle in the form of quanta (see Rae 1986: 3–15).

[3]See, for example, the debate between myself and Stephen Norrie (Williams 2010; Norrie 2010; Williams 2011).

Realism

In Chapter 3 John has shown how the debate around objectivity and subjectivity, in the social sciences, has been largely shaped by theories of the social that have had their origins in the philosophical positions of empiricism or idealism. Empiricist and (in social science) positivist approaches insist that statements of what ought to be cannot be derived from statements of what is, hence the emergent doctrine of value freedom. Opponents of this position, who have mostly embraced or have been influenced by idealism, point out that the separation is not viable because our perceptions of facts derive from ideas. Ernest Nagel (1961: 492–4), an (albeit sophisticated) adherent of the former position, offers a defence of the distinction by attempting to separate 'describing ideas' (what he terms appraising value judgements) from evaluative ideas (characterising value judgements). His example is that of anaemia, its diagnosis derived from a series of characterising judgements based on observable evidence. However, because this condition leads to diminished powers of maintenance of the animal, it may be characterised as a bad thing. Perhaps an initially persuasive contrast, but would this work in a factory or a university? The characterising judgements themselves would almost certainly be contested and we could only move from characterising to appraising if there could be agreement about what constituted the equivalent of anaemia in a factory or university. Nagel's schema can only work when there is agreement about characterising judgements.

The problem with Nagel's position is that it depends on perception and the challenge to it on contrasting ideas of a characterising judgement. An adequate basis for a differentiation between either sense perceptions or contrasting ideas is illusive. However, if we begin from quite a different set of assumptions, that (say) factories or universities are physical entities in which social relations of various kinds are enacted and these social relations have implications for individuals, who in turn create the social relations, it permits us to move from perception or idea and to ask what is the ontological status of that which factories or universities are made of (beyond the bricks and concrete)? That is, they are made of something and that something will have dispositions and (I will argue) causal properties that go beyond sense impressions or ideas.

This implies an altogether deeper task than characterising judgements, because although it may rely on descriptions, these descriptions do not stand on their own. Indeed, we might say that they imperfectly represent an underlying reality that can only be known under particular descriptions. In other words, we have raised the possibility that social reality is not simply captured by description or ideas, but is richer and deeper.

The philosophical position I describe is that of realism. In the philosophy of the natural sciences it has been a mainstream approach for a long while (see, for example, Hacking 1983a; Psillos 1999), but in the social sciences it remains something of a philosophical 'third way'.[4]

The key premise of realism is that there exists an underlying reality, a world where there are things and in which things happen regardless of whether we can, or do, observe them, or even know them. The relationship of this partially hidden world to our attempts to know it is succinctly summed up by Roy Bhaskar, a realist thinker who has been influential in the social sciences in the past 25 years:

> Things exist and act independently of our descriptions, but we can only know them under particular descriptions. Descriptions belong to the world of society and of men; objects belong to the world of nature. ... Science, then, is the systematic attempt to express in thought the structures and ways of acting of things that exist and act independently of thought. (Bhaskar 2008: 250)

Although Bhaskar is talking about the natural sciences, the principle holds for those things that social scientists describe, with the obvious difference that the things described are themselves society and people.

That things 'go on' behind our backs is trivially true. It is easy to think of examples of events unfolding, unbeknown to an individual or group, which will later directly and obviously affect them. Indeed, virtually all of social life is like that and in our everyday lives we see only some of social life. But there is more. What we do not see is not random, unco-ordinated or accidental, but rather it is frequently the operation of, and subsequent effects of, what some realists term 'mechanisms' (Boudon 1998; Elster 1998; Pawson 2000; Bunge 2004).

Although the term 'mechanism' is widely used by realists and others in the social sciences, it would seem to imply a relatively deterministic ensemble of characteristics operating together in a predictable and ordered way. Social mechanisms are not quite like this, though they do exhibit order and have causal properties, but equally they may be complex, multifaceted and contain elements with stochastic properties. Importantly, as Pawson and Tilley (1997: 66) note, they are 'about people's choices and the capacities they derive from group membership'. The mechanism of organised crime, for example, can only exist because criminals exert agency, but agency is only possible within (say) the Mafia hierarchy, which in turn requires other social mechanisms (consisting of rules, norms, values, etc.) to exist.

---

[4]Social science realism has its modern origins in work by Keat and Urry in the early 1970s (Keat and Urry 1975), but gained popularity through the works of Roy Bhaskar. Its influence is uneven. Territorially, it is primarily a British phenomenon, but has widespread popularity in Scandinavia, Australasia and India. It has little influence in North America. Somewhat ironically, though a naturalistic doctrine, it has failed to make much impression on quantitative social science (Williams 2010).

It can be seen from the foregoing that when we speak of the 'real' in the social world, we are primarily speaking of dynamic processes that are known through their effects on people, either actual people or on structures, themselves perhaps thought of as proxies for people. A mechanism in the physical world is not wholly determined because it is subject to greater or lesser modification as a result of internal or external changes, yet because it is often subject to relatively few of these it is has greater longevity and it is more readily identified. This makes for a relatively straightforward identification of causes, perhaps as diagnostics. The causal chain in the failure of a relatively simple mechanism, such as a pump, is easily identified, but a change even in a relatively stable social mechanism is often complex.

While we can hold on to the notion of a social mechanism as exhibiting relative stability, that is, enough to be able to attribute outcomes to an identifiable set of cohering features, the processes and the identifiable features themselves will usually be less enduring or determined. Realism has developed a language to capture this in the social world and will speak of individuals or structures as having 'causal powers', 'liabilities', 'dispositions' (Harré and Madden 1975: 8). Andrew Sayer, for example, speaks of individuals having 'labour power' which they may or may not exercise (Sayer 1992: 105). We could speak of a police officer having the power to arrest anyone within his or her contact, but to actually make an arrest takes place within a context. Such powers or dispositions exist in the physical world, but in the physical world they are underwritten by at least some natural necessity in the final instance,[5] usually grounded in fundamental physical laws (Williams 2010).

For Harré and Madden, natural necessity is:

> When the natures of the operative powerful particulars, the constraining or stimulating effect of conditions and so on are offered as the grounds for the judgement that a certain effect cannot but happen, or cannot but fail to happen, we have natural necessity. (Harré and Madden 1975: 19)

In the social world no such necessity exists and all outcomes are contingent upon earlier events that could have been otherwise. On the face of it this seems a rather sweeping claim. One hears of the necessity of civil or criminal law and it is

---

[5]This is not to imply all events in the physical world are determined. Indeed much of the physical world operates at a local level contingent on the playing out of immediate past events. Though a falling leaf is subject to the laws of gravity, the fall of a leaf will be more immediately subject to the local conditions of wind, pressure and decomposition. But ultimately it will fall. Also the physical world does have some characteristics where the operation of laws will have natural necessity. *Ceteris paribus*, a substance that dissolves in water, once placed in water must dissolve. No such necessity exists in the social world. For a discussion of modes of necessity and their relation to realism, see Williams (2010).

said such facts, as Durkheim observed (Lukes 1973: 12–14), behave like things in nature. They enable and constrain us. If you break certain laws and are caught by the police, a physical loss of liberty may be the result. Laws and their operation are nevertheless contingent upon legislative change or policing practice when seen historically or across societies. For example, today, consensual homosexual acts between adults are illegal in about 70 out of the 195 countries of the world, but this number has changed over time and the number of such countries has diminished. Homosexuality between consenting males was decriminalised in Britain in 1967, following the Wolfenden report. Contingency is captured both spatially and historically: at time *T1* homosexuality was illegal in country A but not B, but at time *T2* the law may have changed in one or both, thus rendering behaviour contingent upon legislation (and indeed its enactment/interpretation) across these times or places.

This is not to suggest that there is an equivalence of probability for events to occur; some things are very much more likely to occur than others, though at a particular time the probability of a specific event occurring will become equivalent to 1 (certain) or 0 (impossible). In this particular example, conviction for homosexuality becomes necessary (1) only when the judge pronounces his or her judgement; up until that point there is only a varying probability of conviction.

What changes that probability? It is perhaps helpful to think of these probabilities as nested (again across time and space). In the homosexuality example, the enactment of laws will produce 0s or 1s locally, but there are other considerations, such as the operation of the criminal justice system, informal judgements or decisions by individuals, or particular behaviours by the person who is accused of an illegal act. The nesting of probabilities is not random because of this relatedness within a mechanism or mechanisms. The law and its operation may be thought of as the mechanism which enables and constrains, increasing or decreasing probabilities and producing outcomes of 1s and 0s.

The above suggests that social reality is rather different from physical reality. This makes a difference to the kinds of mechanisms that exist in them. The physical world will demonstrate varying amounts of contingency, but its mechanisms and structures are ultimately grounded in physical laws. No such grounding is present in the social world. Social reality is contingent.

The only kind of necessity we can find in the social world is that which lies in concepts themselves, or in situations that have come about. In both cases, a thing is something and not something else. A chair cannot simultaneously be a dog – its properties of 'chairness' conceptually necessitate it being a chair and not something quite different. Similarly, the properties of being a police officer, a city council, labour power or a marriage have a conceptual necessity that they are this and not something else, though they may be named different things, or have properties that change rather quickly. It is not necessary that prior states of individuals, entities or processes must become these things, but, equally, we can discover the processes of transformation for them to become these things and to change into other things.

Social objects

Social objects are not like physical objects. You cannot touch them, they do not possess material properties, although, as I will say below, physical objects can also have social properties and are often brought into being through social processes. So what are social objects?

Social objects are socially constructed and real

What 'stuff' is made of in the physical world has occupied philosophers for centuries. The Ancient Greeks, for example, thought everything was made of air, fire or water. Today, physics has trumped philosophy to an extent and many will talk of objects consisting of mass and spin, though there is far more to the debate about physical reality than this, particularly the relationship between what something is and our ways of knowing it.

This latter is central to our conceptions of social reality and is made more complex by a heightened sense of the moral or political nature of what is known, or the knowing. In debates about physical reality there is (what is often derisively known as) the 'death and furniture' argument (Edwards et al. 1995). This is the common-sense view that the world is as it is, regardless of our views about it. The furniture of the world is hard and unyielding, like Dr Johnson's rock, while death is always with us. This should not be dismissed too lightly, at least in so far as contrasting it with the social world, where no such argument can be readily deployed, even at a common-sense level. The physical world contains many things that are beyond our influence or even knowledge, but have real physical consequences (sun spots, geodesic structures, gravity, thermodynamics) and there are those things we make or influence that in turn produce physical consequences (medicines, cars, computers, climate change). While the latter certainly have a moral or political dimension, they are very different from 'stuff' in the social world.

While physical objects that we know of must be socially constructed, they nevertheless have physical properties that transcend the social constructions. Cars can move or kill people, medicines enhance or preserve life, etc. In the social world that is not grounded in physical characteristics, there are only social constructions. For the purposes of the present illustration, we can say that the physical world is 'real', in a material sense, and consists of physical objects related to each other through physical laws, though our relations to them are socially constructed. The social world beyond physical objects is almost, by definition, socially constructed, but can it also be real? Or put it another way, are there social analogues of physical objects?

At a macro-level, physical objects have causal properties, that is, object A in state S, either alone or in concert with other objects, can bring about a change in object X.[6] For some philosophers of science it is the property of making things happen that is the clinching argument for physical causality (Hacking 1983b: 262–75). Can it also be the case that such relations can hold in the social world? I would say yes.

It is obvious that humans change the physical world and might stand in as A (S) in a causal sequence, but can this also be the case where X is also a social property? Again, I say yes. Now, this causal sequence is almost certainly mediated by individual mental processes and these require particular attention (I will turn to these below), but *ceteris paribus*, such processes are manifest at an individual level, or even meso-level. It is easy enough to observe behaviour change in an individual that resulted from the action of another individual, that is agent A would not have done X but for the action of agent B. At a macro-level one can observe the effects (X), but it is rarely possible to closely specify the conditions that brought about X.[7] While somewhat easier at a meso-level, where B is not another individual, but a social process or property, X may be observed, but B may be only partially specified. For example, we can see the effects of stigma on an individual, or of a group decision in a small group, but even in a relatively closed social environment the 'stigma' or 'group decision' will be nested in prior social processes.

Observable effects are real and because we know that effects observed at time *T1* do not exhaust all possible observations and that hitherto unobservable effects might be known at time *T2*, we can also say that there are unobserved effects that are equally real.

The model of social reality I have so far proposed sounds much like a push–pull Newtonian one, whereby an action (or actions) make something else happen, but this is inadequate to capture social reality where those actions result from self

---

[6]For the purposes of the argument here, this is a somewhat simplified statement of what causality is in the physical world and there is a huge literature on the matter (see, for example, Harré and Madden 1975).

[7]Causal statements at a macro-level must inevitably be probabilistic, or at least implicitly so. To say A causes B is to claim that when circumstance C … *n* are held constant in a statistical model, there is a significant directional relationship, whereby B does not occur except when stimulated by A (see Blalock 1961 for a clear account).

awareness and awareness of a perceived reality. Individuals construct their reality and these constructions shape their actions and, most times, those of others.

Individuals construct their reality through mental interpretations derived from prior experience. Such constructions may be based on misinterpretations or partial understandings, they may be based on poor information, they may not be 'rational', but once made will have causal efficacy for them and, often, others. As W.I. Thomas famously said, 'when people define situations as real they become real in their consequences' (Thomas and Thomas 1928: 572).

This view of social construction is at odds with those of 'social constructionists'. As Kenneth Gergen puts it:

> ... all claims to 'the real' are traced to the processes of relationship, and there is no extra-cultural means of ultimately privileging one construction of reality over another. (Gergen 2001: 8)

Gergen and other social constructionists ascribe both a complete autonomy of agency in how individuals construct their world and a complete epistemological or moral relativity in its interpretation. In this physical constraint, social imperatives and moral or aesthetic choices are conflated. The physical world, though often shaped by humans, will enable and constrain what can be constructed as 'real'. In other words, much of our social reality consists of interpretations of the physical world. Secondly, social imperatives (norms, rules, etc.), while not determined, will certainly shape our constructions of reality. In both cases physical and social imperatives will be experienced by people, not just individuals, and will produce the same or similar constructions. Epistemological relativism cannot be sustained because the physical and social worlds enable and constrain us in such a way that interpretations that do not accord with that external reality will be refuted by experience. Put simply – we can't just make it up! Only in the area of moral or aesthetic choices can we see a wide-ranging autonomy or relativity and even these will be shaped by rules or norms.

There is no social reality without social constructions, but equally, social constructions are real. Their reality makes it possible to think of them as objects.

Social objects are real but contingent

The first property of a social object is that it is causal and it is this that makes it real. Social objects can make things happen: a police officer is an individual, but s/he is also a social agent when being a police officer and has powers to bring about change in others. These powers are not necessarily exercised, but when they are we can explain them through the social properties of being a police officer. Social objects are therefore real if, and only if, they have socially causal properties, that is, the existence of an object increases or decreases the probability of the existence of future objects.

A law, rule or convention is a social object, which has causal potential when not exercised, but can be seen to be causally efficacious when it is exercised. Of course, a rule such as 'No Smoking' is enacted by people themselves who would otherwise have smoked and may be embodied in a sign which states 'No Smoking'.

The causal properties of objects make them real, but some objects will possess greater causal efficacy than others, that is, their existence has a greater likelihood of bringing about future social objects than others.

The ontological point I am making here is that while the social world is real, it has objects in it and, indeed, often identifiable mechanisms; the real character of the social world is that it is probabilistic. This ontological claim for probability is not the same as epistemological probability, which is concerned with knowing the world probabilistically as a representation of a non-observable reality. The two are not necessarily mutually exclusive, though beginning from ontological assumptions about probability has methodological consequences (see Williams 1999; Williams and Dyer 2004, 2009).

Social objects are dynamic and invariant

Social objects consist of the actualisation of relationships. And depending on how we choose to look at them, they will look like things or relations between things, but really they are one and the same thing. They are, then, the outcomes of contingent relationships that have a greater or lesser probability of bringing about other social objects. Though they may appear 'thing-like', they are dynamic and continuous. Consider the operation of a law: we can think of a criminal law as a social object, but it implies relationships with other social objects. Different parts of speech are implied. The 'law' is a noun, but it is something that is passed or enforced, implying a doing. The doing itself is enacted by other social 'objects', as individual social agents or rules for its enforcement.

If social objects are dynamic and imply identifiable things and relationships between things, can there be anything in the social world that is not an object? If this question is asked of the physical world, the response might be forces (gravity, etc.). In the social world, this might be thought.

Yet despite their contingent nature, social objects also have the property of invariance. With physical objects invariance exists in (or is reducible to) fundamental laws. While there is plenty of variance (as I noted above, this can even be stochastic), the variance is grounded finally in those laws. An object may exist only for millisecond, but has a real existence, and it may exist in an apparent flux, but the transformations between that flux and its grounding in higher-level invariant objects remains real.

Does the social world have such an analogue? I have already denied that there can be natural necessity in the social world, so invariance must be relative and cannot be grounded in the same way. Nevertheless, we can point to social objects that exist over long periods and even widely across places. Capitalism is an obvious example, but like a biological system that changes over time, it has changed and is different from place to place. Some features possess a conceptual necessity, that is, they make it capitalism and nothing else, while other features may have longevity or are apparent across place, but are not universal. For example, liberal democracy is a feature of most, but not all, advanced capitalist societies. Its existence and relative invariance in (say) Europe, North America and Australasia can be explained by historic mechanisms, such as the development of the political power of the merchant classes in the eighteenth century. Conversely, while China is now a quintessentially capitalist society, its origins in the rapid transformation of a peasant society through Maoist communism in the second half of the twentieth century is an example of a much more recent historic mechanism. One might also venture to say that the former exhibits greater invariance than the latter. Importantly, however, the invariance depends on conceptual, not natural, necessity.

Social objects are continuous with thought objects and physical objects

The causal efficacy of social objects depends on their relationship to other objects. One can say that all of the physical world that is socially available, that is, we can know it intersubjectively, is socially constructed. The form social construction takes varies: it might be our aesthetic appreciation of landscape, the design of a building or how we dispose of the dead. Physical objects that are socially constructed will have no social necessity (that is, they could be otherwise), but they will have physical necessity grounded in physical laws. Actually, much – possibly virtually all – of the social world refers at some point to physical objects, both human created and having an existence which is not human dependent. When we think of social and physical objects there is no radical ontological disjuncture. Similarly, what we might call 'thought objects', that is, mental representations or intentions, will be stimulated by social objects, or physical processes or objects, and they in turn may bring into being social or physical objects. Thought objects may not have any outcomes beyond thought itself, though it is tricky to specify which of our thoughts have no later social outcomes because these may be indirectly socially efficacious via other thoughts.

An objective strategy for discovering social objects

The main message of Chapter 4 was that we live a world of values. Objectivity is one of those values, but a special one because it helps us know things about the world that we could not discover through our own subjective stance. The message of this chapter so far is that there is a dynamic world of objects out there that exist independently of our particular views of them. We may solemnly sign up to seek the truth about objects, but we know we are doing this in a context and we don't know whether that context hinders or helps us. Value freedom promised us a royal road to truth through method, but it was false promise because we cannot separate fact from value and the objects of the world do not present themselves to us complete in appearance and with a traceable pedigree.

But let me clarify. It is not that social objects do not present themselves at all. In fact that is the problem, everywhere we look we can find social objects. The trick is to be able to get beyond appearances to see what the underlying mechanisms are, how those objects are nested in other objects.

We have become obsessed with method in social science. That is not necessarily a bad thing because technically we are very much more sophisticated than we were even 10 years ago and sophistication in method opens up new vistas of possible questions (Williams and Vogt 2011). For example, the advent of multilevel modelling assisted in framing questions about the relationship of local processes in (say) education, to individuals (perhaps pupils), meso- (perhaps schools) and higher level mechanisms (perhaps geographical areas). Possibly we expect too much of method, believing that if we get the method right, we cannot fail to explain or discover? There is a premium on new methods and we are ever exhorted to innovate. Yet there is a fashion in method. I touched upon this in Chapter 4. Fashions change over time and place, even at fundamental levels. I cannot believe, for instance, that the sociological questions of the past 20 years are so different in the USA and the UK, that the former has hugely favoured quantitative methods and the latter qualitative ones (Payne et al. 2004). In the *longue durée*, method will not save or damn us, it might help or hinder, but what is possibly more important, though again not a decider, is methodology.

Social science must have method, but equally it must have methodology as a bridge between a metaphysics of the social world (what this chapter has been about so far) and its methods. The difference between method and methodology is simple at one level, that we can say what each is, but harder at another because they are not discrete. But let us have a working definition.

Methods are the means in which we access the social world as social scientists, the means of obtaining knowledge. The methods one uses may be the best we think we have in the search for truth about social objects and we may be correct in thinking this, but we may be wrong, or more than one method will do the job. The methods may be the means of gathering or analysing data. The two don't always go together. Two researchers using the same survey instrument and testing the same research hypothesis may reach rather different conclusions, depending on the type of analyses conducted. I mention this only to make the point that the way we know the social world goes deeper than method and if we rely only on method, not only will we be scratching our heads when we get anomalous results, but we will fail to be objective.

Methodology is conventionally seen as how we come to decide on those methods and the decisions about methods are, in turn, driven by epistemological assumptions (as I discussed in Chapter 4). But I think it is more than this; it is shaped by the ontology we adopt, or indeed do not adopt.

Positivism tries to work without an ontology. David Hume, the empiricist progenitor of positivism, allowed that we could have sense perceptions of the world and by ordering these perceptions we can show the world to have order, but we cannot know what underlies that apparent order because we are unable to access it. That does not mean that he and later positivists denied underlying structure; rather, that truth claims that move beyond what is empirically verifiable are considered simply speculation. Consequently, positivism claims not to move beyond the observable, or what can be observed through the proxy of our measures. If positivism were right, then the successful operationalisation of measures should demonstrate the regularity of the social world. Manipulating the observable variables will show order, but very little else. Take gender, class, ethnicity, wealth, education, religion, health, location, etc. Decide on a dependent variable, say education, put them all into a big logistic regression model and look for the best fit. Hey presto, class is the biggest 'predictor' of educational success, followed by ethnicity then location. But it doesn't tell us why this is. There may be nothing wrong with this technique, or indeed logistic regression as a method, but it assumes (as realists put it) a 'flat ontology' (Pawson 2000). That is, the variables stand in directly for the social world. Using my language from the previous section, is it the case that the only social objects (and the relations between them) we can talk about are those that are observationally apparent? At common-sense level, we know that many things are not apparent. Education, as measured by achievement at degree, sub-degree, vocational or high school level, is not 'education' as experienced. The qualifications may be evidence for educational achievement, in the way that exhaust fumes are evidence for the presence of a motor car (Byrne 2002: 29), but that is all.

Consider ethnicity as measured and experienced. How we socially construct ethnicity and how we come to use it as a variable in a statistical model neatly encapsulates the difficulties, not simply of measurement, but how we think about ethnicity before we even try to measure it.

The measurement of ethnicity in the social survey is ubiquitous. Usually the survey respondent is presented with eight or nine categories, taken to be the most common. The history of these categories is not one derived from their face validity in pre-pilots, but rather in an historical jumble of race or colonial categories, or political priorities and expediencies (Ahmad 1999). The methodological issues are well illustrated in the use of the 'white' category in UK Censuses and surveys. The 'White' ethnic category usually describes in excess of 90% of the population in most locations and in most analyses of ethnic social disadvantage, 'White' is the reference group. Quite apart of the heterogeneity of the group itself, its actual composition (that is, what counts as 'white') changes. The category was first used in the 1991 England and Wales Census, but since that time it has 'decomposed' with a number of groups formerly subsumed under 'white' being categorised separately (for example, Welsh, Northern Irish, Gypsy, Irish Traveller). The decomposition of the reference category consequently changes analyses of ethnic social disadvantage.

I and others (Williams 2003; Phinney and Ong 2007; Burton et al. 2010) have argued it is possible to improve on such measurement, but here my point is methodological not technical, and hinges on the nature of ethnicity as a social object. Compare, for example, the ethnic categories of 'Greek' and 'White'. When a respondent completing a social survey selects a category labelled 'Greek', it might be assumed that the person would normally identify with that ethnic group as a result of a range of experiences/attributes – not the same ones for all, but many overlapping between those identifying as Greek. The category 'Greek' is a representation of being Greek. Secondly, being Greek is a real property, the outcome of causal processes. Those causal process are rooted in Greek culture, in the Greek language, etc. 'White', on the other hand, is different. Its use in a social survey might even be described as 'not other ethnic groups'. It is different from Greek in that it is used in opposition to other ethnicities, either taxonomically or politically. There is no 'white' language, no 'white' music, no 'white' food, no 'white' literature, no 'white' art and perhaps, most importantly, no shared 'white' cultural norms or rules.[8]

There is a further dimension, that of subjectivity. Two people of the same heritage may differently describe themselves, one as Greek, one as 'White' (or some other category) and this may change over time, with a person identifying with an particular ethnic group at one point, but not at another (or vice versa).

---

[8]Ironically, 'Greek' itself is often subsumed under 'white' in many surveys.

Even when some categories remain the same (say through the UK Censuses from 1991 to 2011), such as 'Black Caribbean', Bangladeshi, 'Pakistani', the people who comprise those categories are not all the same people over time. For example, when such categories were first measured in the 1991 Census, many 'Black Caribbean', 'Bangladeshi', or 'Pakistani' people would have been first-generation migrants to the UK and by ticking those categories were not making a statement of ethnic identity, but just asserting to the countries, or world regions, they originated from. By 2011 the composition of these categories will be different, with many second- and third-generation members of ethnic minorities ticking the boxes to assert membership of an ethnic group.

Good practice in methods will attempt to find the best means of measurement, but this in turn is driven by methodological sophistication that attempts to theoretically grasp the nature of the social objects. Ethnicity demonstrates each of the characteristics that I claim social objects have.

They are socially constructed. Arguably, ethnicity didn't exist before the nineteenth century, and then for a long while it was called 'race' (Carter 2000). It has been constructed positively by those seeking to mark out cultural and community difference and negatively by those who saw this assertion as a threat to their identity or livelihood (the latter often still using the more pejorative 'race'). Its causal consequences, bad and good, from the Yugoslav succession wars to the revival of the Welsh language, are well known. The manifestation of ethnicity is real in these senses, but contingent upon other things in its effects. Not everyone experiences or 'constructs' ethnic identity in the same way (and consequently answers survey questions differently). It is certainly dynamic and changing. The idea that ethnicity somehow preserves traditional identities intact is far from the truth. Witness, for example, the development of hybrid music styles that blend modern western influences, such as hip hop and R&B, with Bangra, Rai, etc. Ethnicity is partially created and affirmed through physical objects, such as dress, music, food, etc., and in some cases through the physical appearance of the individual. At the other end of the scale to physical, awareness and perception of one's identity are thought objects, with which one creates and internalises social objects. Finally, ethnicity is not one kind of object. It comprises many other things, such as language, custom and moral codes. These in turn are shaped by other external objects, such as religion or language. The Arab and Berber ethnic identity of the Maghreb countries in North Africa is inextricably bound to the Muslim faith, but also the colonial legacy of the French language and culture.

Ethnicity, then, implies not just a challenge of a method of measurement for the social researcher, but a methodology of the social objects and their connections that comprise ethnicity. Specifying a battery of methods to help us explain and understand the social objects that comprise ethnicity is insufficient. A methodology of ethnicity that seeks the truth about objects is situated in the context in which that truth is sought. For example, the reasons for measuring ethnicity may lie in a concern about immigration (Migration Watch 2010), they may be about making an ethnic group visible (Southwell 2001), or they may be about explaining comparative disadvantage. What and how it is measured will be shaped by these. We may prefer a more anthropological exploration of an ethnic group, which will suggest quite a different methodological starting point and methods. However, a realist approach in each of these will attempt to seek out the mechanisms and the evidence for those mechanisms.

Middle range realism

This term was coined by Ray Pawson (2000) to indicate a marriage of a realist ontology with the middle range theories of Robert Merton. It is a good example (though not the only one) of a realist methodology that is sensitive to context, but aims to pursue truth about objects. Pawson provides one of the most elegant formulations of the principle of realist methodology: $C + M = O$, where C stands for Context, M for Mechanism and O for outcome (Pawson 2000). Mostly, researchers want to explain outcome, and to do this they must identify the mechanism, but mechanisms operate in contexts (frustratingly often also themselves mechanisms) which may or may not 'fire' the mechanism.

Robert Merton described middle range theories as those:

> [t]hat lie between the minor but necessary working hypotheses that evolve in abundance during day-to-day research and the all-inclusive systematic efforts to develop a unified theory that will explain all the observed uniformities of social behaviour, social organization and social change. (Merton 1957: 39)

Merton can be seen as offering us methodology as a transcending theory that allows the testing of 'minor theories', through research, as a way of building knowledge of the social world. They would be abstract enough to permit testable generalisations from one context to another. As Pawson notes, 'abstraction' is the key here. We need to be able to say that if P holds under circumstances S, then it can also explain Q. The problem with this kind of Mertonian abstraction, as he goes on to argue, is that, like empiricism, it is a 'flat ontology', that is, 'concepts may be said to be "flattened" in the sense that they do not discriminate between the different layers of social reality' (Pawson 2000: 290). To go back to the example of ethnicity above, ethnicity as measured does not capture the underlying processes that it seeks to represent as a variable. Thus a theory about ethnicity as an explanatory variable in social mobility (for example) will only be empirically generalisable if the 'mechanisms' of ethnicity in contexts $c - n$ are the same as in C.

Middle range realism rests on the principle of the existence of a multilay-ered reality that coheres into mechanisms. Actions and intentions can only be understood when they are located in these 'layers'. Ethnic identity is a product of such mechanisms, which themselves overlap and exist within contexts. To successfully use ethnicity as an explanatory variable in different localities or times requires us to understand the mechanisms in the production of such identity. To be Pakistani (say) in the UK in 1991 may be underwritten by the mechanisms of migration and colonialism, but in 2010, among second and third generations of people of Pakistani origin these mechanisms may be more to do with identity politics or religion. According to Pawson, only by under-standing these mechanisms in context can we successfully produce middle range theories. There is much more to both Merton's proposals and Pawson's revision, but what is important to the argument here is that they offer a meth-odology that permits theory building over time that is relatively context-free and pluralistic about method. Pawson's middle range realism is an improve-ment on middle range theory because, although it is applicable in different contexts, the specific context of its application is crucial.

Pawson's middle range realism offers a methodology for social science. It can be read as advocating good practice, but equally it can be read as a characterisa-tion of good social science. While 'middle range realism' is influential in evalua-tion research (Pawson and Tilley 1997; Pawson 2006), there are many examples of research and, more particularly, research programmes that have the characteristics of both middle range theory and realism. Take, for example, 'counterurbanisation'. This term was coined by Berry in 1976 and arose from the serendipitous discovery that many rural areas in the United States had begun to experience a 'population turnaround', that is, that population movement from rural to urban areas of the kind that had dominated migration for more than a century were now supplanted by movement the opposite way from urban to rural areas.

This provided a number of puzzles: Structural (what was going on that pro-duced this population trend?); What were individual motivations? and finally; Taxonomic/methodological. The last concerned whether this was one kind of phenomenon or different phenomena and what 'counts' as urban or rural?

The subsequent history of counterurbanisation research has been marked by a number of phases and theories, which have not always been obviously sequential in building an understanding of mechanisms, but now, looking back over nearly four decades, we can detect a gradual identification of different kinds of migra-tion mechanism, though the individual motivations are rarely straightforward.

In the early days, researchers in the UK and USA claimed to have identified clear evidence of population movement from urban to rural areas (Roberts and Randolph 1983), though surprisingly this was contested (Vining and Kontuly 1978), but the contestation itself arose from issues of measurement. Is moving

20 kilometres from a city counterurbanisation, or must it be 100 kilometres? What population density is 'rural' and what is 'urban'? Nowadays two definitions are routinely applied and give rather similar results: those of 'clean break', where a migrant is moving beyond a defined near metropolitan area (Coombes et al. 1989); and population deconcentration, where movements in the whole country (initially the UK) were measured according to functional zones and areas of metropolitan influence. The typology served as the basis for much of the subsequent comprehensive analyses of counterurbanisation in Britain.

This classification then permitted the analysis of the kinds of migration mechanisms to do with relocation for work purposes, or as a result of lifestyle choices and, indeed, the complexity of the relationship between these motivations. But these do not exist in a vacuum. For example, Perry et al. (1986) undertook a study of migration to Cornwall, UK, and demonstrated the links between migration choices and the growth of tourism. Other studies have shown how lifestyle and migration for work-related reasons are mediated by house price differentials. The history of counterurbanisation research, to the present, is far from tidy, but one can discern tangible progress towards identifying causal mechanisms, some of which (the relationship to other mechanisms, such as house prices) could only become apparent once earlier mechanisms and the context of their operating became known.

The understanding of the processes of counterurbanisation and its changing status as a (realist) middle range theory was not the work of a social scientist, or scientists, at one time. It was not the formulaic application of methodological principles that led to a steady development of the theory. Indeed, as I indicated, it retains many important puzzles. However, over time and across many research programmes, there was a gradual discovery of mechanisms and contexts, and there were revisions to the overall theory of 'counterurbanisation' (it is very different now from when Berry coined the term), but there remain anomalies and puzzles.

Can one apply the same kind of theorising to ethnicity? Can there be a middle range theory of ethnicity? Probably not. Ethnicity and counterurbanisation are both social science constructs, but that is where the similarity ends.

Counterurbanisation is a theory or heuristic that explains certain kinds of population movements that cohere into mechanisms. It is only a social object to the social scientists that use it and is meaningless to those who experience counterurbanisation, either as migrants or the long-term population. We can distinguish ethnicity on two grounds: first, that it does not describe one kind of thing in a particular historic context, as counterurbanisation does. Ethnicity is much more of a social object than counterurbanisation,[9] but unlike

---

[9]However, it would presumably be legitimate to think of counterurbanisation as a social object for those social scientists who work with it. I prefer to think of it as describing processes linking objects.

counterurbanisation, a specific historic phenomenon, ethnicities will be grounded in different historic and cultural mechanisms. Secondly, counterurbanisation, though it will embody individual-level subjective action, is not subject to individual redefinition and construction, as is ethnicity. Ethnicity and counterurbanisation are both social scientific concepts, but the latter is *only* a social scientific concept.

Continuity, change, theories and models

The development of a middle range theory of counterurbanisation and, indeed, a recognition that the development of such a theory in respect of ethnicity would be very much more difficult, indicates the possibilities and limitations of the differentiation of continuity and change.

While I was writing this chapter, the British Prime Minister, David Cameron, made a speech claiming that multiculturalism, for some decades an important element in British social policy, had failed. The grounds for this claim were primarily that cultures (and he was mainly referring to those of ethnic groups originating in the Indian subcontinent) had become separate and alienated from British society. Cameron may or may not be correct in this assertion, but what he failed to articulate is that the cultures themselves are not the same thing as they were 20 or 30 years ago. A policy approach which may have been appropriate then, may not be so now. If the policy is wrong now, it does not follow that it was wrong then. Manifestly, the experience of an Asian British person who was born and grew up in Britain will not be the same as an earlier generation Asian person who grew up in the subcontinent and migrated to Britain. There will be many elements of cultural continuity between generations, but there will also be change.

Mechanisms and the social objects[10] that constitute them are not static. They are static enough for their causal properties to be differentiated, but those differentiations will hold for varying periods. An explanatory mechanism for the emergence of (say) a present-day Pakistani identity in Bradford will not be the same as the explanatory mechanism that would have been appropriate in respect of a Pakistani identity in Bradford 30 years ago. Now it may be that some key elements hold for both mechanisms, such as religion and an experience of racism, and these deeper mechanisms will explain emergent ones that also incorporate elements of British culture, such as education, sport and dress. The social scientist seeks to establish the transformation rules between the emergent

---

[10]As a heuristic and methodological convenience, we can separate out 'objects' from 'mechanisms', but ontologically each is an object, in the way that a clock mechanism is both a mechanism and a physical object.

mechanisms and the deeper ones, by theorising the continuity and change between them. For example, is it possible to describe mechanisms of disadvantage in several ethnic communities (that may have quite different features), but to seek similar transformation rules in each from earlier states, or indeed vice versa?[11]

Realism in the natural sciences is predicated on the ability of a theory to accurately explain phenomena and indeed to predict outcomes on the basis of the explanation (Hacking 1983a). A theory is real if and only if it can achieve this. Historically, theories developed; some were abandoned because they were wrong, or superseded by a better theory. A better theory would often incorporate elements of the theory it replaced, but explain a further range of phenomena. A key historical example is that Einstein's theories of relativity incorporated earlier Newtonian laws. The earlier laws still explained phenomena within their range, so remained real. In many cases such theoretical development took place over a very long period, decades or centuries in the case of the Newtonian model being superseded by the Einsteinian one.

Finding an analogue of this in social science is hard because physical laws depend on a level of invariance, which is simply not present in the social world. If there are laws in the social world, then social science has not been very good at identifying many of them. Laws that are identified are either at a level of generality in that they are little more than taxonomic, or, like Duverger's law,[12] require a large number of *ceteris paribus* clauses in their specific instances.

The logical structure of a middle range theory in social science is the same as that in the natural sciences. It is a propositional statement, but its structure is more likely to be an approximation of reality, rather than an expression of reality itself. That is, our theories are more likely to be heuristics or models (methodological or statistical) that approximate reality, so while we may remain realist about objects and mechanisms, our theories may be cruder approximations of reality. Of course, natural scientists too use models, but the key difference is that those models will have mathematical expressions that relate to actual measures of the physical world, such as temperature, density, pressure, etc. The social sciences will use statistical models which will show relationships between terms in the model, but the measurements will be social constructions, which are more or less proxies for social reality.

---

[11]Statistically, we can think of invariance as goodness of fit in a model and variance, that part of the model that is unexplained. The challenge is to find new models that explain the latter, though as I have said here, a statistical model is merely indicative.

[12]Duverger's law is a principle which asserts that a plurality rule election system tends to favour a two-party system. However, it operates only *ceteris paribus* to the extent that important exceptions themselves have relatively stable characteristics (Riker 1982).

However, it does not follow from this that there is no growth of knowledge in social science, because even though our models are approximate they are capable of producing realistic approximations. Ontologically, a model will contain different kinds of variables. It may (for example) contain measurements of migration from A to B, of the type of housing one lives in, earnings, age or hours worked each week. These kinds of measurements are analogous to those in natural science and, while subject to inaccuracy of measurement, they can have a constancy over time and between places. While there may be variance of behaviour in those that are measured by these concepts, the concepts themselves can remain the same, or if they change (say, in the way housing is measured), they are often translatable (in the same way as measures of temperature might be) one to another. Models built on these kinds of concepts, while informative, tell us very little about motivation, beliefs or behaviour. Sociological concepts, such as ethnicity, social class, well-being, etc., are necessary in order to develop models of the social world that have explanatory adequacy, but they will have a more limited sphere of applicability (Williams 2003) through time and between places, partially because what they represent changes quite quickly across time and space, but also because, as measurements, they can only imperfectly capture the aspects of the social world they represent.

Yet, even though our models are imperfect representations of mechanisms, they will nevertheless represent empirical reality enough for them to be *realistic* (as opposed to *real*). We know this to be the case because the empirical testing of models will frequently reveal unanticipated effects (for example, in counterurbanisation research, the link between migration motivated lifestyle choices and tourism). These in turn have empirically testable consequences.

Conclusion – objectivity and social objects

For there to be objectivity in social science we need to have a culture of investigation that seeks the truth about the social world in context. To do this it must differentiate between things in the world, but I have argued in this chapter that differentiation cannot be simply on the basis of manifest, observable and apparently measurable properties. Objectivity as an epistemological concept implies an ontology of objects. Taken together, an objective social science requires a bridging methodology between the epistemological goal of objectivity and the character of the world itself.

In this chapter I have set out a version of a realist ontology. It is realist in the sense that there is a belief in the existence of social objects that have causal properties. But these properties, though they may often exhibit stability – what I have termed invariance – will also be contingent on the probabilistic outcomes of earlier processes and the manifestation of earlier objects. That is, there is no underlying natural necessity in the social world; rather, objects have varying probabilities of coming into existence and causing new objects. They do cohere into identifiable mechanisms; indeed, if they did not, social life would be an unpredictable flux.

This presents methodological challenges. First, we must separate out method from methodology. Methods are tools or technologies, but methodology must make the bridge between our epistemology, expressed as theories of what the world is like and its reality. Because social reality has much more variance than physical reality, a realist methodology for the social sciences will be different from that of the natural sciences. The latter have established laws which ground phenomena in natural necessity in the final instance. While the social sciences may theorise mechanisms and what links those mechanisms to deeper mechanisms, laws are rare and cannot be grounded in the necessity which grounds physical laws. This has implications for the models of the social sciences, which are much more likely to be approximations of social reality.

Nevertheless, the social world exhibits enough invariance to allow generalisations from one context to another, and we can specify the rules under which particular variances are captured by invariance. But also the social world (like the physical world) has the ability to produce refutations of our theories.

Objectivity is situated in social contexts and these are both external to the investigation in a discipline (what shall be investigated) and internal (how shall we investigate), what counts as evidence, concepts, measures, etc. These things will change over time, as will the social world that is investigated and, moreover, the kind of knowledge we have, derived through measurement, will have differing epistemological statuses. Yet we might say that our best methodological efforts are captured in our best practices. These will include the individual and collective commitment to truth, openness to scrutiny and an awareness of our own subjectivity, intellectual and personal history. But not withstanding these and the contingent nature of the social world, our objectivity is finally underwritten by the character of the social world itself.

Discussion

————Gayle ————

I ACCEPT THAT METHODS AND methodology are often conflated in research writings and we need to remember that methods are the tools we use to collect data. Methodology should involve describing and analysing the methods we have chosen, evaluating their value, reflecting on the dilemmas their usage causes and exploring the relationship between our use of methods and our 'results'. It seems a truism to say that researchers, of the physical and the social world, should always pick the method most relevant to the question – the issue in hand – but not all of us are equally skilled in all methods, and teamwork, including multidisciplinary teamwork, may be necessary.

I agree with Malcolm that the methods we choose and our methodological reflection of them are in turn driven by epistemological assumptions, but because epistemology is concerned with what counts as legitimate knowledge as well as what can be known, our methodological reflection on the relationship between the process and the product of social research is also an epistemological act. This presents a challenge, I think, to what some social scientists call the 'obsession' with methodology and epistemology; a critique that some may make of this book. As Malcolm says, for researchers of the social, rather than the physical, defining an object we might be objective about is harder not least because everywhere we look we can find social objects. We not only have to consider how objects are nested, but it is especially important for us to make it clear that the methods we use and the way we use them affects the knowledge we produce or, as the Fun Boy Three and Bananarama once put it, echoing Ella Fitzgerald's hit from the 1930s: 'It ain't what you do it's the way that you do it. And that's what gets results.'

——John

I HAVE JUST ONE POINT where some clarification might be useful. Many people may accept that social objects exist independently of the social scientist, but will have doubts about whether social objects can truly be regarded as 'existing' independently of the consciousness and meanings of participants. This might be the position taken by many postmodernists, who question the whole idea of a 'social reality'. This is not a position that I would accept, but I wondered how you would justify the idea of a social object against such a comment. You say that social objects are 'socially constructed but real', and I guess that this is tied in to your emphasis on the constraining power of social objects – much as Durkheim described social facts as being both external and constraining. Perhaps you could just elaborate a little bit on this.

——Malcolm

GAYLE IS RIGHT, THE RELATIONSHIP between epistemology, methodology and method is a complex one and our positioning will shape the first and, by extension, the second. To some extent, in the history of social research, there has been a relative independence of method. In one sense this is good, in so far as whatever our epistemological position is, we can agree on many technical aspects of method, particularly statistics, survey and experimental design. The downside is either a naïve realism, in which somehow it is believed our measures directly represent the social world, or epistemological relativism, which gives up on trying to represent social reality and instead simply represents locally situated interests. Ontological grounding, of the kind I advocate here, is far from easy, but it is possible because of the relative invariance of mechanisms in the social world. A moderate realism, which begins from contingent, yet nested social objects, is necessary and desirable for situated objectivity.

John also raises a reasonable point. Many realists think in terms of levels of accessibility. I would not want to push this too far, but it is the case that we inevitably have some awareness of some 'social objects' because we are able to act upon that awareness. Indeed, for social objects to have causal properties there must be reducibility to agency eventually. It does not follow, however, that social objects are merely objects of consciousness. A second level of social object comprises those things that we may become aware of and are enabling or constraining (much as Durkheim's social facts). These might be civil/criminal laws, rules or, crucially, aspects of physical world that we both physically and socially construct, for example, a bicycle or a castle. Finally, and of perhaps greatest interest to social scientists, there are mechanisms of cohering social objects. The most well-known, in economics, is the 'pricing mechanism', but in sociology we might think of mechanisms of deprivation/opportunity, for example. Mechanisms not only operate independently of any given individual, they can be difficult to discover even through social research, though once discovered have explanatory value for social objects at the other levels. One last thing, though, that I want to stress (the enabling/constraining properties of physical objects aside) is that social objects have varying probabilities of existence; none are determined and all are contingent upon other social objects.

SEVEN
Objectivity and Subjectivity in Practice

Having explored and extended philosophical debates surrounding the possibility and desirability of objectivity in social research and the meanings and possibilities of subjectivity, the focus in this chapter is objectivity and subjectivity within and beyond the research process and product.

──Gayle's argument ─────────────────────────────

IN 1959 TALCOTT PARSONS ARGUED: 'the term sociology is coming increasingly to be a central symbol in the popular ideological preoccupations of our time' (Parsons 1959: 553). Parsons insisted that as the profession of sociology came more under the public eye it would 'be exposed to more distortion and misunderstanding than ever before', and because of this sociologists should take care 'to maintain high standards of scientific competence and objectivity' (ibid.: 559).[1] In the same year, C. Wright Mills, arguing for the necessity of a 'sociological imagination' to truly understand the social world, said that the sociologist must be able to look at the familiar in social life and see it afresh. He wrote:

> The sociological imagination enables us to grasp history and biography and the relations between the two within society. That is its task and its promise. To recognise this task and this promise is the mark of the classic social analyst. … No social study that does not come back to the problem of biography, of history, and of the intersections within a society, has completed its intellectual journey. (Mills 1959: 12)

For Mills, the sociological imagination is a tool that enables those who use it to understand individual experience with reference to time and place. It also enables an explanation of the relationship between 'the personal troubles of milieu' and

---

[1]As a sociologist, many of my examples in this chapter come from my own discipline, though much of the argument is relevant beyond this.

'the public issues of social structure'. In other words, it allows us to question whether those problems and experiences that are sometimes defined as private, and thus the responsibility of the individual, are really the result of wider issues relating to society and societal norms and values. Later, in another, different consideration of the relationship between the personal and the public, Alvin Gouldner (1970) suggested that sociology was becoming increasingly technocratic and subservient to the state in terms of its funding, choices of topics and methodological principles and practices. Gouldner argued for a morally responsible, reflexive, radical, critical sociology that 'would recognise that knowledge of the world cannot be advanced apart from the sociologist's knowledge of himself [sic], and his position in the social world, or apart from his efforts to change them' (Gouldner 1970: 489, see also Hollands and Stanley 2009 for further discussion). Mills' and Gouldner's work has been widely influential and can be seen to represent the beginnings of a 'new sociology', a 'public sociology' 'committed to the classical values of citizenship, namely liberty, human dignity, Socratic reason, democracy and moral virtue' (Ossewaarde 2007: 800, drawing on Mills 1959 and Simon 1995).

More recently, Anthony Giddens (1990) and John Scott (2005) have written in support of sociology as necessary to understanding and changing the social world:

> The practical impact of social sciences is both profound and inescapable. Modern societies, together with the organisations that compose and straddle them, are like learning machines, imbibing information in order to regularise their mastery of themselves ... only society reflexively capable of modifying their institutions in the face of accelerated social change will be able to confront the future with any confidence. Sociology is the prime medium of such reflexivity. (Giddens 1990: 21)

> The core concerns of the sociological imagination have to be sustained within the sociology curriculum. There is a general framework of ideas about social relations that may be the common concern of the social sciences but is the particular concern of sociology. Professional sociology is the specific guardian of these intellectual concerns. ... This intellectual task centres on the idea of what it is to talk about human 'society' in all its complexity. (Scott 2005: 7.2)

All of these writers suggest that sociology has a particular responsibility in terms of understanding the social world and with this responsibility comes a need for a reflexive (which involves critical (self) reflection) approach. Additional calls for reflexivity come from Pierre Bourdieu (1990), who, like Gouldner (1970), argues for a 'sociology of sociology', and Loic Wacquant (1992: 40), who urges for reflexivity to 'extend beyond the experiencing subject to encompass the organizational and cognitive structure of the discipline'. The view here is that by aiding the 'progress of science' reflexivity makes for not only a more responsible process but produces more responsible knowledge (Bourdieu 1992: 194). None of this is neutral. Rather, as Tim May (2011: 49) suggests, '[a] clear intent to work with reflexivity to produce an improved science exists alongside the wish to deploy science to improve social conditions'.

However, this view is not universal. Instead, some argue that an approach which engages with political agendas (both within the process and with reference to the product) is less than desirable. For example:

> ...there is ... much pressure among researchers themselves, in many areas, to define their goal in practical or political terms. We see this in the demands of some commentators on educational research that it should be designed to serve educational purposes. We also find it in those forms of social research which are committed to emancipatory political projects, to the fight against sexism or racism or against discrimination on grounds of sexual orientation or disability. ... To the extent that such developments amount to redefining the goal of enquiry as the promotion of some practical or political cause, we see them as sources of motivated bias, and believe that they must be resisted by social researchers. They threaten to destroy the operation of the research communities on which the pursuit of scientific knowledge necessarily depends. (Hammersley and Gomm 1997: 3.3–3.4)

Others argue that even if practical and/or political impact is appropriate and desirable, it is very unlikely:

> The idea that social scientists might influence public policy provides an inspiration for many young social scientists. In most English-speaking countries the sad truth is that things have never worked in this way. (Silverman 2000: 273)

I return to the issue of impact later in this chapter with reference to the politics of the research product and to recent and current debates on the reach and value of sociology and other social sciences. First, I turn to a consideration of the politics of the research process.

The politics of the process

In 2003 I wrote:

> When we enter a field we make footprints on the land and are likely to disturb the environment. When we leave we may have mud on our shoes, pollen on our clothes. If we leave the gate open this may have serious implications for the farmers and their animals. All of this is also relevant to what we find out about the field and its inhabitants. Thus, when doing research (fieldwork) we need to be sensitive to respondents and to the relevance to our own presence in their lives and in the research process. (Letherby 2003c: 6)

I stand by this and continue to argue that not only does who we are affect what we do, but what we do affects who we are and of course the process of research affects the research product(s). So, the methods we decide for and against, the research populations we choose and are able to access, our behaviour when entering and leaving the research field and all other research choices and experiences influence our 'findings', our 'results', our products. Furthermore, we need to acknowledge and theorise the embodied experience of research during data collection and in analysis and with reference to funder/researcher/respondent roles and relationships and identities – including reference to the significance of class, 'race' and ethnicity, age, gender, dis/ability, dress, accent and other social differences – and the impact of this on the process and the product. For me, then, as I argued in Chapter 5, any attempt at an objective social science must involve theorisation of all of these subjective influences whether or not we utilise quantitative methods with their focus on measurement and comparison, qualitative methods with their emphasis on the experiential or a mixture of both.

As noted at various points in this book, in earlier times the 'scientific' method was unquestioned as the best way to study both the physical and the social world. From this perspective the view is that the 'expert neutral knower' (the researcher) can be separated from what is known, that different researchers exposed to the same data can replicate results and that it is possible to generalise from research to wider social populations and physical properties. In other words, the 'scientific' method allows for the 'objective' collection of facts within a linear and orderly research process executed by a value-neutral researcher (Stanley and Wise 1993; Kelly et al. 1994; Letherby 2003c). Sometimes this approach is associated with quantitative methods and with positivism (although this represents a misunderstanding of quantitative approaches and of quantitative researchers (e.g. see Oakley 1999 for further discussion)) and there has been and is much criticism of the use of numbers to 'prove facts' in social life.

Those who advocate qualitative methods have argued that the best way to find out about people is to let them 'speak for themselves' (e.g. Stanley and Wise 1993). Qualitative research is also seen by some as more participatory, giving respondents more control over the research process. Qualitative researchers, then, are concerned to generate data grounded in the experience of respondents. For example, Tina Koch and Debbie Kralik, writing about their research, which focused on the experience of living with chronic illness, argue:

> Story telling has engaged researcher attention as a method of accessing the personal world of illness. ... For the purpose of our inquires, verbal accounts are more than vehicles for collecting personal information; they are the very processes of identity construction. Asking people to tell their story of chronic illness is the most appropriate way to explore how identity is constructed when people are in 'transition'. (Koch and Kralik, 2001: 34)

Criticising what she calls the 'paradigm wars' Ann Oakley (1998: 709) warns us of the danger of representing quantitative and qualitative approaches as 'mutually exclusive ideal types'. Cautioning against choosing favourite methods without proper consideration of the research aims and objectives, Liz Kelly et al. (1994) argue that appropriate methods should be chosen to suit research programmes rather than research programmes being chosen to 'fit' favourite techniques. Similarly, Oakley (2004: 191) suggests: 'The most important criteria for choosing a particular research method is not its relationship to academic arguments about methods, but its fit with the question being asked in the research'. Kelly et al. add:

> Rather than assert the primary of any method, we are not working with a flexible position: our choice of method(s) depends on the topic and scale of the study in question. Whenever possible we would combine and compare methods, in order to discover the limitations and possibilities of each. (Kelly et al. 1994: 35–6)

As I argued in Chapter 5, I believe that as researchers we need to be aware of our own personal and intellectual personhood and our *presence* in both the research process and product, and to appreciate that our research activities tell us things about ourselves as well as about the people we are researching (Steier 1991). 'First-person' research accounts and acknowledgement of the significance of personhood is necessary if the knowledge produced is to be 'accountable' and the processes of research need to be clear and available to critique (Stanley 1991). Researchers are more willing than ever before to acknowledge that empirical research, particularly qualitative research, is '... complex, often chaotic, sometimes messy, even conflictual' (Hallowell et al. 2005: 2). However:

> ... despite what could be called the 'reflexive turn' in research reporting, the realities of doing empirical research are generally glossed over in methods textbooks, research reports and journal articles, which still provide fairly sanitized accounts of the research process. (Hallowell et al. 2005: 2, drawing on Bryne-Armstrong et al. 2001: vii)

This 'cleaning up' of research accounts is unfortunate not only because the research process is a complex endeavour, but also because this complexity is relevant to any discussion of objectivity and subjectivity (and highlights the need to theorise the subjective) in social research. The researcher's status as 'insider' and 'outsider' may be subject to constant negotiation between all parties, or an 'insider' status may be assumed/taken for granted by the respondent(s) and/or the researcher if the researcher shares an identity or experience with respondents or works with similar others in a professional or voluntary capacity (Letherby and

Zdrodowski 1995; Collins 1998; Homfray 2008). Some researchers are explicit about their insider status and about where their loyalties lie:

> Any notion that I am, or could be 'objective' with regard to the question of gay and lesbian equality, or could approach the research as a dispassionate outsider is simply not a possibility. To that extent, I 'take the side' of the wider gay and lesbian community and wanted my research to assist them in their emancipatory aims. As someone who has been intimately involved in this area of campaigning since the mid-1980s, and whose personal identity is that of a gay man, to 'step outside' would simply be impossible... (Homfray 2008: 3.4)

As Mike Homfray (2008) notes, involvement is often seen as synonymous with researcher bias (e.g. see Hammersley and Gomm 1997 above) but, as I and others have suggested, issues of self and other are always a part of research and thus should always be reflected upon (Fine 1994; Wilkinson and Kitzinger 1996; Temple 1997; Letherby 2003c, 2004). Furthermore, if we acknowledge its existence, rather than attempt to deny it, reflecting on bias can lead to useful data.

One core dimension in any research project is that of power. Increasingly, researchers are concerned with challenging a balance of power in favour of the researcher. One approach which attempts to do this is participatory action research (PAR) (e.g. Koch et al. 1999; O'Neill 2008), an approach which draws on Ernest T. Stringer's (1996) four guiding principles of PAR:

- democratic, enabling participation of all people;
- equitable, acknowledging people's equality of worth;
- liberating, providing freedom from oppressive, debilitating conditions;
- life-enhancing, enabling the expression of people's full human potential.

Others *insist* that the choice of method of data collection should meet participatory and emancipatory criteria as well as epistemological ones. So, for example, as noted above, some argue that 'story telling' methods enable a respondent to 'make sense of her [sic] thoughts and experiences through the reliving and retelling of them' (Kralik et al. 2000: 913; see also Letherby and Zdrodowski 1995). In an attempt to research young people with learning difficulties, Tim Booth and Wendy Booth (1996: 65) argued that 'the only way of collecting their stories is to lend them the words'. As Vicky Lewis and Mary Kellett (2004: 199) suggest, this 'putting words into mouths ... rings ethical alarm bells' but as they add 'constructing a narrative via sensitive interpretation' is likely to be more valid than less informed observations. With reference to our concerns in this book, participatory and emancipatory approaches and 'lending' words to respondents both challenges traditional definitions of objectivity and demonstrates the need for careful scrutiny of the significance of the politics of the research process:

for theorised subjectivity. It also raises questions regarding the politics of the research product, as discussed further below.

Some researchers argue that involvement in research can be beneficial in its own right. Indeed, Homfray (2008: 3.5) suggests that, given the limited impact that social research has, this should be our main aim when conducting research:

> ...I would share the views of Truman who casts some doubt upon the empowering or emancipatory function of much social research on the wider stage, and looks towards the experience of participation as something benefi- cial in itself, as opposed to the impact of the future publishing of research findings. ... I would hope that those who took part in the research were able to feel that their contribution was worthwhile on at least the level of being able to express their own views, and thinking through their own position. For if there is any semblance of political gay and lesbian community, and those working for change are important in its development, then opportuni- ties such as this can only be of value. (Homfray 2008: 3.5)

Interestingly, the National Institute for Health Research (www.crncc.nihr.ac.uk/ ppi/ppi_how) also stresses the value of being involved as a participant in a clinical trial or in wider clinical research activities (for example, acting as a research advisory group member, helping develop 'Participant Information Sheets', etc.). Patients and the public may benefit from being actively involved:

- by having a say in research;
- through sharing their experience;
- by getting research started that is important to them;
- by learning more about research activities;
- through meeting new people – researchers, members of the public and other people from different networks;
- by gaining confidence and new skills;
- by having the chance to make a contribution. (www.crncc.nihr.ac.uk/ppi/ppi_how)

But although research might be beneficial, therapeutic even, it should not be confused with therapy or counselling (Cotterill and Letherby 1994) and we need always to be clear about who benefits the most:

> The ethical or moral base of the relationship between researcher and researched cannot be adequately captured by the language of contractual consent or of care. In other contexts, when we contract or ask someone for help or assis- tance, we think in terms of gratitude and obligation rather than informed consent. Roberts and Sanders (2005) see the willingness of participants to be researched as a gift, one of immense value for the studies and subsequent careers of researchers; there may be little direct or immediate benefit for the subjects nor financial or material gain. ... (Pérez-y-Pérez and Stanley 2011: 4.3)

On the other hand, although there is a long held assumption that the researcher always holds the balance of power, research is often more complicated than this in reality and respondents are not always the most vulnerable within research relationships. Sometimes we research 'up' rather than 'down' and respondents do not feel disempowered by either their life experience or by the research relationship and it may be patronising of the researcher to assume that the respondent needs to be empowered by the process (Letherby 2003c, 2004). In addition, there is no script for respondents (despite 'Participant Information Sheets' and 'Consent Forms') and respondents have the right to be unco-operative (Davis et al. 2000) and demanding.

I suggest that, like power, emotion is integral to the research process (see Chapter 5 for more here). Displays of emotion with research can be dangerous for both researcher and respondent, and provide another example of the need to be concerned with researcher (as well as respondent) safety and well-being:

> Mrs S was a twitchy participant, becoming highly animated to the point of belligerence. She smoked throughout the interview. Her answers were disconcerting and contradictory. When I asked about her family relationships, she told me that she had a good relationship with her husband. She went on to say: 'I threw a cup of tea at him this morning because he wouldn't get up'. I became increasingly nervous when she admitted that 'yes' she did have a temper… . [T]he part of the interview that I found most chilling was in response to my questions about her friendships. Mrs S said that she kept herself to herself, but told me that she had at one time been friendly with one neighbour but that was all over now. Mrs S no longer trusted the woman and became suspicious of her to the point where she believed the neighbour wanted to harm her. She leaned towards me confidentially: 'She is trying to poison me by putting ground glass in my tea'. (from Alice Lovell's vignette about aspects of her research experience when studying women's health and their personal relationships, in Hallowell et al. 2005: 118–19)

Clearly then, the research process is a political endeavour and if we deny this and the need to constantly reflect on the significance of the researcher's *presence*, our accounts are less than complete, dishonest even. Furthermore, as Liz Stanley and Sue Wise (1990: 22) note, 'researchers do not have "empty heads" in the way that inductivism proposes', so one must acknowledge the gendered, classed, racial and so on, intellectual and physical presence of the researcher. Thus, the personhood of the researcher is relevant to the selection, explanation, interpretation and judgement we deploy in our theoretical analysis just as it is to research design and fieldwork. Miriam Glucksman (1994: 150) heeds us to remember that 'a concern with the internal dynamics of the research situation' should not take 'precedence over what the research is ostensibly about'. I agree but would suggest that reflexivity – both descriptive (the description of one's reflection) and analytical (involving comparison and evaluation) – are essential parts of the research process. Furthermore, both researchers and respondents engage in it

(Letherby 2002b). Yet, despite the dynamic nature of the research process – as highlighted above – as researchers we are in a privileged position not only in terms of access to resources and access to multiple accounts, but also in terms of discipline training which enables us to engage in 'second order theorising', or what Giddens (1984) calls the 'double hermeneutic'. This involves 'interpretation', not just 'description' of respondents' and researchers' analytical processes (Letherby 2002b). All of this is fundamental to the production of responsible, accountable knowledge and anything even close to 'good enough objectivity'.

The politics of the product

Thus far in this chapter I have been concerned with what happens within the research process. A few years ago I was engaged in a project with Paul Bywaters and colleagues from the Centre for Social Justice, Coventry University, within which we considered the possibility and the value of researcher involvement beyond the traditional end point of research (Letherby and Bywaters 2007a). Suzanne Hood and colleagues (1999: 3) describe the stages of the process as 'design, funding, access, fieldwork, analysis and output'. But we argued for an 'extending social research' model which not only involves a further stage – 'continued involvement and further developments' – but also involves at every aspect of the process a reconsideration of what we mean by the research product(s) and academic involvement and responsibility in the production of these:

1. Extending social research places a spotlight on the impact of the research process and the research product.
2. Extending social research expands the research process to include reporting, applying, publicising and implementing research findings.
3. All stages are extended. Extending social research requires rethinking the whole process.
4. Research relationships are extended as funders, partners, expected beneficiaries and end users are engaged as partners in the change process.
5. Researchers' roles are extended as they take responsibility for what happens with their findings.
6. Researchers' skills are extended as they focus on the change process. (Bywaters and Letherby 2007: 5)

In making our case we suggested that there were three main sets of arguments for an 'extending social research' model:

- Ethical arguments – research as inevitably political: social scientists as 'public intellectuals';
- Pragmatic arguments – changing research agendas: government concerns, evidence-base and 'excellent' applied research;
- Methodological arguments – the process and the product: the relationship between the process and the product.

Similar arguments are relevant to our discussion of objectivity and subjectivity in practice. I have outlined my methodological position already in this chapter (and in Chapter 5) and in the remainder of this chapter I focus on ethical and pragmatic arguments. Of course we (Letherby and Bywaters 2007a) were not the first to argue for an overtly political agenda. In 1994 Norman Denzin suggested that '[i]ncreasingly the criteria of evaluation will turn ... on moral, practical, aesthetic, political and personal issues – the production, that is, of texts that articulate an emancipatory, participative perspective on the human condition and its betterment' (Denzin 1994: 501). Others argue for (not least) community-based research, participatory research, collaborative research, action research, which all aim for the democratisation of the knowledge process, and for social change (Stoeker, 1996; also see calls for reflexive sociology as briefly outlined at the beginning of this chapter). With specific reference to the politics of the product, Michael Huberman (1987) calls for 'sustained inter-activity' throughout the research process, from the definition of the problem to the application of the findings. Similarly, Sandra Nutley (2003: 12) argues that researchers who want their work to be used must pay attention to the gap between research and the policy or practice worlds, which have 'different priorities, use different languages, operate to different time scales and are subjected to very different reward systems'.

Some argue that their own discipline should start with/is best suited to taking an overtly political stance. For example:

> [social work research] ... aims not only to support practice but also to transform it. Social work, with its ethical imperative towards challenging social injustice, requires social work researchers to examine both the socially excluded and the powerful elites who decide upon their social exclusion. (McLaughlin 2007: 13)

> Nowhere, perhaps, is the production of knowledge more enmeshed with social policies and the political agenda than in criminology. Criminological research either feeds criminal justice policies and practices, participating in their exponential growth, or it critiques them. (Martel 2004: 179)

> Within the School of Social Policy, we undertake innovative, exciting, applied research. We believe in research making an impact and we aim to build into the research process itself, communities, policy makers and practitioners, so as to ensure that our research travels and impacts upon people's everyday lives. Our research is ethically driven and sensitive, and deeply resonates with local, national and international issues. (Dr Basia Spalek, Director of Research and Knowledge Transfer, University of Birmingham, www.birmingham.ac.uk/schools/social-policy/research/index.aspx)

Feminist researchers, from disciplines across the academy, aim for research findings, and subsequent theory, which is grounded in the experience of women (and men), validates the experiential, attempts to challenge mainstream ('malestream') knowledge and leads to positive change (e.g. Cook and Fonow 1980; Stanley 1990; Ramazanoglu with Holland 2002; Letherby 2003c; Hesse-Biber 2007b). As Caroline Ramazanoglu and Janet Holland (2002: 169) note, 'the inseparability of epistemology, ethics and politics encourages feminists to imagine how human relationships could be different, and how a better social world could work'. However (and this argument is relevant to anyone who makes claims for their discipline and/or a research approach they share with others), feminism is not a unitary category which encapsulates a consistent set of ideas within an identifiable framework; rather, it is under continual negotiation and there is not one feminism but many (Griffin 1989). So, for most women, the identification of oneself as feminist is not straightforward and involves social, political and personal decisions and choices (Letherby 2003c: 136). This necessitates the need to be sensitive to 'the conundrum of how not to undercut, discredit or write-off women's consciousness as different from our own' (Stanley 1984: 201). In addition: '[f]eminism remains inherently contradictory because gender is only part of people's lives. In order to transform unjust gender relations, more than gender must change' (Ramazanoglu with Holland 2002: 68).

All of the above arguments focus on the *need to make a difference*. Another way to look at the issue is to start from the view that social research cannot avoid impacting not only on respondents but on its funders, its audience and on others, even if as researchers this is not our main goal. With this in mind, it is necessary to pay attention to the external (to the research process) factors that influence the impact which research activity and research findings have (Letherby and Bywaters 2007a; Homfray 2008).

Arguably, funders are the dominant influence in the drive for 'evidence-based practice'. The use of social science knowledge for both understanding and transforming social policies and political systems has come to be taken for granted: '[t]he 'gold standard' Randomised Control Trial focuses attention on how the research is set up and data is analysed, but it is then often just assumed that good enough evidence will lead to good enough implementation' (Letherby and Bywaters 2007: 27). The UK Labour Governments of 1997 and 2001 and the Conservative–Liberal Democrat Coalition Government (elected in 2010) have all pressed for a call for evidence to support policy development, the delivery of policy objectives and the evaluation of policy outcomes. In 2000, David Blunkett, the then Secretary of State for Education and Employment, said: 'Good government is thinking government … rational thought is impossible without good evidence … social science research is central to the development and evaluation of policy (Blunkett 2000: 4). However, he continued by identifying what he saw as a disjunction between what research was needed and what research was actually done:

> It is disappointing that some of the most gifted and creative researchers seem to have turned away from policy-related issues, preferring to work on questions of little interest to those outside of the research community. There is a danger of too much concentration on the micro level – what is the point of research which becomes narrower and narrower, with small groups of people responding to each other's writing in esoteric journals, read only by themselves and relevant only to themselves? (Section 21)

And:

> What policy makers find most frustrating and least useful are, at one extreme, a refusal to venture out from behind the safety of the data and the methodology to draw out any policy implications at all; and, at the other extreme, recommendations which may represent the ideal but take no account, whatever of issues of costs, achievability, the interaction with other priorities and possible unintended consequences; or conclusions which are just not sufficiently backed up by the evidence. This is ivory-towerism at its worst. (Section 49) (from a speech by David Blunkett to the Economic and Social Research Council (ESRC) 2000, cited by Locock and Boaz 2004: 376)

Blunkett's successor as Secretary of State, Charles Clarke, was also critical of the 'medieval concept of the university as a community of scholars unfettered by the difficulties and problems of the wider society' (2003 speech, cited by Locock and Boaz 2004: 376). These views are reflected in the 'Modernising Government' White Paper (1999), which called for better use of evidence and research in policy making and led to the establishment of the National Institute for Clinical Excellence and the Social Care Institute of Excellence (Letherby and Bywaters 2007b: 25). Such concerns are now central in the calls and practices of major research funders (in the UK at least) and in the practices of both the RAE (Research Assessment Exercise) 2008 and REF (Research Excellence Framework) 2014, in terms of the greater recognition, assessment of and credit for applied research and of *impact*. In preparing for RAE 2008, the concern was with acknowledging the importance of applied research:

> Where researchers in higher education have undertaken applied and practice-based research that they consider to have achieved due standards of excellence, they should be able to submit it to the RAE in the expectation that it will be assessed fairly against appropriate criteria. As proposed by the review group, we will ask main panels and sub-panels in all disciplines where this may be an issue to ensure that their criteria statements make clear how they will assess practice-based and applied research, according to criteria reflecting appropriate characteristics of excellence. (RAE 2004 (February) para 47)

In the run up to REF 2014 *impact* has received much more attention. During 2010 the REF team ran a pilot exercise to test and develop proposals for assessing the impact of research in REF 2014. The pilot exercise involved 29 UK higher education institutions and five REF units of assessment. Following scrutiny of these submissions by expert panels, it has been acknowledged that the measurement of impact still needs development and, in recognition of this, impact will have a lower weighting in 2014 than originally suggested. But the intention is to increase this for future REF exercises (www.hefce. ac.uk/research/ref/impact/). Here, impact directly connects with an overtly political approach in that:

> It is essential that impact should be defined broadly to include social, economic, cultural, environmental, health and quality of life benefits. Impact purely within academia should not be included in this part of the REF...

And:

> Submissions should:
>
> Show a distinctive contribution of the department's research to that public engagement activity. Make a case for the benefits arising from the public engagement activity. This must go beyond showing how the research was disseminated. (National Co-ordinating Centre for Public Engagement, Public Engagement, Impact and the REF Workshop, 29 March 2011, www.publi cengagement.ac.uk/sites/default/files/March%2029th%20REF%20 Workshop.pdf)

As noted above, there is further support for impact from funding councils. The Economic Social Research Council (ESRC) expects researchers to embed impact in their research and give advice on how to do this:

> ESRC Pathways to Impact for [grant] applications
>
> As part of your ESRC application you will be asked to complete an Impact Summary (4000 characters max) and Pathways to Impact attachment (maximum 2 × A4 pages)...
>
> The Impact Summary should be an outline of the pathways to impact attachments and answer the two following questions:
>
> • Who will benefit from this research?
> • How will they benefit from this research?
>
> The Impact Summary may be published to demonstrate potential impact of Research Council funded research...

The Pathways to Impact Toolkit gives you everything you need to achieve the maximum impact for your work. The toolkit includes information on developing an impact strategy, promoting knowledge exchange, public engagement and communicating effectively with your key stakeholders. (ESRC www.esrc.ac.uk/funding-and-guidance/tools-and-resources/impact-toolkit/ what-how-and-why/pathways/index.aspx)

And further, in answer to the question 'What is impact?':

Research Councils UK defines impact as 'the demonstrable contribution that excellent research makes to society and the economy'.

Impact embraces all the diverse ways that research-related skills benefit individuals, organisations and nations. These include:

- Fostering global economic performance, and specifically the economic competitiveness of the United Kingdom
- Increasing the effectiveness of public services and policy
- Enhancing quality of life, health and creative output.

A key aspect of this definition is that impact must be demonstrable. It is not enough just to focus on activities and outputs that promote impact, such as staging a conference or publishing a report. You must be able to provide evidence of research impact, for example, that it has been taken up and used by policy makers, and practitioners, has led to improvements in services or business. (www.esrc.ac.uk/funding-and-guidance/tools-and-resources/impact-toolkit/ what-how-and-why/what-is-research-impact.aspx)

And with reference to 'Types of impact':

The ESRC aims to achieve impact across its whole portfolio of activities. This can involve academic impact, economic and societal impact or both:

- Academic impact – the demonstrable contribution that excellent social and economic research makes to scientific advances, across and within disciplines, including significant advances in understanding, method, theory and application.
- Economic and societal impact – the demonstrable contribution that excellent social and economic research makes to society and the economy, of benefit to individuals, organisations and nations...

The impact of social science research can be categorised as:

- Instrumental – influencing the development of policy, practice or service provision, shaping legislation, altering behaviour
- Conceptual – contributing to the understanding of policy issues, reframing debates
- Capacity building – through technical and personal skill development...

To plan impact effectively you need to:

- Identify your key stakeholders – for example, other researchers; public sector; business/industry
- Identify how they will benefit from your research – types of impact might include: improving social welfare/public services; influencing public policy; contributing to operational/organisational change
- Identify how you will ensure they have the opportunity to benefit – for example, through organising public events; conferences; interaction with the media. (ESRC Guidance notes on the Impact report www.esrc.ac.uk/_images/Impact_Report_guidance_tcm8-3992.pdf)

There is recognition that making an impact is not an easy task:

> Determining the impact of social science research is not a straightforward task. Policy and service development is not a linear process, and decisions are rarely taken on the basis of research evidence alone. This makes it difficult to pin down the role that an individual piece of research has played. The timing of evaluation also presents challenges. Too soon after the research ends may mean that any impact has yet to fully develop. Too late, and the impact may no longer be traceable as people involved have moved on. (www.esrc.ac.uk/funding-and-guidance/tools-and-resources/impact-toolkit/what-how-and-why/what-is-research-impact.aspx)

And also an acknowledgement that the ESRC itself is still learning how to 'measure' the impact of social research:

> We are exploring new methods for assessing the impact of the research we fund on policymakers and practitioners, in order to demonstrate its broader contribution to society and the economy. This forms part of the new strategic emphasis on impact assessment alongside our work on bibliometrics and international benchmarking. As part of this initiative, we began to commission a series of impact case studies aimed at identifying the impact from ESRC research, and testing evaluation approaches. (www.esrc.ac.uk/funding-and-guidance/tools-and-resources/impact-toolkit/what-how-and-why/what-is-research-impact.aspx)

Recently in the BIS (Department for Business, Innovation and Skills) the blog of David Willetts, the current minister for Universities and Science, reports on the speech he gave at the ESRC's 2011 *Festival of Science*. The posting includes the following:

> Social science is a global science, with enormous impact on how we live our lives worldwide. And the UK is a world player – ESRC's *international benchmarking exercises* have judged the UK to be second only to the US in anthropology, economics, political sciences, psychology and sociology…

Social science shapes public policy and services, informs welfare reform and enhances civil liberties...

...looking ahead, the social science community also faces a series of challenges:

The 'fruits' of social science: We need to get better at showing the relevance of our quality research...

Data-mining: We must look for ways to use more data from existing research...

Transparency: I very much welcome ESRC's continued commitment to work with Research Councils and others to meet the issues around open access facing the wider research community.

Evidence-based policy: I want to see us build on social science's already excellent record of informing and shaping Government policy...

The social sciences vastly improve our understanding of the world around us – our society, our economy, our quality of life and public health – and most importantly they help us improve the outcomes of people from all backgrounds and areas of society. (http://blogs.bis.gov.uk/blog/2011/11/08/celebrating-the-value-and-relevance-of-the-social-sciences/, 8 November 2011, original emphasis)

So 'relevance' and 'usefulness' are increasingly important in defining what research should be done, what knowledge should be produced and how said knowledge will be assessed. Although encouraging to those who argue for research praxis (practice informed by research and theory), this approach does raise concerns, not least in terms of the fact that it can distract us from actually doing the research and making an impact in its generation of another layer of research and debate concerned with how best to improve research impact (see above and Locock and Boaz 2004; Letherby and Bywaters 2007b). Another concern for some is just whose interests are really being served? If we only do research that focuses on government priorities, this makes for a very narrow research agenda (Locock and Boaz 2004; Letherby and Bywaters 2007b) and we need to take care not to become the servants of government:

Assisting in the extension of outreach work to new populations, or suggesting ways to increase the effectiveness of therapeutic community practice, are each alike, analysable as endeavours which tighten the disciplinary grip of experts on citizens. In a new twist on Becker's old 'whose side are we on?' question, it may be argued that sociology should be assisting not in the extension of power, but in the extension of resistance – resistance to meddlesome interference in prostitutes' street dealings, and resistance to expert orchestration of patients' private lives. The opposite of power is not absence, but the resistance it provokes; sociologists, so the argument goes, should be laying the groundwork for citizen resistance rather than fostering the extension and effectiveness of expert power. (Bloor 1999: 323)

There are different ways, then, to view the focus on 'evidence-based' research and its subsequent impact. On the one hand, there is a concern that as universities increasingly adopt the entrepreneurial spirit of the market, as higher education becomes a 'product' delivered in service industries and as external demands for 'evidence' increase, there is much less support for 'curiosity-driven research' and much more support (including material resources) for research that meets the needs of government and industry (see Esptein 1995; Jary and Jones 2006; Trowler 2008; the special issue of *Contemporary Social Science* 2011, and many more for the critique of change in higher education; see Bate 2011 for a recent critique of impact in the arts and humanities; and see Hessels and van Lente 2010 for a similar debate in the physical sciences). On the other hand, an agenda that advocates making a difference and supports the extension of the process beyond the traditional end point of publication and presentation has the potential for social benefit. Whether we view the current drive for impact as something to celebrate, approach with cautious optimism or something to be wary of it is clearly contrary to the concerns of those who argue that objectivity is an epistemological virtue and necessity:

> ...our preoccupation with clarifying the meaning of 'bias' is not an idle one. It seems to us that we live in dangerous times for research. There are attempts outside of research communities, on the part of funders, including governments, to define the goal of research in terms other than the pursuit of knowledge. In Britain, this can be seen in the increasing contractual restrictions on research financed by government departments, which seem to be designed to ensure that published findings will support current policy and in the growing emphasis on the role of 'users' in the pronouncements of funding agencies, such as the Economic and Social Research Council. The latter organization now requires the research it finances to help 'the government, businesses and the public to understand and improve the UK's economic performance and social well-being' (ESRC Annual Report 1993/94, back cover). At the very least, this looks like the thin end of a wedge. (Hammersley and Gomm 1997: 5.2)

Obviously Hammersley and Gomm were writing several years ago and a lot has happened since then (some of which is recorded in this chapter). Recent and current changes in the academy and in related external agencies and bodies makes, I think, the case for theorised subjectivity even stronger. The influences on research funding and the expectations of research in terms of impact alongside the motivation of many (most?/all?) social scientists to make a positive difference to the lives of real people all strongly imply the need for critical scrutiny of the self and the other within the (extended) research process and product.

Brave new social scientists

Social scientists have always had to defend the status of the methods they use and the knowledge they produce from serious (and not so serious) critique. Here follows just two small examples (some might say extreme examples), but of course there are many more:

> Well quite honestly, I said I hope this research is worth it. I said to my mum, I've got this lady coming to see me this morning. She said 'What about?' I said, I hope it's not a load of old rubbish. Because there's been so much research on such rubbishy things I feel money's been wasted. So she said 'Oh it probably is... . Well, it's a bit indulgent isn't it, really, just talking about yourself all the time? (Oakley 1979, cited by Roberts 1992: 176)

> An ology. He gets an ology and he says he's failed. You get an ology, you're a scientist! (1980s British Telecom advert, voted no. 14 in the Top 100 Adverts of All Time. Grandmother speaking on phone to grandson who has passed only two GCSEs, one of which is Sociology, www.uktvadverts.com)

Rather than shy away from the critique, social scientists have always engaged in the debate. This book, with its critical concern about the status of the knowledge we produce, is part of the discussion. Recently sociologists (and other social scientists) in North America, Australia and Britain have become focused on what we do with the presentation of academic work beyond the academy. Michael Burawoy, in his 2004 Presidential Address to the American Sociological Association (and in his subsequent publication in 2005), argued for 'public sociology'. Burawoy (2005) suggests that while professional sociology has an academic audience, public sociology has an extra-academic audience and is reflexive. Thus:

> The bulk of public sociology is indeed of an organic kind – sociologists working with a labor movement, neighbourhood associations, communities of faith, immigrant rights groups, human rights organizations. Between the organic public sociologist and a public is a dialogue, a process of mutual education. The recognition of public sociology must extend to the organic kind which often remains invisible, private and is often considered to be apart from our professional lives. The project of such public sociologies is to make visible the invisible, to make the private public, to validate these organic connections as part of our sociological life. (Burawoy 2005: 8–9)

According to Burawoy (2005: 7): '[p]ublic sociology brings sociology into a conversation with publics, understood as people who are themselves involved in conversation. It entails, therefore, a double conversation.' This implies the need for sociologists to operate as 'public intellectuals' working beyond the academy, which overlaps and intersects with the call for *impact*. But, just like the impact agenda, 'public sociology' promotes critique, not least because: '[a]s well as providing an opportunity to reach a wider audience, stepping out in public as a sociologist can also involve vulnerability and political compromise' (Back 2007: 161). Furthermore, 'public sociology' can contribute to processes of inclusion or exclusion depending on how it is presented and by whom and how it is received (Skeggs 2004; Back 2007; Taylor and Addison 2011).[2]

One further critique of Burawoy's vision by Robert Hollands and Liz Stanley is that it reduces critical sociology to auto-critique and 'a sociology of sociology', which diminishes Gouldner's view of critical sociology, which:

> ... provides a way of thinking about the connections between sociologists and the various publics they study, which recognises hierarchies and inequalities in society ... whilst also maintaining a moral, ethical, non-partisan stance and a critical appreciation of theory and methodology... (Hollands and Stanley 2009: 3.12)

In many ways this takes me back to where I started in this chapter and leads me to reflect back on what I argued in Chapter 5. I do of course support arguments for a reflexive approach to sociology, to social science, to social research. This, I believe is fundamental to the production of robust and useful knowledge. It must be clear, however, that my position is partisan; indeed, I assert that we are all partisan. Current research drivers – everything from the importance of evidence and impact to the value of working in interdisciplinary teams and alongside commissioners – added to the acknowledgement of the importance of the personhood, the auto/biographies of all concerned in research, supports an approach which starts with a critical focus on subjectivity.

---

[2]Since 2005 there has been a phlethora of responses to Burawoy's (2004, 2005) call for 'public sociology'. This has come from the sociological community and others in the social sciences (who have adapted the concept to other disciplines). Responses range from individual pieces (e.g. Holmwood 2007; Hollands and Stanley 2008; Butler 2009; Farrar 2010; Taylor and Addison 2011) to debates and special editions within journals (e.g. The 'Future of Sociology' debate in *Sociological Research Online*, 10 and 11 (2004/2005); a symposium in the *British Journal of Sociology*, 56 (3) (2005); some pieces in the special issue of *Sociology* on 'Sociology and its Public Face(s)', 41 (5) (2007); four different debates in the *American Sociologist* (2005, 2006, 2007, 2009); plus many books and even a website, *A working bibliography of public sociology*, compiled by Albert Tzeng (http://sociologicalimagination.org/archives/author/alberttzeng).

A personal conclusion

I, alongside other colleagues in my institution, have recently been asked to consider whether I am able to put forward in Impact Statement for REF 2014. In thinking back to the beginnings of my academic career, it makes me smile to think how when starting my doctoral research on the experience of 'infertility' and 'involuntary childlessness' I was excited about what a difference I could make. My doctoral research was invaluable to me. It taught me a lot about the whole process of research, it fuelled my fascination in methodological and epistemological debate, it enabled me to say some useful (I hope) things about childlessness, parenthood and identity, it gave me the resources to work in an environment I continue to find rewarding and challenging. What my PhD did not do was have the impact I hoped it would. I spoke about my work at conferences, wrote some articles and chapters and a few small pieces for non-academic audiences, and I am gratified that I am still sometimes asked to speak, write, examine on the topic. I could have done more but at that time I did not have the skills or the support to do so. More recently with colleagues from Coventry University, I was involved in a series of projects concerned to explore the experience of teenage pregnancy and young parenthood. All of this work was commissioned by practitioners, themselves responsible for the care and support of young women, their partners and their children. In addition to positive responses to our calls for the need for further research in specific areas (e.g. violence and abuse in the lives of pregnant teenagers and young mothers, antenatal care, father's experience), as a research team we have been, and continue to be, involved in activities that could be described both as *impact* and as 'public sociology'. We have, for example, developed and delivered (with young mothers) training packs for health and social care professionals; trained young mothers to become peer researchers; and developed a questionnaire for young women entering and leaving semi-supported housing. In addition, we have presented and published our findings within and beyond the academy (for example, at local and regional meetings of those responsible for the delivery of the UK *Teenage Pregnancy Strategy*, in the local and national press and in practitioner-focused publications) (see Brady et al. 2007; and Letherby et al. 2007 for more detail on all of this). This is the area I will focus on in preparing my REF Impact Statement.

In comparing these two areas of work, I know that the methodological lessons I learnt as a postgraduate influenced the approach my research team and I adopted in our work on teenage pregnancy/young parenthood. Of course the development of our work was influenced too by the personal and intellectual identities of us all. Also relevant was the political motivation of (almost) all of our respondents and of the commissioners of our research and their keenness to work with us to make things better. Because of this we shared the big disappointment when some of our recommendations were rejected by those concerned with the national development of the UK *Teenage Pregnancy Strategy*.

Reflecting on my personal research experience I acknowledge that the increased external value on evidence and impact has led to further opportunities for social research to make a difference. Furthermore, these, and other related research drivers, are likely to increase rather than diminish, which demands the continued critical reflection of the significance of these changes to the doing of social research and of the place and possibilities of objectivity and subjectivity within this. This brings with it the need to extend our reflexive, critical lens, which includes constant critical scrutiny of the self, the other and all the rest within research.

Discussion

——Malcolm

GAYLE TOUCHES ON MANY DILEMMAS social scientists feel, not the least on whether 'impact' can really capture those things we have done that make a positive difference, or whether it simply measures a narrow range of effects that are germane to a contemporary and particular ideology. This kind of problem, I think, has long been the problem for the social scientist who rejects the position of neutrality advocated by those such as Martyn Hammersley. Is it our role to be advocates for emancipation and, if it is, what counts as emancipation and for whom? Critical realists and some Marxists have argued that better knowledge of our social conditions will itself emancipate. They may or may not be right, but that better knowledge is worth striving for because it allows us to make more informed decisions. Knowledge is not a sufficient condition for power, but it is a necessary one.

There is, I think, a subtle difference between specific advocacy for one cause or another and the willing acceptance that our work will be shaped by a commitment to values. Perhaps they are first-order and second-order values. It is the difference between doing research that is founded on a commitment to a set of values about the health and welfare of children (first-order) and doing research that narrowly seeks to demonstrate the efficacy of one family form over another (second-order).

Similarly, and I'm not sure that this is always clear in Gayle's writing, there is a difference between participation in research, in its extended form, and emancipation. Indeed, as she indicates, participation may be therapeutic and 'emancipate' as an unintended consequence, but I do not believe that we should ever set out to emancipate through our research. The social world is too complex and contested to risk such a strategy. Of course, like the engineer who is given the task of producing an energy-efficient pump, much of our bread and butter research is involved in problem solving at a meso-level.

For many years I have pondered whether 'public sociology' is a quite separate activity from that of social research. Maybe, to use an example from popular science, public sociology is rather like the work cosmologists such as Stephen Hawking or Brian Cox do. It is very much informed, but separate from, the empirical work undertaken by their less visible colleagues. My only plea would then be that public sociology is so informed!

———John

I WANTED TO HIGHLIGHT AN issue in public sociology that is often ignored: the question of the role of the audience or public. Discussions of impact tend to stress that social researchers must make huge efforts to get their work out into the world and to engage with policy makers, social movements, and others in order to ensure that their work can make a real difference to how we live. They hold that we must not simply write for academic audiences, but write in a style and in publications that will speak to the publics to whom our knowledge relates. That is, of course, quite correct and important to stress. But is the responsibility solely that of the social scientist? What do we do if the public and our audiences ignore us or, perhaps worse, denounce us (without reading us) as being unworthy of support. We can speak out and try to engage our audiences, but can we make them listen to us? As the old saying goes, you can take a horse to water but you can't make it drink. In our case, I often feel that the horse won't even let us take it to the water and may deny that it is thirsty.

So, I wondered what Gayle's view was of the role of the public in the process of engagement and impact. Can a sociology be a public sociology if the public won't listen?

———Gayle

AS I ARGUED ABOVE, ALTHOUGH research can have therapeutic value for those involved, it is important to remember that it is research, not therapy, and we must always be as clear as we can about the expectations from and consequences of research involvement for respondents. A key concern of ethics committee is that of informed consent, that is, that respondents are consenting to involvement in research from a position of a full understanding of what this involves. Yet, it is often difficult to assess whether consent is 'really' informed (Wiles et al. 2005). Furthermore, ethics committees do not allow for change and development within the research process which suggests that there needs to be 'a shift in our common-sense understanding of ethics ... [and] requires a much broader set of activities than is associated with conventional professional ethics' (Rossiter et al. 2000, cited by Truman 2003: 3.25). Thus, in aiming to be ethical researchers, we must return to issues of ethics throughout the process of research. Participatory methods respect respondents – as people and as individuals capable of reflexivity – and respondents may experience their research involvement as emancipatory. Also, research that aims to make a difference, to make things better and involves researchers in work beyond the traditional boundaries of the research process can have emancipatory outcomes. In my own work I support all of this, for, after all, if we do not act on the political findings of our research, somebody else probably will. I do not believe, though, that we should invite and include respondents in our projects with the *intention* of emancipating them through involvement in the research. This is, I think, both patronising to potential research respondents and is not an appropriate methodological or epistemological motivation for doing research.

With reference to what we do and what happens with our research products, I think we still have more to do in working with different audiences. As Erving Goffman (1959) tells us, we need to present ourselves differently to different audiences and attempting to improve the *impact* of our research and the doing of 'public sociology' brings us into contact with different audiences. There are many examples of social research not having the impact it should because key members of the 'audience' have not been receptive. There are also examples of research having unexpected impact, contrary to researchers' hopes. As I say, there is more to do.

EIGHT

Objectivity Established? A Trialogue

We have come to the end of our argument. One implication of what we have been arguing is that no conclusion can ever be final and absolute. This is certainly true of our own book. We have indicated some areas of debate at the end of each chapter and it is now time to assess the consistency of our whole argument and the areas that might still remain in need of development.

——John——————————————————————————————

I BEGAN OUR DISCUSSIONS BY setting out a starting point that recognised the intellectual gap that exists between the world as human scientists are able to experience, perceive and describe it, and the world as it really is. I showed that because the external world is knowable only through the concepts, categories and sensory apparatuses of human beings, we cannot assume any simple 'correspondence' between theoretical ideas and reality. Our knowledge of the world is always related to the physical and social position from which we are able to view it. Whatever 'objectivity' may be, it cannot be seen, in naïvely empiricist terms, as knowledge that 'reflects' the structure of the external world in the way that our bodies are reflected in a mirror.

   I then argued, in Chapter 3, that a first approximation to an objective representation of the world must be based upon a recognition and acceptance of this diversity and relativity of subjective experiences. Each person's view of the world is related to their standpoint but, if free from technical error, it can be regarded as an authentic expression of their particular embodied perspective. Because it is authentic, this knowledge has a 'truth' and an 'objectivity' for the individual or group that formulates it. For this reason, objectivity and truth can be more adequately approached through bringing together the diversity of perspectives and attempting to combine them into a single and more complex representation. Such a representation is more adequate than those produced from any of the separate viewpoints, but it is not the kind of absolute truth and objectivity that many have, misleadingly, sought. The social scientist must forge an intellectual 'synthesis' of divergent viewpoints, recognising that this is tentative and partial and that it must be constantly refined. We require techniques for assessing the practical adequacy of any intellectual synthesis, and we must recognise that practical engagement with the world means that any synthesis is likely to change the world that it describes and so will be in need of further revision.

————Malcolm ————

IN CHAPTER 4 I SET out the case for an objectivity that is situated in particular periods and the practices of the disciplines in those periods. Unlike the empiricist approach of 'value free' objectivity, which assumes an ahistorical context-free evaluation of research and practice, situated objectivity acknowledges that science and social sciences (and specifically sociology) are themselves social practices that take on different forms in different periods and practices. Objectivity, like other scientific values, is a social construct. However, while objectivity is a value that is socially situated, it has (and indeed must have) values that can transcend period and context.

All investigation must have purpose. That is not to say that purpose dictates outcomes, but it does provide context and can shape methodological approaches. It is the decision to investigate (say) health variations, rather than community cohesion. Focusing on the former may actually lead us to a conclusion about the latter (or vice versa), but the nature of the question will shape what counts as evidence and the kind of conclusion reached. This is equally true in the natural sciences where the scientific community's enthusiasm, combined with a willingness to fund an area of investigation, will shape where a branch of science, or which branch of science, progresses. A particular purpose may be abandoned through lack of investigative progress or the will of wider society to pursue it, but purpose embodies values that may be social or methodological. In this respect I agreed with Helen Longino, that the presence of values is therefore inevitable and often to the benefit of investigation.

The second transcending value, that of differentiation, is pursued in greater depth in Chapter 6, and in Chapter 4 I simply noted that a minimal differentiation between things in the world is a prerequisite for investigation. That is, a thing or event has a particular set of characteristics (at least at an observational level) and not others. We might counterpose this to an extreme form of social constructionism which sees all phenomena as perhaps the product of social discourse, where there can be no privileging of one account over another.

The last of these values is the search for truth about the world and is, in my view, the core value of science and that which marks out the scientific enterprise from faith or ideology. I emphasise that it is the search for truth that is important and it comes with the acceptance that finding a correspondence between our theories and the world may not be achieved, and especially in the social world. In this respect, in particular, John and I are in agreement. I add one caveat to this, that in the search for truth we are able to eliminate error and at least find partial correspondence between our theories and the world as it presents itself (otherwise investigation would have no purpose).

———Gayle

IN CHAPTER 5 I MADE a case for starting with and theorising on the subjective when considering issues of objectivity and subjectivity. As social research involves individuals who are socially situated, 'theorised subjectivity' acknowledges that research is a subjective, power-laden, emotional, embodied experience, and considers the positive and the negative aspects of this. Starting with subjectivity, though, does not mean that we give in to the subjective, indulging in our subjectivities. Rather, it requires the constant, critical interrogation of our personhood within the knowledge production process. 'Theorised subjectivity' relies on a recognition that there is a 'reality' 'out there', but the political complexities of subjectivities are always part of the research process and impact on the research product. It is a reflexive approach that acknowledges the significance of both the intellectual and personal auto/biography of researchers and of respondents but does not privilege involvement. I argue that theorised subjectivity moves us closer to a positive, which we might call objective, and is an attempt at what others have called 'good enough objectivity' or 'collaborative objectivity' and accepts that objectivity is value-laden, 'situated'. The starting point is different, though, as rather than advocating objectivity as an obtainable epistemological virtue or 'struggling' to find a way to justify the use of the term, I suggest that we should begin from a position that acknowledges what reflecting on subjectivity can do for the research process and product.

———Malcolm

GAYLE'S ARGUMENT THAT A THEORISATION of our subjectivity is a necessary condition for later objectivity is, in my view, entirely correct. Nevertheless, this and two of my own necessary conditions for objectivity, purpose and truth, are epistemological in nature. In Chapter 6 I argued that the further necessary condition of differentiation introduces an ontological dimension. This was present in John's discussion in Chapter 2 and again highlighted above when he said the 'external world is knowable only through the concepts, categories and sensory apparatuses of human beings'. Indeed, this must be the case, but I have argued further that objectivity requires 'objects'. The social objects I refer to are socially constructed but, once they come into existence, they are real, because they have causal powers – they make other things happen and create other social objects, which themselves cohere into identifiable mechanisms.

My argument is, then, for a contingent realism, that is, I do not believe that, despite the identifiable existence of objects and mechanisms, there is any natural necessity for the existence of any particular object or mechanism. The very nature of social objects is that their existence is contingent upon the earlier existence (or coexistence) of other social objects. Nevertheless, there is what Robert Nozick termed 'invariance', even in the social world. That invariance is captured in the relative stability of social conditions, rules, norms and values through time and place. That there is such stability is evidenced by our methodological ability to measure and explain change. A methodology that seeks the truth about objects is situated on the context in which that truth is sought. I showed, through the example of ethnicity, how that methodology must arise from our understanding of ethnicity as a dynamic social object.

We can know the social world directly, but we can theorise from our best knowledge of what certain aspects appear to be. We can build models of what we think the world is like and we test these models. In social research they may be theoretical, methodological or statistical. They are not the world itself, but often they are good enough representations of it to permit novel discoveries that change or falsify the original models. It might be said that in devising the most rigorous model we can, we preserve the value of truth in our investigation, but the rigour of the methodology (and method) must be tested through a clash with reality. That is, even in social science, we may propose, but it is reality that disposes!

————Gayle ——

THERE ARE THINGS WE CAN know but much that we can't be sure of. If we don't make knowledge claims, what is the point in doing any of it? However, any claims we do make need to acknowledge the relationship between the process and the product – how what we do affects what we get. In accepting this we acknowledge our epistemic privilege (not that we necessarily know more or know better, but that we have access to more resources, including more accounts and more time to reflect on them). For me, starting from a position that acknowledges and interrogates the significance of our subjectivity gives us a better chance of saying 'something about something' that is meaningful. Writing in the first person (an issue we have discussed in the preparation of this book) is, I believe, both academically and politically appropriate and is an essential part of the production of accountable knowledge. First-person research accounts not only highlight the 'person in the researcher', but also involve the researcher taking responsibility for what is written, for the knowledge being produced.

In Chapter 7 I considered objectivity and subjectivity in practice, objectivity and subjectivity within and beyond the research process and product. Again, I suggest that both the process and the product of research are inevitably political and that this necessitates an acknowledgement of the significance of the subjective in the knowledge. Social research is influenced by internal and external demand for evidence and impact and by calls for 'public intellectualism', all of which involves us in speaking and working with others outside the academy in ways beyond those defined in the traditional research process. This leads us to ask once again what and who is social research for, and brings with it the need to extend our reflexive, critical lens, which includes constant critical scrutiny of the self and of all the others involved in social research.

————Malcolm ——

WHILE I THINK WE ARE in agreement that whatever objectivity is, it has a significant social component, I am also inclined to agree with Gayle that a necessary starting point is an examination of one's own subjectivity. However, this is not a sufficient condition and while we all might agree on this, I have some concerns about what John sees as the social component. Philosophically, I think John wishes to defend a form of social constructionism, whereas I have opted for realism. In characterising John's position thus, I may be wrong, but I think there are three elements with which I am concerned.

First, the idea of a standpoint. What might be termed a 'strong' version of a standpoint was advocated by some feminists in the 1980s (e.g. Donna Haraway and Sandra Harding), whereby the subordinate position of women in an androcentric social setting (such as science) could confer a privileged knowledge upon them. I assume that John is not advancing a 'privileged knowledge' argument? Indeed, I understand John to be arguing for multiple perspectives as standpoints occupied, in which case the question is begged about the relationship of one standpoint to another. If we take a standpoint to be a theory or observation, then how will we choose one over another? Epistemologically, it seems hard to escape some kind of minimum privileging, whereby I say my view is X, yours is Y and I believe X to be correct for Z reasons.

I think John would wish to avoid such an epistemological position and argues for a synthesis of standpoints. This is my second worry, not because I oppose epistemological synthesis *per se*, but in practical terms I don't understand what the mechanism would be for such a synthesis. In matters of politics, I would concede the synthesis might be a consensus, but (to take an example from an area of research that interests me) how would we choose between competing agency and structural theories of homelessness?

This brings me to my third worry, that John is advocating a coherence theory of truth, whereby truth is achieved through social agreement. If this is the case, then truth is in danger of being subsumed to fiat, whether this is consensual, democratic or, worse, imposed by a powerful elite who controls the means of communication. We have seen this in the case of the infamous Lysenko affair in the Soviet Union and we are seeing it now, to some extent, in the almost complete epistemological monopoly of liberal free market capitalism. How, in a synthesis of standpoints, do we preserve the concept of error and that of truth existing outside such a synthesis? To answer my own question about homelessness, the answer lies not in perspective but in analysis. Data on 'homelessness' indicate that it is heterogeneous – different outcomes with different causes. Perspectives that begin from the taxonomy of 'homelessness' as relatively homogeneous will inevitably opt for one or other (or even a synthesis!) of perspectives, but the data indicate that that was the wrong place to begin.

——John

MALCOLM HAS RAISED SOME INTERESTING questions, but I think they need to be addressed to the author of some other book and not to me. I don't recognise what I was arguing in much that Malcolm has said, though I do recognise that someone might possibly read some parts of my chapters in that way. Let me try to deal with the points he raises.

My argument is definitely and decidedly not an argument for social constructionism and against realism. Knowledge *does* involve a constructive process on the part of a socially situated observer, but in order to count as knowledge that construction must be assessed in terms of its empirical adequacy as a means of grasping the *real* world. My argument is that the nature of the real world is unknowable without the presence of a socially situated and embodied human observer who strives to give that world meaning and significance. For this reason, there can be no question of any need to 'choose' between standpoints on anything other than empirical grounds. I do not seek to privilege any standpoint other than that (or those) that help us to understand the real world by virtue of their practical adequacy.

This is the basis of my argument about synthesis. I am not saying that we choose some standpoints and then synthesise them in order to produce a consensus. I don't think I even implied that anywhere in either of my chapters. I certainly did not state or imply that synthesis was the basis of a coherence theory of truth. Neither consensus nor coherence is at all important for my argument. I argued that synthesis is a creative act on the part of the social scientist, who must recognise the potential validity of all authentic viewpoints, including those that may contradict his or her own partial viewpoint. We must identify all those standpoints that have generated knowledge that has a degree of empirical support in relation to a particular scientific problem and must strive to bring these together into a coherent synthesis. We do this not because the synthesis is thereby validated as 'true', but because this synthesis is likely to provide the most fruitful basis for further scientific investigation. The nature of this further scientific investigation is precisely what Malcolm and Gayle explore in their subsequent chapters. I fear that Malcolm's comments ignore the division of labour that was established among the three of us as authors!

──── Gayle ──

I AM CONCERNED ABOUT SOME aspects of Malcolm's argument on situated objectivity and by some of his responses to theorised subjectivity. I accept that in the research that I do my own subjective position is often relevant/related to the topic in hand. Indeed, in many of my projects the question (from respondents) 'what do you think?' is common. I also see and accept the importance of 'sociological variables'. This has become more significant for me recently as I've become involved in more multi/interdisciplinary work where my sociological voice is only one among many. What I'm not sure about, though, is the recognition that in different kinds of research, objectivity and subjectivity play different roles – surely theorised subjectivity is as relevant to one's position on concepts and issues as it is to one's 'relationship' to the project and the data? What I do accept is that objectivity and subjectivity mean different things in different disciplines and that in some academic spaces it would be hard, even impossible, to even have this debate.

Also, social locations are sometimes understood differently by respondents than they are by us as researchers. As I have argued with Pamela Cotterill (Cotterill and Letherby 1994), respondents may position us as 'kindred spirits', 'strangers', 'experts', and so on in ways that do not tally with our understandings of ourselves. Similarly, respondents may see connections between our experiences and theirs, and expect us to agree just because we share an aspect of our identity.

Discussions about research production/research products inevitably involve discussions of power. Power shifts and changes throughout the whole process, does it not? While negotiating research questions with commissioners, arguing with the ethics committee and recruiting through gatekeepers, we as researchers may feel powerless. While in the field, we may be surprised and humbled by the expertise of the 'lay' people we talk too or shocked by the seeming vulnerability of the elites in our study. But, finally, eventually it is us who usually decide what we have to say and we need to acknowledge the significance of our personhood in all of this. I accept that we might need to say different things to different audiences, which is interesting and relevant to any discussion of objectivity and subjectivity. But challenge is possible. One of the commissioners of one of the teenage pregnancy projects I was involved in was concerned primarily for us to discover why young women engaged in such 'risky' behaviour – risky sex, risky choices (e.g. smoking and drinking) during pregnancy, etc. Drawing on the data, we were able to say that the biggest risk to this group was non-access of services that they were entitled to, often because of perceived or actual prejudice. I accept and acknowledge, though, that a different group of researchers, who were less politically motivated, less concerned to consider the holistic experience of teenage pregnancy and young parenthood, could have focused more narrowly on the prescribed task. Whether or not this made our research any less objective is something we might like to discuss further. I do not think it did as we did report faithfully on the data collected. What this example does do, however, is highlight subjectivity, both in terms of the perspective and wishes of the research commissioners and the responses to this by the research team. All the more evidence, then, for a critical consideration of such issues.

——Malcolm

I THINK GAYLE'S CLARIFICATION INDICATES the fundamental compatibility of theorised subjectivity and situated objectivity. Interestingly, it also helps to contextualise what John is saying about perspectives. While in the physical world nature will 'kick back' and falsify a theory, yet even in the natural sciences, theory proposed will make a difference to the empirical findings. In social science this is even more the case and made more complex by the feedback loop between us and our respondents. The orientation of our research, our sampling and the subsequent data analysis and presentation of findings can each be otherwise and sometimes our understanding of a topic or a population can only be achieved in the longer term as a result of research projects which may vary the research question, sample, analysis or the selection of findings.

Gayle mentions 'sociological variables' as important and I think these are what save us from relativism. Though there may be definitional and measurement issues around such things as gender, ethnicity, class, etc., these are grounded in real relationships experienced possibly in different ways by individuals, but experienced enough in common to provide a level of what I have called invariance. Added to these, we have those characteristics that are related to the physical world (health, biological sex, housing conditions) and provide levels in invariance. Empirically, and especially in survey research, we can separate out characteristics such as these from attitudes and beliefs. I'm not saying the latter have no invariance, but they are much more volatile and subject to social and psychological modification.

————Gayle ————————————————————————————————

I ACCEPT THAT IT MAY be easier to separate out/account for some sociological variables when using some methods rather than others. I acknowledge that the use of some methods may leave us feeling overwhelmed by the experiences of our respondents which likely make it harder for us to even separate ourselves from the data. This is why we always need to think carefully about the methods we chose, and why mixed methods, methodological pluralism, reflexive social science and accountable knowledge are all phrases that should be within any social researcher's lexicon.

————John ————————————————————————————————

THAT CLARIFIES A LOT OF the issues about the situated character of knowledge and its relation to values. I think there may still be some issues in relation to Malcolm's argument about social objects in Chapter 6. I wonder how Malcolm would respond to critics, especially perhaps those who come from a social constructionist or postmodernist position, who might claim that the very idea of social objects as 'objects' implies a rather crude empiricism in which the adequacy of knowledge is to be assessed in terms of a naïve idea of 'correspondence' with the real world. That is, doesn't his realism amount simply to a failure to recognise the dependence of knowledge on a human subject? Doesn't he resort to an inadequate picture theory of truth, according to which the mind is simply a pin-hole camera that records a complete and accurate image of the world as it really is, independent of all human intervention?

In order to convince his critics, Malcolm needs to clearly show the difference between his realism and a brute empiricism. If he does not do this, he may be held to emulate Dr Johnson, who believed that he could reject Bishop Berkeley's views that our knowledge of the world reflect our ideas about it simply by kicking a stone and exclaiming 'I refute it thus!'

————Malcolm ————————————————————————————————

ONE OF THE INTERESTING THINGS about this project is the realisation that however hard we try to clarify our arguments, there is the possibility of an alternative reading. This was the case in my reading of John's position on standpoints and synthesis (which he clarified with alacrity). Similarly, here John plays the role of the sceptic and offers an alternative interpretation of my argument.

The pin-hole camera analogy is actually quite a good one. We are constrained to see the world in such a way, metaphorically through the pin-hole, but our past experiences lead us to believe that there is much more than what the eye can capture. So it is with social objects. They are nested in other social objects and they are dynamic. We do not know them directly, but we can know their outcomes because they have the property of making things happen. The office of president or prime minister might be thought of as a social object, but it is nested in others and given its causal character only because of the dispositions of the objects within which it is nested. We might even describe this as a mechanism, albeit a complex one. Nestings, or mechanisms, may have some identifiable properties, but much is unobservable and those mechanisms we do identify are likely to be no more than good enough explanatory models.

An empiricist does not necessarily rule out the existence of unobservables, but gives them no credence in any account of the world. Realists do. Nevertheless, I would not want to embrace a position where the noumenal world of unobservables is reified ever beyond our empirical reach. Possibly through the elimination of error, and indeed some correspondence between our theories and that which we can observe, we can come to know that which was once noumenal. An analogy I once heard is that the process is much like opening one Russian doll to reveal another, but unlike actual Russian dolls, the process of revealing is infinite and, moreover, we know that the hitherto uncovered dolls have the property of transformation that we cannot see. Analogies, like models, are never wholly accurate, but this seems like a good enough way of thinking about social objects.

I can but remind the sceptical reader of the properties of social objects as I understand them: they are real, but they are contingent upon the existence or character of other social objects. They are socially constructed, but real because they cause other things to happen. They are dynamic, yet they may exist over long periods and even widely across places (e.g. democracy, incest taboos, gloves, a wink). Finally, while we socially construct social objects, they may not be reducible to but are contiguous with physical objects and thought objects.

——John ————————————————————————————

I THINK THAT GAYLE VERY usefully relates the argument of the book to current concerns over the 'impact' of social research, especially in so far as it figures in national and international assessments of research. I wonder, however, if in responding to immediate concerns about impact, the social science community may be distorting the aims and goals of scientific investigation. I do not want to argue for returning to the idea that all knowledge is important for its own sake, but are we in danger of saying that no knowledge can be important for its own sake? That is, in making the case for the need to engage with our audiences and publics outside the academic system, might we not be in danger of losing our impartiality – our 'objectivity' – in deciding what is important and interesting to study? How do we ensure that we remain equal participants in a dialogue with our public rather than becoming a mere servant of the powerful?

━━━Malcolm ━━━━━━━━━━━━━━━━━━━━━━━━━━━━━━━━━━━

DESPITE OUR BEST ATTEMPTS TO achieve objectivity through an examination of our subjectivity, to achieve a critical synthesis of evidence through a commitment to truth-seeking, it remains that our purposes are situated not just in our research, but in the concerns and priorities of a wider society. Alvin Gouldner's critique of US sociology in the 1960s, though if not entirely justified, is a valid 'meta sociological' point. I can see no better way than a situated objectivity, but I do sometimes worry that despite our best efforts we can be co-opted into societal projects that history will come to judge as serving a particular ideology. But to dwell too long on this worry leads us into deeper issues of the relationship of social science to moral choice.

━━━Gayle ━━━━━━━━━━━━━━━━━━━━━━━━━━━━━━━━━━━━━

AS THE DRIVE FOR EVIDENCE and impact continues, we need to continue to keep a critical eye on its development. There is a huge danger that only particular types of projects, with a particular type of focus, using particular types of method will be funded. This is all the more likely as many of the major funding councils are moving towards a position of 'demand management' where they will likely limit the number of applications received. Additionally, as league tables and Research Excellence Framework exercises (or the equivalent) move us further towards the measurement of both input (e.g. money) and a particular type of output (e.g. impact), this could very definitely limit the type or research that is valued. It is ironic, I think, that after decades of researchers arguing for research 'with' and 'for' people rather than research 'on' and 'about' them, we still have to make this point in an era that supports work that 'makes a difference'. What I mean is that we need to keep a watch over who it makes a difference to.

A Final word from the three of us

We hope that our discussion throughout this book has highlighted the areas of agreement and disagreement among us without undermining our shared position on the meanings and necessity of both objectivity and subjectivity in social research. It is fair to say that when we started this project we were each in a different place from where we are now. In our face-to-face meetings, email correspondence and in the three presentations we have given together over the last couple of years, we have listened to each other's views and maintained some of our differences while moving closer on other issues and concerns. Although we did write our first drafts of early chapters independently of each other, inevitably as the project progressed our joint discussions began to influence our writing, if only subtly. Writing the book in the way we have has revealed differences in presentation and style as well as epistemological differences. Again, some negotiation has taken place. Fundamentally, of course, or at least it seems to us, there are more similarities between us than differences. Perhaps it would have been much harder to write this book if we had been further apart? Following a recent presentation of our ideas, we were criticised for 'sticking to traditional definitions of objectivity and subjectivity' rather than challenging objectivity and subjectivity as concepts. As a threesome, we found this criticism both frustrating and confusing. As three practising social researchers, we are required to engage with these concepts continually – with ethics committees, with commissioners and funders, with journal reviewers and so on. Our aim in this book was to critically explore the meanings and values of these concepts in the work that we, and others like us, do. We hope that you, the reader, have found the debate as interesting as we have. We hope, too, that the debate will continue and that you will join in it with us.

References

Where two dates are shown, the first date is that of original publication (as cited in the text) and the second date is the date of the translation, edition, or reprint actually used.

Abbott, A. (2001) *Chaos of Disciplines*. Chicago, IL: Chicago University Press.

Abbott, P., Wallace, C. and Tyler, M. (2005) *An Introduction to Sociology: Feminist Perspectives* (3rd edition). London: Routledge.

Ahmad, W. (1999) 'Ethnic statistics: better than nothing or worse than nothing?' in Dorling, D. and Simpson, S. (eds), *Statistics and Society: The Arithmetic of Politics*. London: Arnold, pp.124–31.

Alcoff, L. and Potter, E. (eds) (1993) *Feminist Epistemologies*. London: Routledge.

Antonio, R.J. (1995) 'Nietzsche's antisociology: subjectified culture and the end of history', *American Journal of Sociology*, 101 (1): 1–43.

Appleyard, B. (1992) *Understanding the Present: Science and the Soul of Modern Man*. London: Pan.

Atkinson, P., Delamont, S. and Housley, W. (2008) *Contours of Culture: Complex Ethnography and the Ethnography of Complexity*. Plymouth: AltaMira Press.

Babbie, E. (1995) *The Practice of Social Research* (7th edition). Belmont, CA: Wadsworth.

Back, L. (2007) *The Art of Listening*. Oxford and New York: Berg Publishers.

Bate, J. (2011) *The Public Value of the Humanities*. London: Bloomsbury Academic.

Baudrillard, J. (1977/1988) *Forget Foucault*. Los Angeles: Semiotext(e).

Baudrillard, J. (1983) *Simulations*. New York: Semiotext(e).

Bauman, Z. (1987) *Legislators and Interpreters*. Cambridge: Polity Press.

Beck, U. (1992) *Risk Society: Towards a New Modernity*. London: Sage.

Beck, U. (1995) *Ecological Politics in an Age of Risk*. Cambridge: Cambridge University Press.

Becker, H. (1963) *Outsiders*. Glencoe, IL: The Free Press.

Becker, H. (1967) 'Whose side are we on?', *Social Problems*, 14 (3): 239–47. Also reprinted in H.S. Becker (ed.) (1970) *Sociological Work*. Chicago, IL: Aldine.

bell hooks (1981) *Ain't I a Woman? Black Women and Feminism*. Boston, MA: South End Press.

bell hooks (1986) 'Sisterhood: political solidarity between women', *Feminist Review*, 23: 125–38.

Berkeley, G. (1709/1910) *A New Theory of Vision*. London: J.M. Dent.

Berry, B. (1976) 'The counterurbanisation process: urban America since 1970', in B. Berry (ed.), *Urbanisation and Counterurbanisation*. New York: Arnold.

Bhabha, H. (1994) *The Location of Culture*. London: Routledge.

Bhaskar, R. (1975) *The Realist Theory of Science*. Leeds: Leeds Books.

Bhaskar, R. (1998) *The Possibility of Naturalism* (3rd edition). London: Routledge.

Bhaskar, R. (2008) *A Realist Theory of Science* (3rd edition). Hemel Hempstead: Harvester.

Blalock, H. (1961) *Causal Inference in Nonexperimental Research*. Chapel Hill, NC: University of North Carolina Press.

Bloor, M. (1999) 'Addressing social problems through qualitative research', in D. Silverman (ed.), London: Sage.

Blunkett, D. (2000) 'Influence or irrelevance: can social science improve government?' Secretary of State's ESRC Lecture Speech, 2 February. London: Department of Education and Employment.

Bohannan, P. (1961/1966) *African Outline*. Harmondsworth: Penguin.

Booth, T. and Booth, W. (1996) 'Sound of Silence: narrative research with inarticulate subjects', *Disability and Society*, 11 (1): 55–69.

Boudon, R. (1998) 'Social mechanisms without black boxes', in P. Hedstrom and R. Swedborg (eds), *Social Mechanisms: An Analytical Approach to Social Theory*. Cambridge: Cambridge University Press, pp. 172–203.

Bourdieu, P. (1972/1977) *Outline of a Theory of Practice*. Cambridge: Cambridge University Press.

Bourdieu, P. (1980/1990) *The Logic of Practice*. Cambridge: Polity Press.

Bourdieu, P. (1990) *In Other Words: Essays Towards a Reflexive Sociology* (translated by M. Adamson). Cambridge: Polity.

Bourdieu, P. (1992) *The Logic of Practice*. Cambridge: Polity.

Bourdieu, P. and Wacquant, L.J. (1992) *An Invitation to Reflexive Sociology*. Cambridge: Polity Press.

Brady, G., Bywaters, P., Kynspel, M., Letherby, G. and Steventon, G. (2007) 'Outcomes', in M. Burawoy (2005) 'For Public Sociology', *American Sociological Review*, 70: 4–28.

Braidotti, R. (1991) *Patterns of Dissonance*. Cambridge: Polity Press.

Brown, T. (2001) *Action Research and Postmodernism*. London: McGraw Hill.

Bruun, H.H. (1972/2007) *Science, Values and Politics in Max Weber's Methodology*. Aldershot: Ashgate.

Bryne-Armstrong, H., Higgs, J., and Horsfall, D. (2001) *Critical Moments in Qualitative Research*. London: Elsevier Health Sciences.

Bunge, M. (2004) 'How does it work?', *Philosophy of the Social Sciences*, 34 (2): 182–210.

Burton, J., Nandi, A. and Platt, L. (2010) 'Measuring ethnicity: challenges and opportunities for survey research', *Ethnic and Racial Studies*, pp. 1332–49.

Butler, J. (1990) *Gender Trouble: Feminism and the Subversion of Identity*. London: Routledge.

Butler, K. (2009) 'Blurring public and private sociology: challenging an artificial division', *Sociological Research Online*, 14 (4). [http://www.socresonline.org.uk/14/4/2.html]

Byrne, D. (2002) *Interpreting Quantitative Data*. London: Sage.

Bywaters, P. and Letherby, G. (2007) 'Extending Social Research', in G. Letherby and P. Bywaters (eds), *Extending Social Research: Application, Implementation, Presentation*. Buckingham: Open University.

Carolyn, E. and Bochner, A.P. (2000) 'Autoethnography, personal narrative, reflexivity: researcher as subject', in N.K. Denzin and Y.S. Lincoln (eds), *Handbook of Qualitative Research* (3rd edition). Thousand Oaks: Sage.

Carter, B. (2000) *Realism and Racism*. London: Routledge.

Chalmers, A. (1990) *Science and Its Fabrication*. Buckingham: Open University Press.

Chatterjee, P. (1986) *Nationalist Thought and the Colonial World*. London: ZED Books.

Chatterjee, P. (1993) *The Nation and Its Fragments*. Princeton, NJ: Princeton University Press.

Chodorow, N. (1978) *The Reproduction of Mothering: Psychoanalysis and the Sociology of Gender*. Berkeley, CA: University of California Press.

Cicourel, A.V. (1964) *Method and Measurement in Sociology*. New York: The Free Press.

Clark, M. (1990) *Nietzsche on Truth and Philosophy*. Cambridge: Cambridge University Press.

Coffey, A. (1999) *The Ethnographic Self*. London: Sage.

Collins, P. (1998) 'Negotiating selves: reflections on "unstructured" interviewing', *Sociological Research Online*, 3 (3). [www.socresonline.org.uk/3/3/2].

Contemporary Social Science Special Issue (2011): 'Challenge, Change or Crisis in Global Higher Education', 6 (2) June.

Cook, J.A. and Fonow, M.M. (1980) 'Knowledge and women's interests: issues of epistemology and methodology in feminist sociological research', in J. McCarl Nielsen (ed.), *Feminist Research Methods: Exemplary Readings in the Social Sciences*. Boulder, CO: Westview Press.

Coomber, R. and Letherby, G. (2011) 'Reaching "sensitive topics" and "vulnerable populations" and accessing the "hidden" and "hard-to-reach": challenging some assumptions', Methods @ Plymouth 2011, University of Plymouth (May).

Coombes, M., Dalla Longa, R. and Raybould, S. (1989) Counterurbanisation in Britain and Italy: a comparative critique of the concept, causation and evidence', *Progress in Planning*, 32: 1–70.

Corrigan, O., Letherby, G. and Brennan, N. (under review) 'Experiences of becoming a doctor: doing emotion labour', *Sociology of Health and Illness*.

Cotterill, P. (1992) 'Interviewing women: issues of friendship, vulnerability and power', *Women's Studies International Forum*, 15 (5/6): 593–606.

Cotterill, P. and Letherby, G. (1994) 'The person in the researcher', in R. Burgess (ed.) *Studies in Qualitative Methodology Vol VI*. London: Jai Press.

Cotterill, P. and Letherby, G. (1994) 'Weaving stories: personal auto/biographies in feminist research', *Sociology*, 27 (1): 67–80.

Couvalis, G. (1997) *The Philosophy of Science: Science and Objectivity*. London: Sage.

Davis, J., Watson, N. and Cunningham-Burley, S. (2000) 'Learning the lives of disabled children', in P. Christensen and A. James (eds), *Research with Children: Perspectives and Practices*. London: Routledge Falmer, pp. 201–24.

Delamont, S. (2007) 'Arguments against auto-ethnography', *Qualitative Research*, 4. [www.cardiff.ac.uk/socsi/qualiti/QualitativeResearcher/QR_Issue4_Feb07.pdf].

Delamont, S. (2009) 'The only honest thing: autoethnography, reflexivity and small crises in fieldwork', *Ethnography and Education*, 4 (1): 51–63.

Denzin, N.K. (1994) 'The art and politics of interpretation', in N.K. Denzin and Y.S. Lincoln (eds), *Handbook of Qualitative Research*. London: Sage.

Denzin, N.K. (2003) 'Performing [auto] ethnography politically', *The Review of Education, Pedagogy, and Cultural Studies*, 25: 257–78.

Denzin, N.K. and Lincoln, Y.S. (eds) (1994) *Handbook of Qualitative Research*. London: Sage.

Dilthey, W. (1883/1989) *Introduction to the Human Sciences*. Princeton, NJ: Princeton University Press.

Di Stephano, C. (1990) 'Dilemmas of difference: feminism, modernity and postmodernism', in L. Nicholson (ed.), *Feminism/Postmodernism*. London: Routledge, pp. 63–82.

Douglas, M. (1992) *Risk and Blame: Essays in Cultural Theory*. London: Routledge.

Drew, D., Fosam, B. and Gilborn, D. (1995) 'Race, IQ and the underclass: don't believe the hype', *Radical Statistics*, 60: 2–21.

Du Bois, W.E.B. (1903/1986) 'The souls of black folk', in *W.E.B. Du Bois: Writings*. New York: Viking Press.

Durkheim, E. (1895/1982) *The Rules of the Sociological Method*. London: Macmillan.

Durkheim, E. (1897/1952) *Suicide: A Study in Sociology*. London: Routledge and Kegan Paul.

Edwards, D., Ashmore, M. and Potter, J. (1995) 'Death and furniture: the rhetoric, politics and theology of bottom-line arguments against relativism', *History of the Human Sciences*, 8: 25–49.

Eichler, M. (1988) *Non-Sexist Research Methods*. London: Allen and Unwin.

Elias, N. (1983) *Problems of Involvement and Detachment*. Oxford: Basil Blackwell.

Elster, J. (1998) 'A plea for mechanisms', in P. Hedstom and R. Swedborg (eds), *Social Mechanisms: An Analytical Approach to Social Theory*. Cambridge: Cambridge University Press, pp. 45–73.

Engels, F. (1886/1964) *Dialectics of Nature*. Moscow: Progress Publishers.

Epstein, D. (1995) 'In our (new) right minds: the hidden curriculum in the academy', in L. Morley and V. Walsh (eds), *Feminist Academics: Creative Agents for Change*. Taylor and Francis: London.

Erben, M. (1998) 'Biography and research method', in M. Erben (ed.), *Biography and Education: A Reader*. London: Falmer, pp. 1–17.

Etzioni, A. (1993) *The Spirit of Community: Rights, Responsibilities and the Communitarian Agenda*. New York: Crown.

Evans, M. (1997) *Introducing Contemporary Feminist Thought*. Cambridge: Polity Press.

Exley, C. and Letherby, G. (2001) 'Managing a disrupted lifecourse: issues of identity and emotion work', *Health*, 5 (1): 112–32.

Fanon, F. (1963) *The Damned* [*The Wretched of the Earth*]. Paris: Présence Africaine.

Farrar, M. (2010) 'Cracking the ivory tower: proposing an interpretive public sociology', in J. Burnett, S. Jefffers and G. Thomas (eds), *New Social Connections Sociology's Subjects and Objects*. London: Palgrave Macmillan.

Feuerbach, L. (1841/1957) *The Essence of Christianity*. New York: Harper & Row.

Feyerabend, P. (1975) *Against Method*. New York: Verso.

Fine, M. (1994) 'Distance and other stances: negotiations of power inside feminist research', in A. Gitlin (ed.), *Power and Method: Political Activism and Educational Research*. London: Routledge, pp. 13–35.

Flax, J. (1987) 'Postmodernism and gender relation in feminist theory', *Signs: Journal of Women in Culture and Society*, 12: 334–51.

Foucault, M. (1966/1973) *The Order of Things*. New York: Vintage Books.

Foucault, M. (1971/1972) *The Archaeology of Knowledge*. New York: Pantheon.

Foucault, M. (1982/1994) 'The subject and power', in J. Scott (ed.), *Power: Critical Concepts* (Vol. 1). London: Routledge.

Friedan, B. (1962) *The Feminine Mystique*. New York: Dell.

Friedrichs, R.W. (1970) *A Sociology of Sociology*. New York: The Free Press.

Fry, E.F. (1966) *Cubism*. London: Thames & Hudson.

Fuller, S. (1997) *Science*. Buckingham: Open University Press.

Fuller, S. (2000) *The Governance of Science*. Buckingham: Open University Press.

Gergen, K. (2001) *Social Construction in Context*. London: Sage.

Giddens, A. (1984) *New Rules of Sociological Method*. London: Macmillan.

Giddens, A. (1990) *The Consequences of Modernity*. Cambridge: Polity.

Giddens, A. (1993) *New Rules of Sociological Method* (2nd edition). Cambridge: Polity Press.

Giddens, A. (1998) *The Third Way: The Renewal of Social Democracy*. Cambridge: Polity Press.

Giddens, A. (2000) *The Third Way and Its Critics*. Cambridge: Polity Press.

Gigerenzer, G. (2002) *Reckoning with Risk: Learning to Live with Uncertainty*. Harmondsworth: Penguin.

Gilman, C.P. (1911/2001) *The Man-Made World, or Our Androcentric Culture*. New York: Humanity Books.

Glucksmann, M. (1994) 'The work of knowledge and the knowledge of women's work', in M. Maynard and J. Purvis (eds), *Researching Women's Lives from a Feminist Perspective*. London: Taylor and Francis.

Goffman, E. (1959) *The Presentation of Self in Everyday Life*. New York: Anchor Books.

Gouldner, A. (1962/1973) 'Anti-minotaur: the myth of a value free sociology', in A. Gouldner (ed.), *For Sociology: Renewal and Critique in Sociology Today*. Harmondsworth: Penguin.

Gouldner, A. (1968) 'The sociologist as partisan: sociology and the welfare state', *American Sociologist*, 3 (2): 103–16.

Gouldner, A. (1970) *The Coming Crisis of Western Sociology*. London: Heinemann.

Gramsci, A. (1929–35/1971) *The Prison Notebooks* [*Selections From*]. London: Lawrence and Wishart.

Gray, B. (2008) 'Putting emotion and reflexivity to work in researching migration', *Sociology*, 42 (5): 935–52.

Griffin, C. (1989) "I'm not a women's libber but ...": feminism, consciousness and identity', in S. Shevington and D. Baker (eds), *The Social Identity of Women*. London: Sage

Griffin, S. (1983) 'Introduction', in J. Caldecott and K. Leland (eds), *Reclaim the Earth*. London: The Women's Press.

Guha, R. (1982/2000) 'On some aspects of the historiography of colonial India', in V. Chaturvedi (ed.), *Mapping Subaltern Studies and the Postcolonial*. London: Verso.

Guha, R. (1983) *Elementary Aspects of Peasant Insurgency in Colonial India*. Delhi: Oxford University Press.

Guha, R. and Spivak, G.C. (eds) (1988) *Selected Subaltern Studies*. Delhi: Oxford University Press.

Gusterson, H. (2009) 'Project Minerva and the militarization of anthropology', *Radical Teacher*, 86 (Winter): 4–16.

Habermas, J. (1970) 'Towards a theory of communicative competence', in H.P. Dreitzel (ed.), *Recent Sociology, Number 2*. New York: Macmillan.

Habermas, J. (1981/1984) *The Theory of Communicative Action. Vol. 1: Reason and the Rationalisation of Society*. London: Heinemann.

Hacking, I. (1983a) *Representing and Intervening: Introductory Topics in the Philosophy of Natural Science*. Cambridge: Cambridge University Press.

Hacking, I. (1983b/2002) 'Making up people', in I. Hacking, *Historical Ontology*. Cambridge, MA: Harvard University Press.

Hall, S. (1992) 'The question of cultural identity', in S. Hall, D. Held and T. McGrew (eds), *Modernity and Its Futures*. Cambridge: Polity Press.

Hallowell, N., Lawton, J. and Gregory, S. (eds), (2005) *Reflections on Research: The Realities of Doing Research in the Social Sciences*. Buckingham: Open University.

Hammersley, M. (2000) *Taking Sides in Social Research: Essays in Partisanship and Bias*. London: Routledge.

Hammersley, M. (2011) 'Objectivity: a reconceptualisation', in M. Williams and W.P. Vogt (eds), *The Sage Handbook of Innovation in Social Research Methods*. London: Sage, pp. 25–43.

Hammersley, M. and Gomm, R. (1997) 'Bias in social research', *Sociological Research Online*, 2 (1). [www.socresonling.org.uk/socresonline/2/4/7.html]

Haraway, D. (1991) *Simians, Cyborgs, and Women*. London: Free Association Books.

Harding, S. (1986) *The Science Question in Feminism*. Milton Keynes: Open University Press.

Harding, S. (1993) 'Rethinking standpoint epistemology: what is "strong objectivity"?', in L. Alcoff and E. Porter (eds), *Feminist Epistemologies*. New York: Routledge, pp. 49–82.

Harré, R. (1972) *Philosophies of Science*. Oxford: Oxford University Press.

Harré, R. and Madden, E. (1975) *Causal Powers*. Oxford: Blackwell.

Hartsock, N. (1983a) *Money, Sex and Power: Toward a Feminist Historical Materialism*. Boston, MA: Northeastern University Press.

Hartsock, N. (1983b) 'The feminist standpoint: developing the ground for a specifically feminist historical materialism', in S. Harding and M. Hintikka (eds), *Discovering Reality: Feminist Perspectives on Epistemlogy, Metaphysics and Philosophy of Science*. Dordrecht: Reidel.

Hemmingson, M. (2009) *Auto/Ethnographies: Sex and Death and Symbolic Internationalism in the Eight Moment of Qualitative Inquiry*. San Bernadino, CA The Borgo Press.

Henderson, L.D. (1983) *The Fourth Dimension and Non-Euclidean Geometry in Modern Art*. Princeton, NJ: Princeton University Press.

Henderson, L.J. (1932) 'An approximate definition of fact', in B. Barber (ed.), *L.J. Henderson on the Social System*. Chicago, IL: University of Chicago Press, pp. 159–80.

Herman, D. (1994) *Rights of Passage*. Toronto: University of Toronto Press.

Herrnstein, R. and Murray, C. (1994) *The Bell Curve: Intelligence and Class Structure in American Life*. New York: The Free Press.

Hesse-Biber, S.N. (ed.) (2007a) *Handbook of Feminist Research: Theory and Praxis.* Thousand Oaks, CA: Sage.

Hesse-Biber, S.N. (2007b) 'Feminist research: exploring the interconnections of epistemology, methodology and method', in S. Hesse-Biber (ed.), *Handbook of Feminist Research: Theory and Praxis.* Thousand Oaks, CA: Sage.

Hesse-Biber, S.N., Gilmartin, C. and Lydenberg, R. (eds) (1999) *Feminist Approaches to Theory and Methodology: An Interdisciplinary Reader.* New York: Oxford University Press.

Hesse-Biber, S.N., Leavy, P. and Yaiser, M.L. (2004) 'Feminist approaches to research as a *process*: reconceptualizing epistemology, methodology, and method', in S.N. Hesse-Biber and M.L. Yaiser (eds), *Feminist Perspectives on Social Research.* New York: Oxford University Press.

Hessels, L.K. and van Lente, H. (2010) 'The mixed blessing of Mode 2 knowledge production Science', *Technology and Innovation Studies*, 6 (1): 65–59.

Hill-Collins, P. (1989) 'Black feminist thought', *Signs: Journal of Women in Culture and Society*, 14 (4): 745–73.

Hill-Collins, P. (1990) *Black Feminist Thought: Knowledge, Consciousness and the Politics of Empowerment.* London: Harper Collins.

Hochschild, A.R. (1983/2003) *The Managed Heart: Commercialization of Human Feeling* (20th anniversary edition). Berkeley, CA: University of California Press.

Hochschild, A.R. (ed.) (2008) *The Sociology of Emotion as a Way of Seeing.* London: Routledge.

Hollands, R. and Stanley, L. (2009) 'Rethinking "Current Crisis" Arguments: Gouldner and the legacy of critical sociology', *Sociological Research Online*, 14 (1). [http://www.socresonline.org.uk/14/1/1.html]

Holmwood, J. (2007) 'Sociology as public discourse and professional practice: a critique of Michael Burawoy' *Sociological Theory,* 25 (1): 46–66.

Homfray, M. (2008) 'Standpoint, objectivity, and social construction: reflections from the study of gay and lesbian communities', *Sociological Research Online,* 13 (1): 7. [www.socresonline.org.uk/13/1/7]

Hood, S., Mayall, B. and Oliver, S. (1999) *Critical Issues in Social Research: Power and Prejudice.* Buckingham: Open University.

Horowitz, I.L. (ed.) (1967) *The Rise and Fall of Project Camelot: Studies in the Relationship between Social Science and Practical Politics.* Cambridge, MA: MIT Press.

Housley, W. and Smith, R.J. (2010) 'Innovation and reduction in contemporary qualitative methods: the case of conceptual coupling, activity-type pairs and auto-ethnography', *Sociological Research Online*, 15 (4): 9. [www.socresonline.org.uk/15/4/9]

Huberman, M. (1987) 'Steps towards an integrated model of research utilization', *Knowledge*, June: 586–611.

Hume, D. (1772/1927) *Enquiry Concerning Human Understanding.* Oxford: Oxford University Press.

Iles, T. (1992) *All Sides of the Subject: Women and Biography.* New York: Teachers' Press.

Jackson, S. (1992) 'The amazing deconstructing woman', *Trouble and Strife*, 25: 25–31.

Jary, D. and Jones, R. (eds) (2006) *Widening Participation in Higher Education – Issues, Research and Resources for the Social Sciences and Beyond.* Birmingham: C-SAP.

James, C.L.R. (1938/1963) *The Black Jacobins: Toussaint L'Ouverture and the San Domingo Revolution.* New York: Vintage.

James, N. (1989) 'Emotional labour: skill and work in the social regulation of feelings', *Sociological Reviews*, 37: 15–42.

James, W. (1902/1947) *Varieties of Religious Experience.* London: Longmans Green.

Jenkins, R. (2002) *Foundations of Sociology: Towards a Better Understanding of the Human World.* London: Macmillan Palgrave.

Jewkes, Y. and Letherby, G. (2001) 'Insider and outsiders: complex issues of identification, difference and distance in social research', *Auto/Biography*, IX: 1 and 2.

Jones, T. (1998) 'Interpretive social science and the "native's" point of view', *Philosophy of the Social Sciences*, 28: 132–68.

Kamin, L. (1981) *Intelligence: The Battle of the Mind.* London: Pan Books.

Kant, I. (1781/1934) *Critique of Pure Reason.* London: J.M. Dent. (A translation of the 2nd edition of 1787.)

Kant, I. (1788/1997) *Critique of Practical Reason.* Cambridge: Cambridge University Press.

Katz-Rothman, B. (1996) 'Bearing witness: representing women's experiences of prenatal diagnosis', in S. Wilkinson and C. Kitzinger (eds), *Representing the Other: A Feminism and Psychology Reader.* London: Sage.

Katz-Rothman, B. (2007) 'Writing ourselves in sociology', *Methodological Innovations Online*, 2 (1). [http://erdt.plymouth.ac.uk/mionline/public_html/viewarticle.php?id=40&layout=html]

Keat, R. and Urry, J. (1975) *Social Theory as Science.* London: Routledge and Kegan Paul.

Kelly, L., Burton, S. and Regan, L. (1994) 'Researching women's lives or studying women's oppression? Reflections on what constitutes feminist research', in M. Maynard and J. Purvis (eds), *Researching Women's Lives From a Feminist Perspective.* London: Taylor and Francis, pp. 27–48.

Kettler, D. and Meja, V. (1995) *Karl Mannheim and the Crisis of Liberalism.* New Brunswick, NJ: Transaction Books.

Kincaid, H. (1996) *Philosophical Foundations of the Social Sciences: Analyzing Controversies in Social Research.* Cambridge: Cambridge University Press.

Kirkman, M. and Letherby, G. (2008) 'Some 'Grimm' reflections on mothers and daughters: a fairy tale for our times', *Journal for the Association for Research on Motherhood*, 10 (2): 196–201.

Koch, T. and Kralik, D. (2001) 'Chronic illness: reflections on a community-based action research programme', *Journal of Advanced Nursing*, 36 (1): 23–31.

Koch, T., Kralik, D. and Sonnack, D. (1999) 'Women living with type II diabetes: the intrusion of illness', *Journal of Clinical Nursing*, 8 (6): 712–22.

Kralik, D., Koch, T. and Brady, B.M. (2000) 'Pen pals: correspondence as a method for data generation in qualitative research', *Journal of Advanced Nursing*, 31 (4): 909–17.

Kuhn, T.S. (1962) *The Structure of Scientific Revolutions* (2nd edition, 1970). Chicago, IL: University of Chicago Press.

Kuhn, T.S. (1970) 'Postscript – 1969', in T.S. Kuhn (ed.), *The Structure of Scientific Revolutions* (2nd edition). Chicago, IL: University of Chicago Press.

Lakatos, I. (1970) 'Falsification and the methodology of scientific research programmes', in I. Lakatos and A. Musgrave (eds), *Criticism and the Growth of Knowledge*. Cambridge: Cambridge University Press.

Lee-Treweek, G. and Linkogle, S. (eds) (2000) *Danger in the Field: Risk and Ethics in Social Research*. London: Routledge.

Lenin, V.I. (1909/1976) *Materialism and Empirio-Criticism*. Peking: Foreign Languages Publishing House.

Lennon, K. and Whitford, M. (eds) (1994) *Knowing the Difference: Feminist Perspectives in Epistemology*. London: Routledge.

Letherby, G. (1993) 'The meanings of miscarriage', *Women's Studies International Forum*, 16 (2): 165–80.

Letherby, G. (1994) 'Mother or not, mother or what?: problems of definition and identity', *Women's Studies International Forum*, 17 (5): 525– 32.

Letherby, G. (1999) 'Other than mother and mothers as others: the experience of motherhood and non-motherhood in relation to "infertility" and "involuntary childlessness"', *Women's Studies International Forum*, 22 (3): 359–72.

Letherby, G. (2000) 'Dangerous Liaisons: auto/biography in research and research writing', in G. Lee-Treweek and S. Linkogle (eds), *Danger, Gender and Data in Qualitative Inquiry*. London: Routledge.

Letherby, G. (2002a) 'Challenging dominant discourses: identity and change and the experience of "infertility" and "involuntary childlessness"', *Journal of Gender Studies*, 11 (3): 227–88.

Letherby, G. (2002b) 'Claims and disclaimers: knowledge, reflexivity and representation in feminist research', *Sociological Research Online*, 6 (4). [www.socres online.org.uk/6/4]

Letherby, G. (2003a) 'I didn't think much of this bedside manner but he was very skilled at his job: medical encounters in relation to "infertility"', in

S. Earle and G. Letherby (eds), *Gender Identity and Reproduction: Social Perspectives*. London: Palgrave.

Letherby, G. (2003b) 'Reflections on where we are and where we want to be: response to "Looking back and looking forward: some recent feminist sociology reviewed"', *Sociological Research Online*, 8 (4). [www.socresonline.org.uk/8/4]

Letherby, G. (2003c) *Feminist Research in Theory and Practice*. Buckingham: Open University Press.

Letherby, G. (2004) 'Quoting and counting: an autobiographical response to Oakley', *Sociology*, 38 (1): 175–89.

Letherby, G. (2011a) 'Auto/biographical reflections on personal and other legacies: much more than money', in A. Sparkes (ed.), *Auto/Biography Yearbook*. Oxford: Clio Press.

Letherby, G. (2011b) 'Feminist methodology', in M. Williams and P. Vogt (eds), *The Sage Handbook of Methodological Innovation*. London: Sage, pp. 62–79.

Letherby, G., Brady, G. and Brown, G. (2007) 'Working with the Community: research and action', in C. J. Clay, M. Madden and L. Potts (eds), *Towards Understanding Community: People and Places*. Houndsmills: Palgrave, pp. 123–36.

Letherby, G. and Bywaters, P. (eds) (2007a) *Extending Social Research: Application, Implementation, Presentation*. Buckingham: Open University.

Letherby, G. and Bywaters, P. (2007b) 'Extending social research: why?', in G. Letherby and P. Bywaters (eds), *Extending Social Research: Application, Implementation, Presentation*. Buckingham: Open University, pp. 19–36.

Letherby, G. and Zdrodowski, D. (1995) 'Dear Researcher: the use of correspondence as a method within feminist qualitative research', *Gender and Society*, 9 (5): 576–93.

Lévy-Bruhl, L. (1921/1966) *Primitive Mentality*. Boston, MA: Beacon Press.

Lewis, V. and Kellett, M. (2004) 'Disability', in S. Fraser, V. Lewis, S, Ding, M. Kellett and C. Robinson (eds), *Doing Research with Children and Young People*. London: Sage.

Lichtheim, G. (1965/1967) 'The concept of idelogy', in G. Lichtheim (ed.), *The Concept of Ideology*. New York: Vintage.

Lincoln, Y.S. and Denzin, N.K. (2000) 'The seventh moment: out of the past', in N.K. Denzin and Y.S. Lincoln (eds), *Handbook of Qualitative Research*. Thousand Oaks, CA: Sage.

Locock, L. and Boaz, A. (2004) 'Research, policy and practice – worlds apart?', *Social Policy and Society*, 3 (4): 375–84.

Longino, H. (1990) *Science as Social Knowledge: Values and Objectivity in Scientific Enquiry*. Princeton, NJ: Princeton University Press.

Lukács (1919–23) *History and Class Consciousness*, London: Merlin Press, 1967.

Lukes, S. (1973) *Emile Durkheim: His Life and Work: A Historical and Critical Study*. Harmondsworth: Penguin.

Lyotard, J.-F. (1979/1984) *The Postmodern Condition*. Manchester: Manchester University Press.

MacIntyre, A. (1967) *A Short History of Ethics*. London: Routledge and Kegan Paul.

Madge, J. (1963) *The Origins of Scientific Sociology*. London: Tavistock.

Manicas, P. (1987) *A History and Philosophy of the Social Sciences*. Oxford: Blackwell.

Mannheim, K. (1922/1982) 'The distinctive character of cultural-sociological knowledge', in K. Mannheim (ed.), *Structures of Thinking*. London: Routledge and Kegan Paul.

Mannheim, K. (1923/1952) 'On the interpretation of "Weltanschauung"', in K. Mannheim (ed.), *Essays on the Sociology of Knowledge*. London: Routledge and Kegan Paul.

Mannheim, K. (1924/1982) 'A sociological theory of culture and its knowability', in K. Mannheim (ed.), *Structures of Thinking*. London: Routledge and Kegan Paul.

Mannheim, K. (1927/1952) 'The problem of generations', in K. Mannheim (ed.), *Essays on the Sociology of Knowledge*. London: Routledge and Kegan Paul.

Mannheim, K. (1929a/1952) 'Competition as a cultural phenomenon', in K. Mannheim (ed.), *Essays on the Sociology of Knowledge*. London: Routledge and Kegan Paul.

Mannheim, K. (1929b/1936) 'Ideology and utopia', in K. Mannheim (ed.), *Ideology and Utopia, Chapters 2–4*. London: Routledge and Kegan Paul.

Mannheim, K. (1931/1936) 'The problem of the sociology of knowledge', in K. Mannheim (ed.). *Ideology and Utopia, Chapter 5*. London: Routledge and Kegan Paul.

Mannheim, K. (1932) 'The sociology of intellectuals', *Theory, Culture, and Society*, 10 (3): 69–80.

Mannheim, K. (1932–33a/1956) 'The democratisation of culture', in K. Mannheim (ed.), *Essays on the Sociology of Culture*. London: Routledge and Kegan Paul.

Mannheim, K. (1932–33b/1956) 'The problem of the intelligentsia', in K. Mannheim (ed.), *Essays on the Sociology of Culture*. London: Routledge and Kegan Paul.

Mannheim, K. (1932–33c/1956) 'Towards a sociology of the mind', in K. Mannheim (ed.), *Essays on the Sociology of Culture*. London: Routledge and Kegan Paul.

Mannheim, K. (1936/1968) 'Preliminary approach to the problem', in K. Mannheim (ed.), *Ideology and Utopia, Chapter 1*. London: Routledge and Kegan Paul.

Marpsat, M. and Razafindratsima, N. (2010) 'Survey methods for hard to reach populations', *Methodological Innovations Online*, 5 (2): 3–16.

Martel, J. (2004) 'Policing criminological knowledge: the hazards of qualitative research on women in prison', *Theoretical Criminology*, 8 (2): 157–89.

Marx, K. (1844a/1959) *Economic and Philosophical Manuscripts*. London: Lawrence and Wishart.

Marx, K. (1844b/1970) 'Theses on Feuerbach', in C.J. Arthur (ed.), *The German Ideology*. London: Lawrence and Wishart.

Marx, K. and Engels, F. (1845/1956) *The Holy Family*. London: Lawrence and Wishart

Marx, K. and Engels, F. (1846/1970) *The German Ideology*. London: Lawrence and Wishart.

Marx, K. and Engels, F. (1848/1967) *The Communist Manifesto*. Harmondsworth: Penguin.

Masterman, M. (1970) 'The nature of a paradigm', in I. Lakatos and A. Musgrave (eds), *Criticism and the Growth of Knowledge*. Cambridge: Cambridge University Press, pp. 59–90.

May, T. with Perry, B. (2011) *Social Research and Reflexivity: Content, Consequence and Context*. London: Sage.

Mayall, B. (2002) *Towards a Sociology of Childhood: Thinking from Children's Lives*. Buckingham: Open University Press.

Maynard, M. (1994) 'Race, gender and the concept of "difference" in feminist thought', in H. Ashfar and M. Maynard (eds), *The Dynamics of 'Race' and Gender: Some Feminist Interventions*. London: Taylor & Francis, pp. 9–25.

McCarthy, G. (2001) *Objectivity and the Silence of Reason*. New Brunswick, NJ: Transaction Books.

McLaughlin, H. (2007) *Understanding Social Work Research*. London: Sage.

Medvedev, Z. (1969) *The Rise and Fall of T.D. Lysenko*. New York: Columbia University Press.

Merton, R.K. (1942/1973) 'The normative structure of science', in R.K. Merton (ed.), *The Sociology of Science: Theoretical and Empirical Investigations*. Chicago, IL: Chicago University Press.

Merton, R.K. (1957/1968) *Social Theory and Social Structure*. New York: The Free Press.

Migration Watch (2010) *Population Growth – Migration or Birth rate?* [http://www.migrationwatchuk.org/briefingPaper/document/180]

Mill, J.S. (1843/1987) *The Logic of the Moral Sciences*. London: Duckworth.

Millen, D. (1997) 'Some methodological and epistemological issues raised by doing feminist research on non-feminist women', *Sociological Research Online*, 2 (3). [www.socresonline.org.uk/socresonline/2/3/3]

Mills, C.W. (1959) *The Sociological Imagination*. London: Penguin.

Modernising Government White *Paper* (1999) Presented to Parliament by the Prime Minister and the Minister for the Cabinet Office by Command of Her Majesty. London: The Stationery Office.

Montmarquet, J. A. (1993) *Epistemic Virtue and Doxastic Responsibility*. Lanham, MD: Rowman and Littlefield.

Morgan, D. (1998) 'Sociological imaginations and imagining sociologies: bodies, auto/biographies and other mysteries', *Sociology*, 32 (4): 647–63.

Morley, L. (1996) 'Interrogating patriarchy: the challenges of feminist research', in L. Morley and V. Walsh (eds), *Breaking Boundaries: Women in Higher Education*. London: Taylor & Francis, pp. 124–45.

Mukherjee, R. (1979) *Sociology of Indian Sociology*. Bombay: Allied Publishers.

Muncey, T. (2010) *Creating Autoethnographies*. London: Sage.

Mykhalovskiy, E. (1996) 'Reconsidering table talk: critical thoughts on the relationship between sociology, autobiography and self-indulgence', *Qualitative Sociology*, 19 (1): 131–51.

Nagel, E. (1961/1979) *The Structure of Science: Problems in the Logic of Scientific Explanation*. Indianapolis, IN: Hackett.

Naples, N.A. (2003) *Feminism and Method: Ethnography, Discourse Analysis and Activist Research*. New York: Routledge.

Newton, I. (1687/1969) *Mathematical Principles of Natural Philosophy*. London: Dawsons.

Nicholson, L. (ed.) (1990) *Feminism/Postmodernism*. London: Routledge.

Nietzsche, F. (1886/1998) *Beyond Good and Evil*. Oxford: Oxford University Press.

Nietzsche, F. (1887/1996) *Genealogy of Morals*. Oxford: Oxford University Press.

Norris, C. (1996) *Reclaiming Truth: Contribution to a Critique of Cultural Relativism*. Durham, NC: Duke University Press.

Norris, C. (2000) *Quantum Theory and the Flight from Realism: Philosophical Responses to Quantum Mechanics*. London: Routledge.

Norrie, S (2011) 'Reality and probability: *Contra* Williams', *Social Epistemology*, 25 (1): 57–66.

Nozick, R. (2001) *Invariances: The Structure of the Objective World*. Cambridge, MA: Harvard University Press.

Nutley, S. (2003) *Bridging the Policy/Research Divide: Reflections and Lessons from the UK*. St Andrews: Research Unit for Research Utilization, University of St Andrews.

Oakes, G. (1980) 'Introduction', in G. Oakes (ed.), *Georg Simmel: Essays on Interpretation in Social Science*. Manchester: Manchester University Press.

Oakes, G. (1988) *Weber and Rickert*. Cambridge, MA: MIT Press.

Oakley, A. (1979) *From Here to Maternity: Becoming a Mother*. London: Penguin.

Oakley, A. (1998) 'Gender, methodology and people's ways of knowing: some problems with feminism and the paradigm debate in social science', *Sociology*, 32 (4): 707–32.

Oakley, A. (1999) 'People's ways of knowing: gender and methodology', in S. Hood, B. Mayall and H. Roberts (eds), (1992) *Women's Health Matters*. London: Routledge.

Oakley, A. (2004) 'Response to "Quoting and counting: an autobiographical response to Oakley"', *Sociology*, 38 (1): 191–2.

Okley, J. (1992) 'Anthropology and autobiography: participatory experience and embodied knowledge', in J. Okley and H. Callaway (eds), *Anthropology and Autobiography*. London: Routledge, pp. 1 –28.

O'Neill, M. (2008) 'Sex, violence and work services to sex workers and public policy reform', in G. Letherby, P. Birch, M. Cain and K. Williams (eds), *Sex and Crime?* Devon: Willan Press.

Ossewaarde, M. (2007) 'Sociology back to the publics', *Sociology*, 41: 799–812.

Outhwaite, W. (1983) *Concept Formation in Social Science*. London: Routledge and Kegan Paul.

Owen, D. (1995) *Nietzsche, Politics, and Modernity: A Critique of Liberal Reason*. Beverley Hills, CA: Sage.

Parsons, T. (ed.) (1930) *Max Weber: The Protestant Ethic and the Spirit of Capitalism*. London: Unwin.

Parsons, T. (1937/1968) *The Structure of Social Action* (3rd edition). New York: The Free Press.

Parsons, T. (1959) 'Some problems facing sociology as a profession', *American Sociological Review*. New York: Free Press.

Parsons, T. (1963a) 'On the concept of influence', in T. Parsons (ed.), *Politics and Social Structure*. New York: The Free Press.

Parsons, T. (1963b) 'On the concept of political power', *Proceedings of the American Philosophical Society*, 107: 232–62.

Parsons, T. (1966) *Societies: Evolutionary and Comparative Perspectives*. Englewood Cliffs, NJ: Prentice-Hall.

Parsons, T. (1971) *The System of Modern Societies*. Englewood Cliffs, NJ: Prentice-Hall.

Parsons, T. and Shils, E.A. (eds) (1951) *Toward a General Theory of Action*. New York: Harper & Row.

Parsons, T. and Smelser, N.J. (1956) *Economy and Society*. New York: The Free Press.

Pawson, R. (2000) 'Middle range realism', *Journal of European Sociology*, XLI (2): 283–325.

Pawson, R (2006) *Evidence-Based Policy: A Realist Perspective*. London: Sage.

Pawson, R. and Tilley, N. (1997) *Realistic Evaluation*. London: Sage.

Payne, G., Williams, M. and Chamberlain, S. (2004) 'Methodological pluralism in British sociology', *Sociology*, 38 (1): 153–64.

Peirce, C.S. (1877) 'The fixation of belief', *Popular Science Monthly*, 12 (November): 1–15.

Peirce, C.S. (1878) 'How to make our ideas clear', *Popular Science Monthly*, 12 (January): 286–302.

Pérez-y-Pérez, M. and Stanley, T. (2011) 'Ethnographic Intimacy: Thinking Through the Ethics of Social Research in Sex Worlds', *Sociological Research Online*, 16 (2). [www.socresonline.org.uk/16/2/13]

Perry, R., Dean, K. and Brown, B. (1986) *Counterurbanisation: case studies in urban to rural movement*. Norwich, England: Geo Books.

Phinney, J.S. and Ong, A.D. (2007) 'Conceptualization and measurement of ethnic identity: Current status and future directions', *Journal of Counseling Psychology*, 54: 271–81.

Platt, J. (1996) *A History of Sociological Research Methods in America 1920–1960*. Cambridge: Cambridge University Press.

Popper, K.R. (1945) *The Open Society and Its Enemies*. London: Routledge and Kegan Paul.

Popper, K.R. (1979) *Objective Knowledge: An Evolutionary Approach* (2nd edition). Oxford: Oxford University Press.

Porter, C. (1934) *Anything Goes*. New York: Warner Brothers, Inc. American Society of Composers, Authors and Publishers (ASCAP).

Poutanen, S. and Kovalainen, A. (2010) 'Epistemic communities facing a new type of agora? Centres of science, technology and innovation as defining the new research landscape in Finland', *Sociological Research Online*, 15 (2): 12. [www.socresonline.org.uk/15/2/12]

Prakash, G. (1990/2000) 'Writing post-Orientalist histories of the Third World', in V. Chaturvedi (ed.), *Mapping Subaltern Studies and the Postcolonial*. London: Verso, pp. 163–90.

Probyn, E. (1993) *Sexing the Self: Gendered Positions in Cultural Studies*. London and New York: Routledge.

Psillos, S. (1999) *Scientific Realism: How Science Tracks Truth*. London: Routledge.

Rae, A. (1986) *Quantum Physics: Illusion or Reality?* Cambridge: Canto.

RAE (Research Assessment Exercise) (2004). Initial decisions by the UK Funding Bodies. February. Ref RAE 01/2004. Higher Education Funding Council for England. Scottish Higher Education Funding Council. Higher Education Funding Council for Wales. Department for Employment and Learning Northern Ireland. [http://www.rae.ac.uk/pubs/2004/01/rae0401.doc]

Ramazanoglu, C. with Holland, J. (2002) *Feminist Methodology: Challenges and Choices*. London: Sage.

Ramsay, K. (1996) 'Emotional labour and qualitative research: how I learned not to laugh or cry in the field', in E.S. Lyon and J. Busfield (eds), *Methodological Imaginations*. Basingstoke and London: Macmillan, pp. 131–46.

Remmling, G. (1975) *The Sociology of Karl Mannheim*. London: Routledge and Kegan Paul.

Renn, O. (1992) 'Concepts of risk: a classification', in S. Krimsky and D. Golding (eds), *Social Theories of Risk*. Westport, CT: Praeger.

Rescher, N. (2000) *Realistic Pragmatism*. Albany, NY: SUNY Press.

Ribbens, J. and Edwards, R. (eds) (1997). *Feminist Dilemmas in Qualitative Research: Public Knowledge and Private Lives*. Thousand Oaks, CA: Sage.

Rich, A. (1980) 'Compulsory heterosexuality and lesbian existence', *Signs*, 5 (4): 631–60.

Rickert, H. (1902/1986) *The Limits of Concept Formation in Natural Science*. Cambridge: Cambridge University Press.

Riker, W. (1982) 'The two-party system and Duverger's Law: an essay on the history of political science', *American Political Science Review*, 76: 753–66.

Roberts, H. (ed.) (1981) *Doing Feminist Research*. London: Routledge and Kegan Paul.

Roberts, H. (ed.) (1992) *Women's Health Matters*. London: Routledge.

Roberts, J. M. and Sanders, T. (2005) 'Before, during and after: realism, reflexivity and ethnography', *The Sociological Review,* 53 (2): 294–313.

Skeggs, B. (2004) *Class, Self, Culture*. London: Routledge.

Roberts, S. and Randolph, W. (1983) 'Beyond decentralisation: the evolution of population distribution in England and Wales, 1961–81'. *Geoforum,* 14: 75–102.

Rose, D. and O'Reilly, K. (eds) (1997) *Constructing Classes: Towards a New Social Classification for the UK*. London: ESRC/Office for National Statistics.

Rubin, G. (1975) 'The traffic in women: notes on the "political economy" of sex', in R. Reiter (ed.), *Toward an Anthropology of Women*. New York: Monthly Review Press, pp. 157–210.

Ruddick, S. (1990) *Maternal Thinking*. London: The Women's Press.

Runciman, W.G. (1972) *A Critique of Max Weber's Philosophy of the Social Sciences*. Cambridge: Cambridge University Press.

Russell, B. (1946/1979) *A History of Western Philosophy*. London: Unwin Hyman.

Said, E. (1978/1995) *Orientalism*. Harmondsworth: Penguin.

Said, E. (1993) *Culture and Imperialism*. London: Chatto & Windus.

Said, E. (1994) *Representations of the Intellectual*. London: Vintage Books.

Sampson, H., Bloor, M. and Fincham, B. (2008) 'A price worth paying? Considering the "cost" of reflexive research methods and the influence of feminist ways of "doing"', *Sociology*, 42 (5): 919–34.

Sarantakos, S. (2005) *Social Research* (3rd edition). Basingstoke: Palgrave.

Sayer, A. (1992) *Method in Social Science: A Realist Approach* (2nd edition). London: Routledge.

Schluchter, W. (1989) *Rationalism, Religion, and Domination*. Berkeley, CA: University of California Press.

Schopenhauer, A. (1818) *The World as Will and Representation*. New York: Dover Publications.

Schreiner, O. (1899/1987) 'The woman question', in C. Barash (ed.), *An Olive Schreiner Reader*. London: Pandora Press.

Scott, J. (1998) 'Relationism, Cubism, and reality: beyond relativism', in T. May and M. Williams (eds), *Knowing the Social World*. Buckingham: Open University Press, pp. 103–19.

Scott, J. (2001) *Power.* Cambridge: Polity Press.

Scott, J. (2005) 'Sociology and its others: reflections on disciplinary specialisation and fragmentation', *Sociological Research Online*, 10 (1). [www.socresonline.org.uk/10/1/scott.html]

Scott, S. (1998) 'Here be dragons', *Sociological Research Online*, 3 (3). [www.socresonline.org.uk/socresonline/3/3/1]

Silverman, D. (2000) *Doing Qualitative Research.* London: Sage.

Simmel, G. (1892/1977) *The Problems of the Philosophy of History.* New York: The Free Press.

Slovic, P. (1992) 'Perception of risk: reflections on the psychometric paradigm', in S. Krimsky and D. Golding (eds), *Social Theories of Risk.* Westport, CT: Praeger.

Smith, D.E. (1987) *The Everyday World as Problematic.* Milton Keynes: Open University Press.

Smith, D.E. (1990) *The Conceptual Practices of Power.* Toronto: University of Toronto Press.

Smith, D.E. (1999) *Writing the Social.* Toronto: University of Toronto Press.

Southwell, J. (2001) 'Count me in?', *Radical Statistics,* 78: 32–39.

Sparkes, A. (1998) 'Reciprocity in critical research? Some unsettling thoughts', in G. Shaklock and J. Smyth (eds), *Being Reflexive in Critical Educational and Social Research.* London: Falmer, pp. 67–83.

Sparkes, A. (2002) *Telling Tales in Sport and Physical Activity: A Qualitative Journey.* Leeds: Human Kinetics.

Spivak, G.C. (1985/1993) 'Can the subaltern speak?', in P. Williams and L. Chrisman (eds), *Colonial Discourse and Post-Colonial Theory.* Hemel Hempstead: Harvester-Wheatsheaf.

Spivak, G.C. (1988) *In Other Worlds.* London: Routledge.

Spivak, G.C. (1990) *The Post-Colonial Critic.* London: Routledge.

Stanley, L. (1984) 'How the social science research process discriminates against women', in S. Acker and D. Piper (eds), *Is Higher Education Fair to Women?* London: Routledge.

Stanley, L. (ed.) (1990) *Feminist Praxis.* London: Routledge.

Stanley, L. (1991) 'Feminist auto/biography and feminist epistemology', in J. Aaron and S. Walby (eds), *Out of the Margins: Women's Studies in the Nineties.* London: Routledge.

Stanley, L. (1992) *The Auto/biographical I: The Theory and Practice of Feminist Auto/biography.* Manchester: Manchester University Press.

Stanley, L. (1993) 'On Auto/biography in sociology', *Sociology,* 27 (1): 41–52.

Stanley, L. (1999) 'Children of our time: politics, ethics and feminist research processes'. Paper presented at 'Feminism and Educational Research Methodologies' conference. Institute of Education, Manchester Metropolitan University (June).

Stanley, L. and Wise. S. (1979) 'Feminist research, feminist consciousness and experiences of sexism', *Women's Studies International Quarterly*, 2 (3): 259–74.

Stanley, L. and Wise, S. (1983) *Breaking Out*. London: Routledge.

Stanley, L. and Wise, S. (1990) 'Method, methodology and epistemology in feminist research processes', in L. Stanley (ed.) *Feminist Praxis: Research, Theory and Epistemology in Feminist Sociology*. London: Routledge.

Stanley, L. and Wise, S. (1993/1983) *Breaking Out Again: Feminist Ontology and Epistemology*. London: Routledge.

Stanley, L. and Wise, S. (2005) 'Putting it into practice: using feminist fractured foundationalism in researching children in the concentration camps of the South African War', *Sociological Research Online*, 11 (1). [www.socresonline.org.uk/11/1/stanley]

Steier, F. (ed.) (1991) *Research and Reflexivity*. London: Sage.

Stoeker, R. (1996) Report to the Community Development Society on the Participatory Research meeting at Melbourne Community Development Society. [http://www.comm-dev.htm]

Stouffer, S. (1949) *The American Soldier*. Princeton, NJ: Princeton University Press.

Stringer, E. (1996) *Action Research: A Handbook for Practitioners*. Thousand Oaks: Sage.

Tarnas, R. (1991) *The Passion of the Western Mind*. London: Random House.

Taylor, C. (1994) 'Neutrality in political science', in M. Martin and L. McIntyre (eds), *Readings in the Philosophy of Social Science*. Cambridge, MA: MIT Press, pp. 181–212.

Taylor, Y. and Addison, M. (2011) 'Placing research: "city publics" and the "public sociologist"', *Sociological Research Online*, 16 (4). [http://www.socresonline.org.uk/16/4/6.html]

Temple, B. (1997) '"Collegiate accountability" and bias: the solution to the problem?' *Sociological Research Online*, 2 (4). [www.socresonline.org.uk/socresonline/2/4/8]

Thomas, W.I. and Thomas, D.S. (1928) *The Child in America: Behavior, Problems and Programs*. New York: Knopf.

Toulmin, S. (1972) *Human Understanding* (Vol. 1). Oxford: Clarendon Press.

Trowler, P. (2008) *Cultures and Change in Higher Education*. London: Palgrave Macmillan.

Truman, C. (2003) 'Ethics and the ruling relations of research', *Sociological Research Online*, 8 (1). [www.socresonline.org.uk/8/1/truman]

Vining, D.R. and Kontuly, T. (1978) 'Population dispersal from major metropolitan regions: an international comparison', *International Regional Science Review*, 13 (1): 49.

Wacquant, L. (1992) 'The structure and logic of Bourdieu's sociology', in P. Bourdieu and L. Wacquant (eds), *An Invitation to Reflexive Sociology*. Cambridge: Polity Press.

Wajcman, J. (1991) *Feminism Confronts Technology*. Cambridge: Polity Press.

Warren, C. (1988) *Gender Issues in Field Research*. Newbury Park, CA: Sage.

Weber, M. (1904/1949) '"Objectivity" in social science and social policy', in M. Weber (ed.), *The Methodology of the Social Sciences*. New York: The Free Press.

Weber, M. (1907/1977) *Critique of Stammler*. New York: The Free Press.

Weber, M. (1919/1989) 'Science as a vocation', in P. Lassman and I. Velody (eds), *Max Weber's Science as a Vocation*. London: Unwin Hyman, pp. 3–31.

Westmarland, N. (2001) 'The quantitative/qualitative debate and feminist research: a subjective view of objectivity', *Forum: Qualitative Social Research*, 2 (1). [www.qualitative-research.net/index.php/fqs/article/viewArticle/974/2124]

Wiles, R., Heath, S. and Crow, G. (2005) *Informed Consent and the Research Process* (ESRC Research Methods Programme: Methods Briefing 2). Manchester: ESRC.

Wilkinson, I. (2001) 'Social theories of risk perception: at once indispensable and insufficient', *Current Sociology*, 49 (1): 1–22.

Wilkinson, S. (1986) *Feminist Social Psychology: Developing Theory and Practice*. Milton Keynes: Open University Press.

Wilkinson, S. and Kitzinger, C. (eds) (1996) *Representing the Other: A Feminism and Psychology Reader*. London: Sage.

Williams, B. (2002) *Truth and Truthfulness: An Essay in Genealogy*. Princeton: Princeton University Press.

Williams, M. (1999) 'Single case probabilities and the social world: the application of Popper's Propensity Interpretation', *Journal for the Theory of Social Behaviour*, 29 (2): 187–201.

Williams, M. (2000) *Science and Social Science: An Introduction*. London: Routledge.

Williams, M. (2003) 'The problem of representation: realism and operationalism in survey research', *Sociological Research Online*, 8 (1). [www.socresonline.org.uk/8/1/williams.html]

Williams, M. (2005a) 'Situated objectivity', *Journal for the Theory of Social Behaviour*, 35 (1): 99–120.

Williams, M. (2005b) 'Definition, measurement and legitimacy in studies of homelessness', in M. Romero and E. Margolis (eds), *Social Inequalities* (Blackwell Companion to Sociology Series). Malden, MA: Blackwell, pp. 190–210.

Williams, M. (2010) 'Contingent realism – abandoning necessity', *Social Epistemology*, 25 (1): 37–56.

Williams, M. (2011) 'Contingent or Necessary: a response to Stephen Norrie', *Social Epistemology*, 26 (2).

Williams, M. and Cheal, B. (2001) 'Is there any such thing as homelessness? Measurement, explanation and process in "homelessness" research', *European Journal of Social Research: Innovation*, 14 (3): 239–53.

Williams, M. and Dyer, W. (2004) 'Realism and probability', in B. Carter and C. New (eds), *Making Realism Work*. London: Routledge.

Williams, M. and Dyer, W. (2009) 'Single case probabilities', in C. Ragin and D. Byrne (eds), *Case Based Methods*. London: Sage, pp. 84–100.

Williams, M. and Vogt, W.P. (2011) 'Innovation in social research methods', in M. Williams and W.P. Vogt (eds), *The Sage Handbook of Innovation in Social Research Methods*. London: Sage, pp. 1–18.

Winch, P. (1958) *The Idea of a Social Science*. London: Routledge and Kegan Paul.

Wise, S. and Stanley, L. (2003a) 'Looking back and looking forward: some recent feminist sociology reviewed', *Sociological Research Online*, 8 (3). [www.socres online.org.uk/6/4/wise.html]

Wise, S. and Stanley, L. (2003b) 'Review article: Looking back and looking forward: some recent feminist sociology reviewed', *Sociological Research Online*, 8 (3). [www.socresonline.org.uk/8/3]

Wollstonecraft, M. (1792/1975) *A Vindication of the Rights of Woman*. Harmondsworth: Penguin.

Young, E.H. and Lee, R. (1996) 'Fieldworker feelings as data: "emotion work" and "feeling rules" in the first-person accounts of sociological fieldwork', in V. James and J. Gabe (eds), *Health and the Sociology of the Emotions*. Oxford: Blackwell, pp. 97–114.

Index